D1498100

Fields of Death

Fields of Death

Retracing Ancient Battlefields

Richard Evans

Pen & Sword
MILITARY ·

First published in Great Britain in 2013 by
Pen & Sword Military
an imprint of
Pen & Sword Books Ltd
47 Church Street
Barnsley
South Yorkshire
S70 2AS

ISBN 978 1 84884 797 2

A CIP catalogue record for this book is available from the British
Library

Typeset in Ehrhardt by
Mac Style, Driffield, East Yorkshire
Printed and bound in the UK by CPI Group (UK) Ltd, Croydon,
CRO 4YY

Pen & Sword Books Ltd incorporates the imprints of Pen & Sword
Archaeology, Atlas, Aviation, Battleground, Discovery, Family
History, History, Maritime, Military, Naval, Politics, Railways,
Select, Social History, Transport, True Crime, and Claymore Press,
Frontline Books, Leo Cooper, Praetorian Press, Remember When,
Seaforth Publishing and Wharncliffe.

For a complete list of Pen & Sword titles please contact
PEN & SWORD BOOKS LIMITED
47 Church Street, Barnsley, South Yorkshire, S70 2AS, England
E-mail: enquiries@pen-and-sword.co.uk
Website: www.pen-and-sword.co.uk

Contents

Acknowledgements

I t is appropriate that here that I should thank the Research Committee of the School of History, Archaeology and Religion (Chair: Professor Josef Lössl) at Cardiff University for providing funds that allowed me to visit some of the sites discussed in this volume, including Sybaris, Heracleia (Siris), Metapontum and Tarentum during the summer of 2012.

I should also like to note my continuing association with the Department of Classics and World Languages at the University of South Africa, Pretoria, in which I hold the honorary position of Academic Associate.

I should also like to extend a warm thanks to Dr Alun Williams (Cardiff) for his permission to reproduce here the picture of Lindos on Rhodes, and to Dr Lea Beness and Professor Tom Hillard of MacQuarrie University, NSW, for their permission to use their slides of Aquae Sextiae and the Fossae Marianae (Arles-Marseilles Canal).

Preface

It is arguably insufficient to try and recreate the military events from ancient history by simply using the available, often fragmentary literary sources and therefore archaeological, and especially numismatic, evidence can be very helpful in trying to understand how episodes unfolded in the distant past. Better still should be the objective, not always fulfilled of course, to visit the relevant sites under discussion and to reach an interpretation of events through as detailed an analysis of the place through thorough empirical investigation. Therefore, the aim in this volume, and the one to follow, is as far as has been possible, to trace a number of scenes of battles by firstly looking at the minutiae of the subject and secondly by employing an on-the-site knowledge to obtain a clarity not hitherto achieved in such discussions; hence the title *Retracing Ancient Battlefields*.

In recent years, I have been fortunate enough to become reasonably well acquainted with the archaeological remains of Sybaris, Motya, Syracuse and the topographical features of numerous other former Greek and Roman cities and towns in Magna Graecia and Sicily, and what is even more important their geographical context. I have also been able to visit Arelate (Arles) and Aquae Sextiae (Aix-en-Provence) and parts of the Rhone valley and Delta, and also several of the main centres in north-eastern Spain (Catalonia) such as Emporion (L'Escala), Barcino (Barcelona) and Tarraco (Tarragona). I regret that I have not yet been able to organize a visit to Alexandria, but have become familiar with the cities of ancient Asia, including Pergamum (Bergama), Ephesus, Miletus and Halicarnassus (Bodrum), which also feature in Chapter 5. The subject of relief columns as a countermeasure to sieges (also Chapter 5) allowed me the opportunity to exploit my familiarity with the geography of South Africa and with its more recent history. In the process of the following discussion not only is the intention to throw some clarity on often misperceived events in the ancient world but also to debunk quite a few myths that have entered not only the ancient but also the modern literature.

Abbreviations and Notes

The abbreviations employed in this work follow the standard and common practice and therefore should be readily understandable. While the ancient sources have been referenced to modern editions, the translations are mine and any errors that remain here are also mine alone.

I make no apology for the almost idiosyncratic use of Latinized names for some of the Greek characters and place names while employing a transliteration of the original Greek for others. However, all should be easily recognizable.

Maps and Plans

List of Plates

(Except for Chapter 4 numbers 1–3 and Chapter 5 number 4, for which see under the Acknowledgements, all others are the author's own)

Chapter 1
1. Sybaris: 'The city quickly grew because the land was so fertile.' (Diod. 12.9.1)
2. Sybaris with the Pollino Massif in the background.
3. The Via Decumana at Sybaris-Thurii Copia.
4. The Bay of Sybaris.
5. Temple of Hera outside Croton.
6. General view of Metapontum.
7. The Argive Heraion at Metapontum.
8. The acropolis (right) at Tarentum (Taranto) and entrance to the harbour.

Chapter 2
1. View of Ortygia and the Great Harbour from the Eurialos Fort.
2. View from Epipolai towards the Megarian Plain with Leon and Thapsos in the foreground.
3. The Temple of Zeus at Polichne with Ortygia and Daskon in the background.
4. View from Lysimeleia to Mount Climiti: the initial route of the Athenian retreat.
5. The small harbour from Ortygia with Akradina in the background.
6. Entrance to the Great Harbour from Ortygia to Plemmyrion.
7. The theatre adjacent to the Temenos of Apollo in the Neapolis District of Syracuse.
8. Entrance to the Great Harbour: the Athenians set up a trophy in front of Plemmyrion (Thucydides, 7.23).
9. The northern end of the ἀκραῖον λέπας or 'High Cliff' in the valley of the Anapos River.
10. The gorge of the Erineos above Noto: a possible way of retreat for the Athenians.
11. Nature of the terrain above Noto, which contributed to the Athenian defeat.

Chapter One

The End of Sybaris (510 BC)

If you were to gaze out through the haze of a summer's day from the Pollino Massif in that part of southern Italy, which is the border between Calabria and Basilicata, where the Tyrrhenian and Ionian Seas are separated by scarcely a hundred kilometres (60 miles) of mountainous terrain, you might find it difficult to grasp that two and a half thousand years ago there should have been visible below towards the east a thriving metropolis. H.V. Morton wrote, in one of his travels to Italy in the mid-1960s, that:

> When I left Castrovillari I could look down over blue hills and woodland to the Ionian Sea and the yellow plain upon which the city of Sybaris once stood. Rich and famous, the parent of Paestum, a city that could put three hundred thousand men into the field, a city whose wealth and luxury excited the envy of the Hellenic world. Sybaris has vanished from the map.[1]

This city is mentioned numerous times in the ancient literature and examples of its coinage illustrate apparently a sophisticated and wealthy community. It is a little more than thirty-four kilometres (21 miles) from the town of Castrovillari to the *Museo di Sibaritide*, which is situated on the edge of an area that has been identified, after prolonged excavation work, as the site of Thurii beneath which lay Sybaris. The landscape is a rather non-descript coastal plain of mostly cultivated fields criss-crossed by roads and irrigation ditches. The museum, a modern building of utilitarian design, constructed some years after Morton came here, is also about three kilometres (¾ of a mile) from the sea and the modern lidos that characterize the landscape of the Italian coastline. This countryside has that timeless quality that is quintessentially Mediterranean although, as is often the case, it hides well the fact that much has changed here since the ancient world, not least it seems the disappearance of so powerful a city of the Greeks. How and why did Sybaris cease to be and how much truth can we attach to the ancient accounts of its end? These questions and a search for answers are the focus of the discussion here in this first chapter of tracing ancient battlefields.

Not least among the intriguing aspects of this subject is the widely reported information that once the city of Sybaris had been occupied by its besiegers the Crotoniates they not only levelled the whole urban area to the ground but they then covered it with water. Indeed the geographer Strabo, writing in the first century AD, states (16.1.14) that the local river or rivers, the Crathis and the Sybaris, were diverted over the site so that its whereabouts would thereafter be completely forgotten. Yet it was not forgotten and in fact tales about Sybaris and its end seem to have quickly sprung up during or soon after the Classical period of Greece, initially perhaps within a generation or two of its apparent demise. The result was that the city's name became forever linked with wealth and unimaginable riches, and its citizens described as devotees of an unparalleled decadent lifestyle. However, scepticism has not surprisingly been voiced and here again it is well worth noting another comment by Morton.

Why Sybaris should be so fascinating is difficult to say. Perhaps the words 'sybaritic' and 'sybarite' give it a certain interest, though when one has read all the references to 'sybaritism', how commonplace they are: the feasts, the street awnings, the honour paid to cooks, the chariots in which men visited their estates, the Maltese lapdogs which women carried, the pet monkeys, the purple cloaks, the scented hair bound by gold fillets ... all this appears merely to reflect a standard of living that one would expect to find in any rich community of the time. Why the writers of antiquity should have picked upon Sybaris as the symbol of excessive luxury is difficult to understand.[2]

Aelian in his *Varia Historia* also pours cold water on the notion that Sybaris was destroyed for its luxurious lifestyle. Aelian (1.19) calls the destruction of Sybaris a widely circulated popular tale (δημώδης λόγος) but says that the Ionian city of Colophon was also destroyed for its attachment to luxury and that this information was much less well known. So too the downfall of the Bacchiadae at Corinth was caused by what Aelian describes as excessive luxury (τρύφη). Aelian was writing about AD 200 and his dismissal of the tale should alert us to the fact that the destruction of Sybaris even if a real event had become embellished by extraneous details.[3] Therefore the discussion here will also focus on why these have entered the tradition and, having advanced some reason for such material dominating what should be a straightforward account of a war between two states, some idea about what occurred in 510 and which brought about disaster to Sybaris will be presented.

Southern Italy was a prosperous region of the ancient Mediterranean world and contained from early times a large population of Greeks. The Greek cities of the southern coast of Italy from east to west were: Taras (Tarentum), Metapontion (Metapontum), Heracleia (Siris), Sybaris (later called Thurii and later still Copia), Croton, Caulonia and Locris Epizephyri ('Locri towards the west wind'), which were roughly fifty to sixty kilometres (25–30 miles) from one another, with finally far-flung Region (Rhegium), which completed this line of cities at the Straits separating Italy from Sicily.[4] Sybaris is said to have been among the first to be established by the Greeks in a region, which became known as Magna Graecia, in the last decades of the eighth century BC. It was therefore among that initial wave of settlements set up by the Greeks as they ventured into the western Mediterranean from mainland Greece at just about the same time as Homer was recounting the stories of the Trojan War and the homecoming – or was it setting up new homes – of the various Greek heroes who had fought in this epic struggle.[5] Other cities founded in this same period include Naxos, Syracuse, Leontinoi, Catane, Messene (Zancle) and Megara Hyblaia in Sicily and Region, Croton and Taras.[6] On account of its antiquity Sybaris naturally held a preeminent place in the communities of the region, but its immediate southerly neighbour Croton – a mere 200 stadia (40 kilometres, 25 miles) separates them – was founded only a very short time afterwards (Strabo, 6.1.12). The founders of Sybaris were Achaeans (Strabo, 6.1.13) and it is possible that a former citizen of Helice, a city which was situated on the southern shore of the Corinthian Gulf, was the leader of the settlers. These were almost certainly looking to trade with the local Italian tribes. The identity of the founder is uncertain because the text of Strabo is not fully intelligible at this point, and a lacuna may be conjectured, but if it was indeed a Helicaean then this provides a link that is perhaps of a considerable significance in the later tradition about the fate of his city and its people (see further below).[7] Considering the fame of Sybaris, Strabo's coverage is surprisingly brief in comparison to the other cities and he merely states that Sybaris became a great power with control extending over four of its neighbouring states and that this included twenty-five satellite towns, that it could muster an army of 300,000,[8] and its city had circuit walls of fifty stadia (ten kilometres, approximately 6 miles), and that it was destroyed by Croton in a campaign that lasted a little more than two months (seventy days).[9] After Strabo relates a rise to dizzy heights of power and wealth he shows an equally sudden disinterest in the general history of Sybaris thereafter in what was said to have been a great power.

Today the generally accepted foundation date for Sybaris is roughly 720 BC, yet there is some internal conflict in Strabo's evidence that makes this date uncertain and seems at odds with the information rendered by a writer known in modern times as Pseudo-Scymnus, who lived in the first century BC.[10] First of all this is because Strabo's account of Croton is far more elaborate than that for the other Italian Greek cities, and contained in it there is also mention of Sybaris. This is not a problem if Croton was founded after Syabaris but Strabo appears to think that it was founded just before Syracuse or about 735. The oikist or founder of Croton is said to have been a certain Myscellus who had sought and received an oracle from the Pythia at Delphi concerning the whereabouts of a new settlement. He was advised to situate the new town at the place where Croton was eventually established, but when he reconnoitred the area he preferred the site of the already established Sybaris. Seeking a second message from Apollo he was told to ignore Sybaris and settle where he was first directed. While on this second visit to Delphi he is supposed to have met Archias, who was to be the oikist of Syracuse, who helped in the settlement of Croton before he sailed down the coast to Sicily. The chronology clearly does not work, and this immediately calls into question either the date of the foundation of Sybaris or that of Croton and Syracuse. The date attributed to Syracuse may of course be rather too early for in a way it is remarkable that the Greeks are described as setting up settlements in Sicily before they did in so in southern Italy, which was closer to mainland Greece.[11] Thus Syracuse's enhanced antiquity may well have been deliberate and an instance of Sicilian pride.[12] Croton too could easily have accepted a series of immigrants over a generation or so and the stories of their arrival were synthesized into one grand tale. To be the first was important and there is clearly some element of one-upmanship in the stories attached to foundations of cities especially those in the western Mediterranean. Syracuse certainly aspired to be the first of the Sicilian Greek cities, a dispute over primacy between Sybaris and Croton, may therefore be exposed in this account and probably had an early origin. The dates themselves were always mere approximations and were recognized as such by most sensible commentators in antiquity. However, that there was some debate about the respective ages of Croton and Sybaris can in part account for the hostility between two states vying with each other for dominance in both territorial extent and respectability in a region where, because of the geographical constraints, the military expansion of one could spell disaster for the other.

In terms of literary evidence, the destruction of Sybaris is first remarked upon by Herodotus writing about seventy-five years after the event. Although it could be supposed that he would have shown a particular interest in the history of this city, especially since he was then living in Thurii,[13] his comments are quite brief and lacking much substance. Sybaris' end was not an episode directly related to Herodotus' main theme of the wars between the Greeks and Persians. Still the writer was also not above going into lengthy digressions when these might suit or enliven his narrative. That he seems to pay scant regard to the Sybarites is curious. Herodotus' history is the literary source that is by far the closest in time to the event in question and the evidence it provides about Sybaris tends to highlight economic or other ties between this and other cities on the Greek mainland and in Ionia rather than military issues. There is a specific recall of a firm relationship between the citizens of Sybaris and Miletus, although the focus of his attention is on the destruction of the latter in 494/3, a decade and half after that of the former.

> The Sybarites, who were living in Laos and Scidros, after the fall of their city did not exhibit the correct form of respect for the people of Miletus following their own disaster, for after the destruction of Sybaris the entire citizen body of the Milesians including the boys shaved their heads and went into deep mourning as a sign of the friendship between the two cities. In fact I am not aware of two other cities that were more closely linked.[14] (Herodotus, 6.21)

This connection has been the subject of scrutiny since Sybaris did not have an ethnic tie with Miletus, which was, however, highly active in setting up trading posts around the Euxine and the northern Aegean.[15] The reason for the distress of the citizens of Miletus is therefore held to have been not one of sentimental origin but of economics for it is implied that the Milesians lost a valuable market for their goods. The Sybarites were apparently very fond of wearing cloth imported from Ionia. When Miletus was ravaged and depopulated by the Persians after a siege in 494/3,[16] Herodotus states that any surviving Sybarites did not respond to the fate of the Milesians with the same sympathy that had been accorded them. It should be noted though that they were no longer living in their own city and this supposed economic bond had long been severed. That link itself may also be associated in a rather more negative way with lifestyle since both cities were considered to have been devoted to luxury. Men who wore their hair long surely had a great deal of leisure time and did not face the drudgery of physical labour. Herodotus may have intended his comment to reflect poorly on the people of Sybaris, although it is rather unfair if any survivors of the fall of the city were living elsewhere. On the other hand, he is not particularly complimentary about the Milesians either in his account of the Ionian revolt against Persia. Moreover, those Sybarites referred to by Herodotus may have left Sybaris even before its capture by Croton and been the supporters of Telys who had made himself tyrant of the city, possibly in emulation of Histiaeus, tyrant of Miletus and prime instigator of the Ionian Revolt. The relationship between the two states may therefore have been both economic and more importantly political since tyrants, if they were not a threat to one another, could often forge alliances.[17] Tyranny which could provide strong and enlightened leadership in due course also acquired as much a negative perception as an addiction to luxury. Therefore, the Sybarites possessed two elements – if useful and enjoyable – which just might be viewed with hostility by later commentators.

Herodotus also mentions that some of the former citizens or their descendants claimed that the Spartan Dorieus (5.43–45) had a hand in the destruction of Sybaris. These informants said that the Crotoniates had enlisted the help of this royal exile, while the citizens of Croton denied his involvement. Dorieus was the second son of the Spartan king Anaxandrides and when the King died in about 520 his elder brother Cleomenes succeeded.[18] Dorieus left Sparta to carve out a kingdom for himself and eventually reached Sicily where, Herodotus says, he was killed in a battle near Segesta having been intent, after receiving an oracle at Delphi, on settling at the town of Eryx. Had Dorieus been employed as a mercenary by the Crotoniates in their war with Sybaris his participation might well have played an important part in their success. But it is also understandable that the Crotoniates would deny such a link because they might have considered that the help of an outsider diminished the magnitude of their victory.[19] Herodotus has a high regard for the Spartan but his participation in a war between Croton and Sybaris is at least unlikely since he was known to be looking to carve out territory for himself. Employing a mercenary, however high born, was a risky business that the Crotoniates might well have sought to avoid.

Religious observances and their neglect evidently played a powerful role in the destruction of Sybaris. Herodotus says (5.43) that there were ominous signs that the Sybarites chose to ignore before they began their war with Croton, which foretold the end of the city. This so frightened a soothsayer named Callias who had been instructed by Telys to make sacrifices preparatory to starting the campaign that he fled to avoid the inevitable disaster. The people of Croton agreed that this Callias had indeed defected to their city just before the war began, and that he was granted estates that had remained in the same family down to the time Herodotus wrote. His other reference to Sybaris seems to accentuate the subject of indulgence and luxury. This occurs in his description of the method by which Cleisthenes, the tyrant of Sicyon, chose a husband for his daughter Agariste (6.127–130). At the Olympic Games where he won the chariot race,[20] he invited any potential suitor to come to Sicyon as his guest for a whole year, where during that time he intended to vet and assess his worth as a possible son-in-law. One of those who came, and failed, was a certain Smindyrides, son of Hippocrates, from Sybaris, described then 'at the height of its prosperity' and the suitor as someone 'especially notable for his delicate and luxurious lifestyle'. Herodotus maintains that although strength and education were considered important facets by Cleisthenes it was the table-manners of the suitor that took precedence; and the Athenian Megacles, son of Alcmaeon, emerged as the preferred choice. Smindyrides, whatever his cultivated background, appears not to have figured highly in Cleisthenes' estimation. The episode itself is also placed at the court of a tyrant who himself was clearly partisan in the matter of luxury, and while the Alcmaeonid Megacles is not remembered as a particular follower of luxury, his grandson was ostracized for precisely this fault in 486 BC.[21] However, an earlier Megacles had also been exiled with the entire family for sacrilege.[22] Luxury and contempt for the gods are therefore inextricably linked as fatal vices. Still it would be unwise to assume from Herodotus' comments that Smindyrides was a fair representative of his *polis* especially since the even more urbane Athenian was preferred as the marriage partner of Agariste.

Herodotus is the first military historian and so he ought to provide some sound material for a study of Sybaris' end but his account has actually only limited use for trying to understand the events of 510. From what Herodotus wrote it could be argued that, although denuded of its population, which had fled elsewhere (6.21), for him the events at Sybaris in 510 were not as sensational as the main focus of his history, which was the war between the Greeks and Persians. Herodotus says only that Sybaris had been captured by Croton, which even suggests no permanent devastation of the site. And yet the fate of Sybaris already became notorious during antiquity and its fame or infamy was reflected upon by many commentators then and ever since. It would therefore seem by a logical process of deduction that our next earliest extant literary evidence after Herodotus would be the source for the views about Sybaris that now dominate modern perceptions.

But it is not as simple as that for, although the *Library of History* composed by Diodorus Siculus, written between about 50 and 20 BC, has several references to Sybaris and will have contained a full account of the destruction of the city, the first discussion of the Sybarites which appears in Book 8 where he must have covered the foundation of the city is largely lost. What we possess are just a few fragments (Book 8. 18–20) preserved through the antiquarian interests of the Byzantine emperor Constantine IX Porphyrogenitus (AD 909–959). These sections may well have formed an introductory section to Diodorus' account of the settlement of the city, but the emphasis here is about the place as a playground for the addict of luxury. Some material is evidently derived from Herodotus since it contains the tale about the search for a husband for Cleisthenes' daughter Agariste and that a Sybarite named Mindyrides (a copyist error rather than the fault of the historian) failed in this quest. The tale is retold almost verbatim from Herodotus. However, not all of Diodorus' material goes back to Herodotus since in its current order, it begins with the assertion that the people of Sybaris were slaves to their appetites and devoted to luxury. Indeed when a citizen of that city visited Sparta, it is claimed that although he had often thought about the bravery of the Spartans once he had seen the wretched poverty of their existence he actually considered that they were little better than animals, and apparently declared: 'For the most cowardly Sybarite would choose to die two times over rather than have to endure their lifestyle.'[23] Moreover, although there is something of confirmation about a special friendship existing between the Sybarites and the Milesians, as related by Herodotus, according to Diodorus, this bond came about only because the former considered the latter to be their equals in their liking of luxurious living.[24] The background is at once unreservedly negative and belongs to a tradition that probably developed in the literature after the fifth century BC. Can its source be identified? Miletus may have had its detractors on account of its role in the rebellion against Persia in 499, which resulted in its sack in 494/3. But the city was quickly re-established and became a major ally of Athens in Ionia in the second half of the fifth century before being regained by the Persians after about 404. It was subsequently besieged and captured by Alexander in 334 at the start of his invasion of Asia Minor. Thereafter the city again became prosperous and, more important, for this discussion highly respected among both cultural and political circles well into the Roman Empire and beyond. A writer inclined to view Miletus with disfavour is therefore likely to have been active in the period between 400 and 334 when it was a city ruled indirectly certainly but ultimately by the Persians. But what about a writer or writers who would have viewed Sybaris negatively?

Although this section of the history is a small indication of a fuller coverage, because of what has been preserved it might still seem provocatively inaccurate not only because it is so remote from the events in the late sixth century but also because of a lack of skill in Diodorus' interpretation of his sources. Thus it could be argued that here Diodorus relays a moral tract without any critical appreciation. The source was probably the fourth century historian Ephorus (ca. 400–330 BC) who wrote an account of Greek affairs from the earliest times down to about 350. Diodorus appears to have closely followed and placed great trust in what he considered to be reputable sources and he may have simply copied down some of the material in front of him. But Ephorus could have provided adverse material about Miletus and is probably the earliest account of what seems to have become the accepted end of Sybaris. Yet from where could Ephorus have obtained his information? Ephorus originally came from Cyme in Ionia but later lived in Athens and included events in Magna Graecia in his account.[25] But there were earlier writers than Ephorus such as Philistus, a prominent Syracusan citizen and supporter of Dionysius I who was an almost exact contemporary of Xenophon. His history was about Sicilian affairs down to shortly before his death in about 354 and must also have possessed allusions to events in southern Italy. Philistus cannot be ruled out as a source for the fall of Sybaris since Diodorus clearly knew his work, but having said that, he is unlikely to have been used by Ephorus who was also another contemporary, if a little younger.[26] Finally there was Antiochus of Syracuse whose work was bound to have included background details of the foundation of Syracuse, including any stories about Sybaris and Croton. The details are very sketchy, but he is attested as a reputable source by several later writers and appears to have lived down to at least about 425. Hence he was also a contemporary of Herodotus, in contradistinction to whom he appears to have adopted the deliberate pose of casting the West as the focus of his history.[27] All trace of his coverage of the fall of Sybaris has disappeared unless this is what has been preserved via Ephorus in Diodorus' account.

Of equal if not of more importance to the transmission of the tradition is a rather later writer, assuming Diodorus did not access the earliest sources directly, and this was the Sicilian Greek Timaeus.[28] This historian wrote about fifty years after Ephorus, between 300 and 250 BC, while he lived in Athens exiled from his home on account of the jealousy of Agathocles then the ruler of Syracuse.[29] Although regarded as a historian of considerable stature who concerned himself with relaying accuracy in many respects he was not only a severe critic of all tyrants except Timoleon and his own father Andromachus, but was also prone to dramatic embellishment of his narrative. He was clearly employed by many later historians for their coverage of the earlier events in Greece, Magna Graecia, Sicily and Italy, and writers such as Polybius, who were in various respects continuators who were heavily influenced by his style and methodology or reacted strongly against it. Either way Timaeus became something of a yardstick against which to measure historical compositions in antiquity. His influence on the development of later Greek and Roman historical prose should not be underestimated. Having said that, what would Timaeus have written about Sybaris? That he recorded its demise cannot be doubted. Something of that content can be gleaned from Diodorus and from Athenaeus who both say that they have used material that they found in Timaeus' history. Timaeus used Ephorus and greatly elaborated the narrative of the earlier Athenian historian.

Diodorus' next discussion of Sybaris is another fragment that deals with Sybaris' end in the generally accepted chronological sequence at or about 510 since it is recorded in the text after a discussion of the last Roman king, Tarquin, whose rule also came to an end in or about this year.[30] The notice is very brief and again appears to have a moralizing message:

The Sybarites went to war with three hundred thousand men against the Crotoniates, and starting an unjust war they stumbled into destruction; and not being skilful enough to bear their prosperity they left their own destruction as a particularly stark example for all men to fear almost as much in times of good fortune as in times of adversity. (Diod. 10.23.1)

After this brief statement, Diodorus provides a fuller account of this war but only very much out of the historical context in a later section of his history (12. 9.1–10.1). In Book 12 he is actually recounting the foundation of Thurii in 445/4 BC and in doing so gives a background to this event. There is therefore probably a degree of repetition from the earlier and complete narrative, which is lost from Book 10. He duly notes the geographical situation of Sybaris between the rivers Crathis (Crati) and Sybaris, and that the city became very wealthy on account of the fertility of its land.[31] He says that the fertile plain around Sybaris allowed such an abundance of produce that it was this that caused the city to prosper rather than through its commercial contacts. This is interesting for it is usually overlooked by modern commentators more keen to emphasize the Sybarites' occupation as traders. That may have been the reason why the Greeks first settled here, but this pursuit clearly was not viable. Moreover, the Sybarites are said to have been very liberal in granting citizenship to immigrants, a practice that resulted in a large population.[32] However, the three hundred thousand citizens claimed for Sybaris is simply not possible for a city contained within the circuit wall noted by Strabo. The origin of the total figure is unknown but exaggeration might be expected from Timaeus.[33] Of course, in its war with Croton Sybaris could perhaps have called on allies for military support, although that is not mentioned by any of the sources.

But was Sybaris really such a powerhouse in the region? Its status would surely have been undermined by the period of *stasis* or internal civil unrest that appears to have occurred towards the end of the sixth century during the course of which the demagogue Telys became tyrant. In order to secure his position and to rid himself of potential rivals, Telys brought accusations against five hundred of the wealthiest citizens of Sybaris who had in former times presumably comprised the oligarchic elite. There was no mass slaughter but rather exile and seizure of their properties. These exiles went directly to Croton and appeared as suppliants at various shrines throughout this city. When Telys heard of this he sent heralds to order the return of these exiles or face the prospect of a war with Sybaris. The citizens of Croton met to decide the fate of these men. It is said that their initial inclination was to surrender these refugees and so avoid a damaging conflict with their powerful neighbour, but the philosopher Pythagoras who was then living in Croton argued that the Sybarite exiles should be protected. A Sybarite army is said to have advanced into the territory of Croton where it was met at or near the River Traeis by the defenders who possessed an army of about one hundred thousand men. It was commanded by the former wrestler Milo,[34] hero of several Olympic Games and said to be a follower of Pythagoras, and who wore his crowns of victory into battle and was among the first to drive the Sybarites from the battlefield.[35] No details of the battle are recounted by Diodorus who jumps immediately to the aftermath (12.10.1) where he describes surprisingly perhaps, given what had transpired before the war, the violent behaviour of the Crotoniates, who killed any enemy they found and, unusually for ancient warfare, took no prisoners. And according to Diodorus, 'on account of their anger ... they plundered and utterly desolated the city'. A plausible reason for this sudden change from civil behaviour to one which was more barbaric than their neighbours is preserved by Athenaeus (12. 521 d–e). He states that thirty envoys from Croton arrived at Sybaris, and although the reason is not given, it was either in connection with the five hundred exiles or to negotiate a truce either before or after the battle. Once admitted to the city they were murdered and their bodies flung from the walls where their bodies were left unclaimed and unburied. The status of envoys in the ancient world was never a comfortable one and there are numerous instances of heralds and messengers being killed when supposedly on diplomatic missions. The killing of such individuals sent out a particularly strong message that no diplomacy was possible and that no quarter could be expected or given in the event of future or current hostilities. Whenever the murder of the ambassadors occurred, it gave Croton as much an excuse to march against Sybaris as the Sybarites had after the request for the return of their five hundred exiles had been declined. Following this affront not only to Crotoniates but also to the gods, omens are described that predicted the end of Sybaris, and which may have been the cause of Callias' flight. In particular, a statue of Hera, the city's patron deity, began to vomit bile while a fountain at the goddess' temple poured blood.

These threatening omens were not the first for an oracle had earlier foretold the doom of Sybaris in response to the question of how long its citizens would remain prosperous. The Pythia, according to Athenaeus (12.520 b), is reported to have said 'Sybarites while you honour the gods you will be abundantly happy but if you show more respect to a human being than to the gods then war and disastrous discord will afflict you.' This turning away from the gods and showing contempt for civic cults is rather laboured in the sources but may well have its origins in the activities of Telys and his role in the fall of the city and may be identified as the subject of the oracle. The issue of sacrilege with a wider contempt for the gods is also noted by Aelian (3.43) who describes how a musician in a contest in honour of Hera caused a riot between some citizens who were his enthusiastic supporters and others not. The performer feared for his life and sought sanctuary at Hera's altar but here even as a suppliant he was murdered. Soon afterwards a bloody fountain was observed in the temple of Hera and so envoys were sent to Delphi to seek a solution to end this phenomenon. The response of the Pythia could not have been worse for no oracle was granted to the Sybarites and they were ordered as polluters of a sacred shrine to leave Delphi at once and since they had been responsible for the death of a 'servant of the Muses' they could soon expect divine retribution for their evil:

> It hovers above their heads and over their children and sorrow after sorrow prowls among them. (Aelian, *VH*. 3.43 = *The Delphic Oracle* no. 74 – Parke & Wormell)

And sure enough, says Aelian, not long afterwards they marched out against the Crotoniates and were defeated and their city was obliterated. The killing of envoys and a musician are both elements in this lack of religiosity among the Sybarites but it is not necessarily a reflection or a result of a luxurious lifestyle but rather an indictment of tyranny as a system of government.

Athenaeus was writing at much the same time as Aelian but unlike the latter he is fully absorbed by the misdeeds and evils of the Sybarites. He gives an account of the end of Sybaris, claiming to have used Phylarchus, which was probably from Timaeus,[36] or perhaps Heracleides of Pontus (*FGrH*. 2.199). In his account Athenaeus (12.521 e–f) not only provides the invaluable information about the murder of thirty Crotoniate envoys, but also that the Sybarites turned on their tyrant Telys and his supporters and all were killed, even those who had taken refuge in temples and shrines. This is obviously meant to contrast with the way the Crotoniates had treated the Sybarite exiles in their midst earlier. The death of the tyrant is likely to have occurred after the defeat of the Sybarite army when the Sybarites were hard pressed during the subsequent siege of the city. This violent act against fellow citizens compounded the crime of sacrilege the Sybarites had already committed, and consequently, this blood lust became all too much for the gods and the statue of Hera in its sanctuary averted its gaze (ἀπεστράθη) from the *polis*, a sure signal of impending destruction.[37] The blood that flowed from Hera's fountain became a deluge that was only contained by throwing up bronze doors to prevent this from engulfing the city, itself a portent of its inundation. Historians such as Timaeus also pointed out the *hubris* of the Sybarites in wanting to establish Games in competition with those established at Olympia and that such a gesture was a further insult to the gods.[38]

Because he must already have told the story of Sybaris' end in Book 10 of his history, Diodorus at this point in his narrative is much more concerned to devote a more detailed account of events in the later settlement of Thurii and a discussion of its constitution and laws (12.11.3–19.3). A citizen named as Charondas was chosen to provide laws for the new community, but this philosopher has been wrongly incorporated into this tale for he is considered a contemporary of Solon and hence lived a century or more before the events with which he is supposedly connected.[39] Diodorus either used Charondas in error or used him as a vehicle to discuss laws that are said to owe something to Pythagorean thought. Diodorus or his source probably intended to drawn attention to the link between the thoughts of this man and those of Pythagoras and his followers who remained influential in nearby Croton and plausibly also over Sybaris for some years after its fall. Philosophical considerations therefore also loom large in the fall of Sybaris, which added a certain complexity to the picture, and so it is worth taking some care with what Diodorus has to say since next to Herodotus he provides the earliest available material and his evidence shows some divergence and development from the views of Sybaris now generally held. Diodorus' account of the war between Sybaris and Croton is the sole continuous narrative, such as it is, from any extant historical prose, and this consists of no more than two sentences. The role of Pythagoras in the end of Sybaris is not mentioned at all by Diodorus yet he had played a prominent part in earlier discussion, and indeed there are no allusions to the activities of his followers such as Milo. It does rather look as if the involvement of the philosopher and his circle was deliberately manipulated in order to obscure on the one hand the actions of the Crotoniates and on the other to place the reputation of Sybaris in as negative a light as possible. It is therefore possible to assume that the narrative went something along the lines of a description of the Crotoniates intercepting the invaders at the edge of their *chorē* and once they routed the hubristic Sybarite army they pursued the defeated enemy right up to the fortifications of their city, forced a siege, followed by the successful assault and sack. There was no great and protracted siege of Sybaris as there was, for example, at Tyre by Alexander in

332, which went on for six months. Missing from Diodorus' evidence is the fate of the tyrant Telys, and most remarkably any detail about the flooding of the city. This is a unique fate and it is puzzling that our main source is silent on the issue.

The end of Sybaris has become the supreme act of finality and it is perhaps surprising that Diodorus refers to the city not long afterwards. Under the date 476/5 during the rule of Hieron I at Syracuse he relates that Sybaris was again besieged by the Crotoniates. The Sybarites sent an urgent appeal to Hieron for aid. Hieron, who feared the popularity of his brother Polyzelus, levied troops and placed his brother in command and ordered him to go to the relief of Sybaris, although Diodorus claims (11.48.3–5) in the hope not of saving Sybaris but that his brother would be killed by the Crotoniates. The focus is Hieron's jealousy of his brother and the fate of Sybaris goes unrecorded. Still the important point to consider is that Sybaris was still an identifiable *polis*.[40] And there was another version, written by Timaeus, of this tale, which stated that Polyzelus was actually successful in his expedition and that Croton was defeated.[41] Timaeus probably related both versions and Diodorus chose to recount only one of these. It is also possible that Ephorus had one version and Timaeus another and that Diodorus preferred to give one on this occasion.[42] Whatever the provenance of the story, if the Sybarites were defeated again in the 470s it suggests a reoccupation of the site rather than as Pearson argues that this military activity was directed against former citizens of Sybaris supported by their allies in Laos (near modern Sapri), Scidros (modern Scalea) and perhaps even Posidonia (Paestum). Now it is conceivable that thirty years after its destruction survivors and their families were in a position to mount an expedition to the Crathis Valley with the intention of reforming their old community and that this attempt was repulsed by Croton, which now held this land. Diodorus, however, gives a diametrically opposite version in that Polyzelos was meant to aid the Sybarites in defending their territory and city from an incursion by the Crotoniates. While there may be some confusion with the events of 510, it is more likely that this passage indicates that Sybaris was actually still standing in about 480 and that its new troubles arose from a Crotoniate expansion north and west into the Crathis Valley. Although Croton is not usually regarded as a city that involved itself in territorial adventures because its government of Pythagoreans has been considered pacifist that view is perhaps incorrect and imperial ventures were initiated at least from the 520s and continued down to after 480. And it is probably crucial here to note that Diodorus (8. 21.1–2) had already dealt with Locrian concerns about Croton when he describes their attempts to seek military aid from Sparta, which, however, appears to have been unsuccessful.

This episode given its position in the text may well have occurred at some stage in the late sixth or early fifth century.[43] Still, conflict in the Crathis Valley may also suggest that the Crotoniates had not established complete ascendancy in the area and having allowed their old rival to remain they now considered it expedient to suppress it again.

Diodorus goes on to write that fifty-eight years after the destruction of Sybaris it was repopulated in part by settlers from Thessaly together with surviving Sybarites but that these were driven out by the Crotoniates (11.90.4). This dates to 453/2 and the lack of any link between this and the earlier reference in the same book suggests that the historian was careless in his composition. In 453/2 the Sybarites sent envoys to Sparta and Athens requesting aid to resettle their city and the latter responded positively but the eventual Greek contingent represented many cities from Greece. The despatch of messengers to cities in Greece also points to a substantial number of Sybarites who were clearly far more than just a small displaced band of wanderers. The new settlers joined the Sybarites and established a new town in 444/3, which they named Thurii after a local spring. Civil unrest soon broke out between those of Sybarite origin and the newcomers and the former were killed or again expelled (Diod. 12.11.2). And it was soon after this latest violent episode that the citizens of the newly established *polis* Thurii chose their lawgiver. The usual view, following Diodorus (11.90. 3 and 12.10), is that the citizens of Sybaris who survived the events of 510, or more likely their descendants, tried to re-found the city in about 453 but were unsuccessful in their endeavours and it was only in 444/3 that Thurii was established.[44] The account is obviously flawed and incomplete and it is possible to conclude that as far as Diodorus was concerned Sybaris continued to exist as an entity until it was renamed Thurii. This is an important issue because Aelian (*VH* 3.43) simply states that Sybaris ceased to be, which is precisely what happened when its name was changed. Here is perhaps the crux of the problem: a simple changing of name, a practice that was uncommon among the Greeks, although the Romans later on neither had little nostalgia nor any attachment to former names.[45] There is little that is sentimental in Diodorus' evidence, so why was it that this, on the face of it, a relatively straightforward historical episode, a dispute between Sybaris and Croton probably associated with their common borders in which one came to grief at the hand of its neighbour, a common enough occurrence, should become so embellished? After all elsewhere other scenes of carnage led almost immediately to rebuilding and repopulation and one has only to cite, for example, the case of Miletus destroyed by the Persians in 494/3, but which became a leading member of the Delian League by 479. Eretria, too, was destroyed in 490 but recovered quickly, Plataea was destroyed on a number of occasions, most famously in 427 (Thuc. 3.68), while Thebes suffered multiple spoliation, most notably in 335. The island community of Melos was infamously depopulated in 418, while Corinth and Carthage were sacked in 146. Both Carthage and Corinth were resurrected and enjoyed a long history and great prosperity.[46] Indeed the underlying cause for the end of Sybaris is more commented on than the event itself, especially the flooding of the city, mentioned only by Strabo (6.1.13). Herodotus says only that it was seized by the Crotoniates (5.43, 6.22), and both Diodorus (12.10.1) and Aelian (*VH* 1.19, 3.43) write of destruction without detail, while Athenaeus (Book 12), so avid in his interest of the social habits of its citizens, does not mention the end of Sybaris at all. Strabo then is the sole source for the drowning of Sybaris. Therefore it is conceivable that the destruction at Sybaris was not a particularly dramatic event and the reason is perhaps not that difficult to discover.

Like Diodorus, Strabo (6.1.13) also notes the presence of survivors who actually reclaimed the site and that they were joined here by Athenians and other Greeks who after a dispute with the original Sybarites moved the settlement to where in his time Thurii stood. The problem ever since has been the precise geographical relationship between Sybaris and 'nearby' Thurii Copia, which Diodorus says was at some distance from the original urban centre. The archaeological evidence does not support Diodorus however, for it does not show two easily discernible settlements but one, with a more or less continuous existence. This followed all the intensive interest in the site in the 1960s.[47] According to Strabo, later on Thurii was a flourishing town but when it was faced with threats from both the Lucanians and the Tarentines to safeguard its future the Thurians sought the help of the Romans under whose influence the community subsequently fell.[48]

Athenaeus, writing what is essentially a work devoted to the sorts of topics discussed during dinner parties or symposia, provides further details of the Sybarite life style. He preserves some mention of a liking for wine in festivals (11.484 f), although that is hardly a phenomenon confined to Sybaris. Smindyrides the suitor for Cleisthenes of Sicyon's daughter Agariste appears only briefly (12.511 c), but later on the subject of Sybaris is again raised but this time in much more detail. This material is said to come from a slightly earlier work from the second century AD by Alciphron, in which the luxuries of the Sybarites were clearly the subject of acute appraisal.[49]

Concerning the Sybarites is it necessary to speak? Among them the first of all they had in irons in the baths the carriers of water and other attendants who poured the water so that they could not walk quickly and burn the bathers in their haste. The Sybarites were also the first to ban from their city any trades which made a noise such as blacksmiths, carpenters so that sleep was not to be disturbed. It was even illegal to have a cockerel in the city. (Athenaeus, 12.518 c)

Athenaeus, quoting Timaeus, says that when a citizen of Sybaris was travelling in the countryside and saw farmers digging that man later said to his friends that the mere sight of this exertion had given him a rupture (Athenaeus, 12.518 d). One of the listeners is supposed to have replied that simply hearing of this phenomenon had given him a pain in the side. On another occasion a man from Sybaris visiting Croton, seeing that a citizen was preparing a wrestling ground for some forthcoming event expressed his surprise that there was no slave available to carry out such work, while another had gone to Sparta and been horrified at the austerity of the lifestyle there.[50] Athenaeus, adding examples of popular personal clothing and the ownership of exotic pets or specialized slaves, clearly used Timaeus *in extenso*, and probably almost verbatim, but this is also a sign of the depth and the length of coverage that his source devoted to Sybaris.[51] Athenaeus also gives details he says (12.521 c) he has obtained from Phylarchus, writing slightly later than Timaeus,[52] about the Sybarite women's excessive preparation for festivals, and on the elaborate steps to invent new cuisine. Timaeus is also known to have stated (*FGrH*. 1.205) that the citizens of Sybaris were particularly fond of Milesian wool, which was known to be of the finest quality, and that this economic tie made for a special relationship between the states. Athenaeus notes the extravagant behaviour and lifestyle of the *hippeis* of Sybaris, who are said to have numbered five thousand.[53] He includes here the now famous information about the training of the cavalry.

They even trained their horses to dance at festivals to the sound of the flutes. Now the Crotoniates were aware of this when they went to war with the Sybarites ... and so had musicians in armour play the appropriate tunes so that when the horses heard these they danced away with their riders on their backs and went over to the Crotoniates.

The Sybarites therefore lost their advantage in numbers of cavalry and the battle itself by a clever trick and not by any mastery of the battlefield by their enemy. This kind of subterfuge was not unknown for Polyaenus (7.2.2) relates that Alyattes, the king of Lydia in the sixth century BC, destroyed the cavalry of Colophon by the clever strategy of appearing to favour them above all others in his army. When he was at Sardis with the Colphonian cavalry he announced a generous bonus for their service. These men therefore left their horses and came on foot into the city where they were surrounded and massacred. The details may be different but the result bears more than a passing relationship to the loss of the Sybarite cavalry delivered at the hands of Croton. It was not just the destruction of an important element in the composition of the army but it was also the loss of a whole socio–political stratum since the cavalry represented the wealthiest section of the community and were often the rulers and their families or were the main supporters or opponents of a tyrant like Telys. Some additional information whether true or not suggests that a Sybarite deserter gave the information to the Crotoniates in revenge for some insult, and that at the sound of the music the horses reared and threw their riders causing havoc in the battle and a resounding victory for Croton.[54] Note nonetheless that the five hundred exiles – if indeed there were so many – will have belonged to precisely this section of the Sybarite army and their absence in Croton will have in any case weakened the Sybarite army and could well account for the defeat especially if they also fought on the side on the Crotoniates. Much of the material offered by Athenaeus is, as Morton suggested earlier, not that shocking either to a modern reader or to an ancient audience which was fully used to slavery and strict social hierarchy. But it is also worth remembering that while Sybaris is cited for the peculiar extent of its luxuries and seems to be regarded as the supreme example of such behaviour it is not the sole city or people discussed. Others such as the Etruscans and the Syracusans are noted and both were famous for the standards of their styles of life. However, some of Athenaeus' information is of a more serious nature and needs to be reintegrated into the outline of events which is contained in Diodorus' disjointed narrative. Not only is he the source for the murder of the Crotionate envoys and the death of Telys, but Athenaeus also states that the wealth of Sybaris was based on its land and not any harbour facility which it always lacked (12.519 e–f).

A particular reason for Sybaris' wealth came from the area in which it was situated since the coast alongside the city does not possess good harbours and therefore the produce of the land is consumed locally. The city lies in a hollow [and] enjoys cool mornings and evenings in the summers but is unbearably hot in the middle of the day and encourage[s] the belief that heavy drinking contributed a great deal to health so that it came to be said that if a citizen of Sybaris wanted to enjoy a long life he should look neither on the dawn nor the sunset.

The possession of good lands could just as easily lead to a corruption in the way of life because it brought prosperity and the wealth with which to turn away from simple pleasures, a theme again noted by Athenaeus (12.526f–527 a) referring to the people of Umbria and Thessaly, here using Theopompus as his source, and elsewhere to other cities such as Miletus and Colophon in Ionia.

The sources for Ionian luxury may ultimately be traced all the way back to the early poet Archilochus. Thus note how the Colphonians also declined into luxury says Athenaeus (12.526 a), quoting Phylarchus, but which had appeared in the poetry of Archilochus and Xenophanes.[55] The descent of these Greeks into a life of vice is considered to have happened because of their contact with the Lydians. The Samians also lost their city at the same time as the sack of Miletus by the Persians in 494/3 and was on account of their lack of civic solidarity, which presumably indicates *stasis* in the *polis*. Athenaeus (12.525 f) refers again to Heracleides of Pontus as one of his sources, although the main details of Samian history were well recounted by Herodotus. However, Samos was not destroyed but a faction of the citizen body departed to set up a new home in Sicily first in Messene (Zancle) later in Tyndaris. The situation may not be on the same scale as the fate of Sybaris except that war engulfed all of these states. The destruction of cities on account of an excessive attachment to luxuries and the accompanying lifestyle becomes commonplace for the Archaic Period of Greece (700–480 BC). Croton did not escape either for it is said to have descended into luxury after its victory over Sybaris (Ath. 12.522 a) and also tried to usurp the position of Olympia by establishing its own pan-Hellenic competitions (Ath. 12.522 c). Perhaps this state of affairs coincided with the expulsion of Pythagoras and his followers.[56] The poet Theognis (1103–1104) also refers to the devastation of Magnesia and the Ionian cities of Colophon and Smyrna,[57] caused by the excessive pride or *hubris* of their citizens. Colophon was noted for its wealth and luxury (Arist. *Pol.* 1290[b] 16–17; Ath. 12.526 a–d) while the words of Xenophanes (*FGrH* 81 F66) draw attention to exactly that notorious way of living which made Sybaris famous and its end equally so.[58] Siris (Heracleia) also succumbed to luxury (Ath. 12.523 c), also perhaps after the removal of its powerful neighbour Sybaris. The Samians were also notorious for their addiction to luxury (Ath. 12.526–a), while the luxury loving Milesians were infamous (Ath. 12.523 e–f).[59] None, however, have the baffling end of Sybaris, so we must look further afield for a reason or a guiding hand on this episode.

There is a clear tradition in the literature for civic decline, which is deemed to start very early in the history of the *polis*; witness the evidence of Archilochus, which then pervades the literature right down into at least the second century AD, and still features strongly in the works of Athenaeus and Aelian. It is in part probably introduced by writers as a caveat or warning to their audience, which was the urban political elite, about the prospect of catastrophe that might occur and did occur if they did not abide by civilized behaviour. But what role did the story of the end of Sybaris play in this message? It is obvious from this same literature that Sybaris was not alone in possessing a high standard of living, so was it in any sense exceptional? The site that is acknowledged to be Sybaris is essentially that of a Roman town but many of the artefacts on display at its museum are archaic Greek but taken altogether do not indicate an exceptional level of civilization beyond that appropriate for the end of the sixth century BC. These do not illustrate the existence of a city of fabulous wealth. Moreover, there are no great temple structures to be seen and if Sybaris had been as wealthy as Syracuse, for example, then one could expect to see early examples of peristyle temples as can be seen on Ortygia or at Polichne, both of which possess temples dated to between 610 and 580. These are easily within the time scale that should have been emulated by Sybaris if it possessed the means to do so. Their absence suggests that Sybaris was a city of much more modest means. This would accord well with the assertion that Sybaris' wealth came from the land because this resource provided less wealth than a city such as Syracuse, which had trade as the basis of its economy. Sybaris' lack of a good harbour again points to a smaller and less affluent community than some of its neighbours in the western Mediterranean. The urban topography is hardly impressive while the geographical context is unfavourable for the development of a great city remaining thoroughly waterlogged as it has been since antiquity. There are similarities here with Metapontum, which was also never a great city, but also with the marshy ground at Lysimeleia at the southern end of Syracuse. The fate of Sybaris also has something in common with another city destroyed at nearly the same time. This was Megara Hyblaia in Sicily, destroyed and depopulated by Gelon the tyrant of Syracuse in 480 BC and which was never re-founded.[60] Megara was also a city of modest means without major cult structures or a particularly wealthy site or situation. Its site close to Syracuse made it vulnerable to attack rather like the site of Siris-Heracleia vulnerable to nearby Metapontum.

The date of the fall of Sybaris should also alert us to the possibility of a construct since the date 510/9 BC coincides with the expulsion of tyrants around the Mediterranean, including the tyrant Hippias in Athens and Tarquinius Superbus, the Etruscan king of Rome. It is certainly possibly that Tarquin featured more prominently in some accounts of Sybaris' misfortunes and that his downfall in part was a result of the philosophical inclinations of the powerful group of Pythagoreans at Croton. The surviving material in Diodorus' account is more focussed on constitutional change in

Sybaris-Thurii than on the military events and this may have formed a wider discussion of governmental changes, including those in Athens and Rome. The prominence afforded to Pythagoras at the start of Book 12 of Diodorus' history certainly suggests this possibility. The Etruscan Tarquinii and the Pisistratidae of Athens were expelled for their tyranny and pride (*hubris*), and constitutional governments were created to replace them: in Athens the democratic reforms of Cleisthenes, in Rome, the senatorial-led government inaugurated by Lucius Brutus. In Sybaris the hubristic behaviour of its people was replaced in due course by similarly constitutional rule through the settlement of Thurii.

Besides this, there are clear echoes of the Atlantis myth in the fall of Sybaris with its inundation by the victors. However it should be noted that Helice, the Achaean metropolis of Sybaris, was destroyed by a tsunami following an earthquake in 374/3 BC (Pausanias, 7.24.6). It is now thought by some to be the subject that prompted Plato's ideas of the demise of a city he named as Atlantis in his dialogue the *Timaeus*.[61] It is not difficult to see how the idea transferred itself to Sybaris; an earlier destruction also associated with sacrilegious behaviour and a dramatic watery end was projected back to 510 BC. It is also possible that the idea of destruction by water was first discussed in the Platonic circle in which Heracleides of Pontus, cited by Athenaeus as one of his sources for Sybaris, was prominent. From Plato and Heracleides, who perhaps found the idea among the recorded thoughts of Pythagoras, the episode was recorded as a historical event by Ephorus, and was later much embellished by Timaeus, to be employed and preserved in Diodorus and Athenaeus. It therefore becomes understandable that the end of Sybaris was not particularly sensational to Herodotus, but after Plato's work had circulated widely that the myth began to gather force so that the idea of a city receiving such an appalling end but one that appealed and became the tradition.[62]

There is also another instance of a city being destroyed by water at roughly the same time as Helice, but this occurred at the climax of a siege and appears to be a fully documented historical event. In 385 the city of Mantinea in the central Peloponnese was besieged by the Spartans, which according to Xenophon (*Hellenica*, 5. 2.3) began in the spring. The Mantineans had taken the precaution of filling their granaries in advance and since the Spartans possessed no siege engines a long siege appeared to be in sight. The Spartan king Agesipolis ordered a circumvallation of the city's walls and so trenches and palisades were constructed but realizing that only a lengthy period of attrition was likely to bring about a conclusion employed a quite different tactic of damming the river that ran through the city where it made its exit (*Hell.* 5.2.4–5). The river was running high and quickly began to flood not only the city's streets but also the foundations of its circuit walls. The water soaked into the lower levels of the brickwork and so undermined the upper levels. The Matineans tried all means to shore up their walls and prevent the waters flooding their town but when they saw that nothing more could be done they sent envoys to the Spartans offering peace. Peace came with a price for they were obliged to move themselves into four ancestral villages away from the urban centre of the *polis* and the walls of Mantinea were dismantled only to be rebuilt after Sparta's defeat near the city in 362. At Sybaris there were no ancestral villages into which to disperse the population, but the Crathis and Sybaris rivers, which probably flowed on either side of the circuit walls, could have been diverted not to flood the site but to undermine the fortifications.[63]

A more critical assessment of the geographical evidence also points to clear misperceptions about the events under scrutiny. In 510 the Sybarites are supposed to have fought the Crotoniates in a battle at the River Traeis, and they were met while advancing into the territory of Croton. When Polybius (2.29.1) records events that he says took place at Sybaris and are dated to the mid-fourth century, this has been taken to mean that following a second re-foundation of Sybaris, with the participation of some Thessalians, about 446/5 and after surviving Sybarites had been forced to leave this new town they tried to set up another Sybaris on the Traeis River. According to Diodorus this was destroyed by the Bruttians (12.22.1–2).[64] Whatever the precise chronology of events in the 440s, what is surely indicated here is that the river Traeis was inside the *chorē* of Sybaris and did not belong to Croton, and that the Sybarites were actually advancing to defend their frontier and lands from an invasion coming from the south. Thus the detail of the military campaign has been turned on its head. If the Traeis is the same stream that is called today the Triunti and which flows into the sea just north of modern Rossano (Roscianum), which might have been the new but short-lived community of Sybaris on the Traeis, then it was situated close to the Crathis River.[65] In fact the Sybarite army marched a mere fifteen kilometres (about 5 miles) to meet the Crotoniates. The Crotoniate version of history therefore triumphed in the tradition, and the destruction of Sybaris, put about as one brought upon itself, was in fact the direct result of its neighbour's territorial expansionism.[66] And that act of imperialism must have been supported if not promoted by the Pythagoreans who comprised the dominant faction in Croton for some years and who controlled its government.[67]

Perceptions about systems of government also appear to be deeply rooted in the story of Sybaris' end. At Sybaris there was a tyranny, and at Croton an oligarchy as there had been at Colophon, Corinth and other cities that had suffered destruction. This is an interesting reversal in the general trend since tyrants although they may be charged with many other shortcomings such as cruelty are not often accused of excessive luxury.[68] It is of course possible that Telys became unpopular because he tried to change the lifestyle of the Sybarites from one of peace to one that sought military adventures. The Sybarites seem to have been reluctant soldiers. This also rather turns the tradition on its head, which has a peaceful Croton attacked by aggressive Sybarites, although the lifestyle of the latter was much less warlike than the Crotoniates led by athletes such as Milo.

In the end therefore the blotting out of the physical Sybaris and the creation of its legend was partly the construct of philosophers. The destruction of Sybaris occurred as destruction of cities and peoples most often occurs: because of territorial disputes. Sybaris' weakness lay not in its citizens' sumptuous lifestyle but in its lack of military resources. It is clear enough that Sybaris had less wealth than its neighbours because it was not able to control the trade routes from Etruria, the preserve of Rhegium, nor did it possess exceptional harbours as many other cities, such as Syracuse or Taras possessed. The foundation of settlements by Sybaris along the Tyrrenhian coast, which is usually argued as a sign that it was taking trade overland from Etruria and avoiding any tribute required in the Straits, makes no sense at all unless the goods concerned were small and valuable to be carried on horseback or by mules. There was no sophisticated road network in this period and slow-moving wagons drawn by oxen whose routes were through difficult mountain passes that lie above Poisdonia, Laos and Scidros do not reasonably seem a more profitable way of moving goods than by ship. Anything that required storage in amphoras – grain, oil, wine, perfumes – is therefore excluded,[69] as indeed are natural resources such as timber, minerals and stone; and even woven material was probably too bulky a commodity to easily carry overland in large quantities. Such an overland trade would almost certainly be restricted to precious metal or perhaps dried spices but even together these hardly represent a major factor in overall trade figures.[70] Sybaris was neither the military nor the economic powerhouse of Magna Graecia.

The demise of Sybaris was actually a long one spanning at least two generations and even then it was not remarkable. However, later Roman writers were able to expand on this theme especially noting the coincidence of the date – real or invented – that placed the end of Sybaris in the same year as the fall of tyranny at Athens and the tyrannical kingship at Rome. This congruence is almost certainly invented but became a useful moralizing passage in the hands especially of the writers of the Second Sophistic (second century AD). The connection with Helice is possibly where the idea of an inundation came from but historians will also have known Xenophon's account of the sack of Mantinea. The penalty for sacrilege was drowning as the unfortunate three thousand Phocian prisoners, captured at the battle of the Crocus Field in 353/2 BC, learned to their cost. The Macedonian king Philip II ordered their drowning in the sea for their leaders' sacrilegious use of the treasures at Delphi.[71] No Greeks were likely to flood temple precincts of even sacrilegious fellow Greeks so the tale of the flooding of Sybaris may be dismissed while at the same time the low-lying and marshy nature of the land here could also have contributed to the myth. In conclusion there was, in fact, no dramatic end to Sybaris merely a name change. The end of Sybaris and causes for its destruction eventually engendered so much comment with heavy moralistic overtones that the real history and the battlefield itself was lost even in antiquity to join the ranks of other fabulous events and in the same league as the end of Atlantis, the end of Troy, or even the end of the Minoan Labyrinth.[72]

Chronology

720	Foundation of Sybaris by Achaean settlers (Strabo, 6.1.13)
735/10	Myscellus establishes Croton (Strabo, 6.1.12)
560?	Smindyrides of Sybaris a suitor for Agariste, daughter of Cleisthenes of Sicyon (Herodt. 6.127; cf. Diod. 8.19)
530	Pythagoras becomes a resident of Croton
520/10	Doreius in Italy as a mercenary and dies at Eryx in Western Sicily (Herodt. 5.43–5)
510	Telys the tyrant at Sybaris (Diod. 12.9.2)
	Five hundred most prominent Sybarites exiled who went to Croton (Diod. 12.9.2)
	Telys demands return of exiles but refused
	Thirty Crotoniate envoys go to Sybaris where they are murdered (Ath. 12.521 d–e)
	Crotoniates advances into Sybarite territory
	Battle at the River Traeis and Crotoniate army led by Milo victorious
	Sybarites defeated and besieged
	Telys and his supporters murdered in a coup (Ath. 12.521 e–f)
	Sybaris taken and destroyed by the Crotoniate army (Diod. 12.10.1)
	Milesians mourn the destruction of Sybaris (Herodt. 6.21)
	Hippias expelled from Athens
	Tarquinius Superbus expelled from Rome

490	Zancle renamed Messene
494/3	Sybarites fail to mourn the destruction of Miletus
476/5	Sybaris attacked by Croton and appeals to Syracuse for aid
454/3	Sybaris receives new settlers from Thessaly (Diod. 12.10.2)
445/4	Sybaris renamed Thurii after the spring Thurium (Diod. 12.10.6)
440/30	Herodotus a resident in Thurii
385	Siege and sack of Mantinea
373/2	Destruction by tsunami of Helice

The cavalry of Sybaris

Athenaeus (12.519 b–c) states that in 510 BC Sybaris had no fewer than 5000 cavalry but how does this figure stand up to those numbers given for other city states and kingdoms then and later, and therefore is this number realistic or a gross exaggeration either by this writer or from his source, most likely Timaeus, to enhance the magnitude of this state's power and hence also its fall?

1. The Persian seaborne expedition against Eretria and Athens in 490 consisted of a large cavalry presence, which illustrates that there was no difficulty in the transportation of men and animals across the Aegean. The number of ships is given by Herodotus (6.95) as six hundred, mostly transports for men and horses, but probably smaller than triremes more commonly used in the conflict between the Greek and Persians later. The losses at Marathon are given as 6400 Persians and 192 Greeks (Herodt. 6.117). There were perhaps 10,000 infantry and half that number of cavalry. The power of Sybaris was possibly meant to equate to the might of the Persian Empire.

2. Syracuse in 414/3 BC could muster 1500 cavalry with allies (Thuc. 6.67), which was roughly the same as the total of cavalry in the Athenian expedition (Thuc. 6.31, 6.71, 6.93–94; Lysias, *Polystrat.* 24–27). It should be noted that the Athenian force was the largest ever sent out by Athens.

3. Alexander the Great had just 5500 cavalry at the battle at the Granicus River in 334 and 7000 at Gaugamela in 331.[73] Demetrius, son of Antigonus Monophthalmos, archetypical Hellenistic king and warrior, had approximately 18,000 cavalry in 288 BC, which Bosworth describes as 'prodigious' and probably exaggerated by ancient writers such as Plutarch.[74]

4. Antiochus III at the Battle of Magnesia ad Sipylum in 190 BC is considered by Grainger to have had about 12,000 cavalry, including 6000 cataphracts out of a total of at least 50,000 in his army. Antiochus, one of Rome's great rivals in the Eastern Mediterranean, might well have stood out as worthy

of comparison with Sybaris. Antiochus like the Sybarite tyrant Telys might well have appeared despotic and hubristic. The Romans are said to have had about 5000 cavalry, most of which were allied troops from Pergamum.[75]

5. In 197 Philip V possessed just 2000 cavalry at Cynoscephalae in an army of 20,000.

6. Perseus at Pydna in 168 had 3000 cavalry in an army totalling nearly 30,000.[76]

MAGNA GRAECIA AND SICILY

N
W E
S

R. Tiber

Rome

A d r i a t i c

S e a

Cumae Neapolis

Posidonia

Elea

Metopontum Taras

Scidros

Heracleia Siris

Laos Sybaris

T y r r h e n i a n

S e a

Temesa Croton

Terina

Hipponium

Messene Medma

Eryx Panormus Tyndaris

Segesta Himera Rhegion Locri

Lilybaeum *Mt Etna*

Selinous Tauromenium

Heracleia Minoa Naxos *I o n i a n*

Akragas Catane *S e a*

Neapolis Leontinoi

Gela Megara Hyblaia

Camarina Syracuse

0   100 km

0   100 miles

MAGNA GRAECIA

N
W E
S

*Adriatic
Sea*

MAGNA
GRAECIA

Cumae
Pithecusae
Posidonia
Elea
Scidros
Laos
Metopontum
Taras
Heracleia Siris
Sybaris
Bay of Sybaris

*Tyrrhenian
Sea*

Croton
Temple of Hera

Hipponium
Lipari Islands
Messene

*Aegades
Islands*
Eryx
Panormus
Locri
Segesta
Rhegion
Lilybaeum
SICILY
Naxos
The Straits
Selinous
Heracleia Minoa
*Ionian
Sea*
Akragas
Catane
Megara Hyblaia
Neapolis
Gela
Syracuse
Camarina

0   100 km
0   100 miles

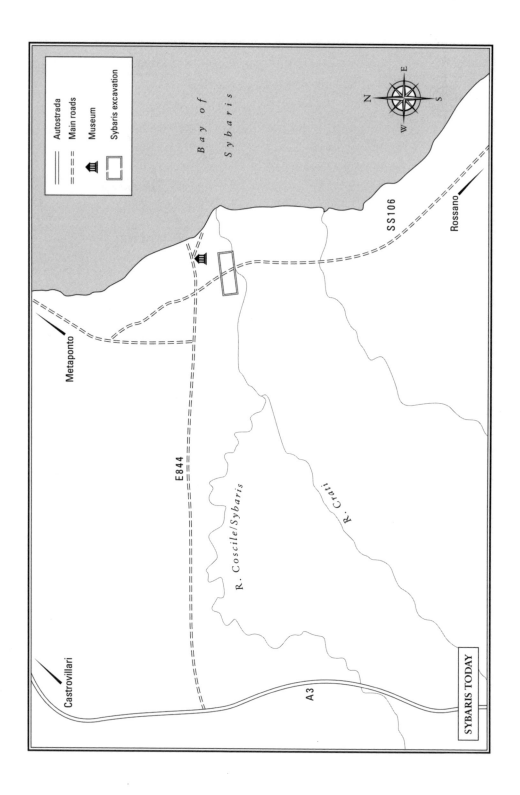

SYBARIS TODAY

Bay of Sybaris

Metaponto

Castrovillari

E844

A 3

R. Coscile/Sybaris

R. Crati

SS106

Rossano

Autostrada
Main roads
Museum
Sybaris excavation

N E
W S

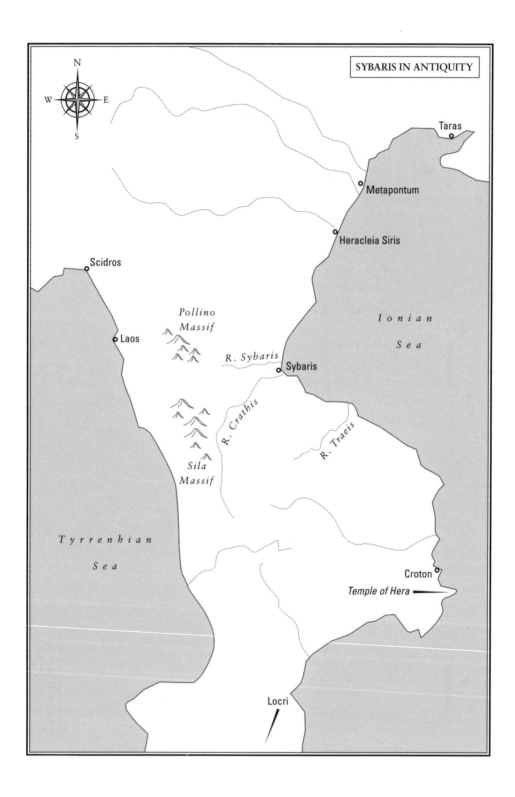

SYBARIS IN ANTIQUITY

N
W · E
S

Taras

Metapontum

Heracleia Siris

Scidros

I o n i a n

S e a

Pollino
Massif

Laos

R. Sybaris   Sybaris

R. Crathis

R. Traeis

Sila
Massif

T y r r e n h i a n

S e a

Croton

Temple of Hera

Locri

Chapter Two

The Athenian Siege of Syracuse (414–413 BC)

In my opinion, this was the greatest achievement of any Greek city in this war indeed in the entire history of the Greeks. It was at once the most glorious event for the victors and at the same time the most catastrophic for the losers. The Athenians were utterly beaten and they suffered on an unimaginable scale. Their destruction was complete and they lost their warships, their army indeed everything was lost and few ever returned to their homes. These were the events in Sicily. (Thucydides, 7.87)

In his history of the Second Peloponnesian War' (431–404 BC) Thucydides devotes a substantial amount of space and detail to an episode that took place far away from mainland Greece or indeed the Peloponnese.[1] This was the expedition of the Athenians – their second – to Sicily. In modern editions this amounts to almost two of the eight books, into which his history of the Peloponnesian war is divided; in research the detail evident reveals a serious historian at work on a composition he wanted to last for all time.[2] The history of Thucydides was never completed and breaks off abruptly in 411 BC towards what would have been the end of an eighth book.[3] Therefore, out of a total of twenty years of warfare between the two greatest states in Greece a full quarter of the content deals with rather less than two years of Sicilian affairs, an extraordinary focus that in itself is a compelling reason to analyse the account in some detail. Even more riveting is the disastrous siege of Syracuse in which the besieging Athenians and their allies were defeated by numerically smaller forces and much less experienced military command and troops. The question here is why were the Athenians thwarted in their objective, and why did the defeat became such a disaster with far reaching consequences for the war? The defeat of the combined forces of the Delian League, in reality those of the Athenian Empire, first in the Great Harbour of Syracuse and then on land when its army of at least 40,000 men endeavoured to escape from outside the city in late September or early October 413 BC has achieved notoriety and become one of the seminal events in ancient history. It brought great fame to the winners of this Herculean contest and caused ultimately the defeat of Athens in its war with Sparta. Why then did this siege fail, should the expedition have begun in the first place, and was there ever a point when the Athenians could have withdrawn with their pride intact, or did the result become inevitable? These questions must also be addressed in this discussion tracing one of the most famous of ancient battlefields.

Sicily and Syracuse, in particular, came to the attention of the Athenians as early as the fifth year of the war when Thucydides (3.86) states that towards the end of that summer they sent a squadron of twenty triremes to Leontinoi in response to a legation from that city complaining of aggression from Syracuse. The Greek cities in Sicily and Magna Graecia were composed of two basic ethnic groups – Ionians and Dorians. The Ionians were related to the Athenians while the Dorians were originally from the Peloponnese; and Thucydides makes the point that the Dorian cities of Sicily and Magna Graecia supported Sparta in the war but had not joined physically in the fighting. In the western Mediterranean this ethnic difference, however, was the source of constant hostility. Thus Leontinoi could draw support from its Ionian neighbours Camarina, Naxos, Messene and Italian cities such as Rhegium, while Syracuse, the largest city on the island, had allies among states such as Akragas in Sicily and the Locrians in Italy. The Athenian generals were Laches and Charoeades, and the ostensible aim to bring aid to the people of Leontinoi who were under siege from the Syracusans. However, the real reason says Thucydides was to prevent the export of grain from Sicily to the Peloponnese. The interior of Sicily was highly fertile and produced a surplus of cereals, which was exported via the harbours of the Greek cities which were mostly situated on the coast.

Leontinoi was an exception to that phenomenon and was one of the few Greek towns to be established to exploit the local agricultural wealth rather than the incoming and outgoing traffic at the coast. Although on a river Leontinoi lay some twenty kilometres inland (roughly 13 miles). It was also a small community and overshadowed by its far more powerful neighbour Syracuse a mere thirty-five kilometres (21 miles) to the south-east. Leontinoi already had a chequered history of domination by the rulers of Syracuse, but the Syracusans had rid themselves of their autocrats in 466 and since then been a democracy like Athens. In much the same way as the Athenians saw themselves as dominant in the Aegean, the Syracusans regarded themselves as the major power in Sicily and beyond. The Athenian generals sent to help the citizens of Leontinoi were also briefed, so Thucydides says, with ascertaining the possibility of supplanting Syracusan primacy with their own. The Athenian fleet went first to Rhegium on the Straits of Messina, which they continued to use as a base, and were involved in an expedition against the people who lived on the island of Lipari who were allied with

Syracuse.[4] The Liparaeans refused to break their alliance with the Syracusans and presumably took measures to withstand a siege. The acropolis at Lipari on a high rocky outcrop would have been well fortified and not easily invested especially if as seems likely the Athenians lacked siege equipment.[5] Although the Athenians and their allies looted and destroyed as much as they could they were unable to gain an outright victory and sailed away as the onset of winter brought an end to the fighting (Thuc. 3.88).

The following spring saw the Athenians actively supporting their Sicilian allies, but Thucydides intimates that there was a great deal of instability on the island at this time. Moreover he also says that he will concentrate only on the events that he considers relevant to his subject. Laches had been obliged to take sole command following the death in battle of his co–general. Rather than relieve Leontinoi, however, the Athenians instead appear to have been intent in strengthening their position at the Straits. The fleet went to Mylae, a town on the north coast of the island and which possessed a population made up mostly of Messenians. During the early part of the fifth century Messene had been united with Rhegium under the rule of the tyrant Anaxilas who named the city after his birth place in the Peloponnese. After his death Messene broke away from Rhegium and seems to have been quite independent in its choice of allies. By 427 Messene was quite clearly an ally of Syracuse hence the Athenian interest not least in that a successful attack on Messene would mean domination of the Straits which would be denied to the Syracusans. The citizens of Mylae with troops from Messene tried to ambush the Athenians when they made land, but the plan backfired and they were defeated, the town was besieged and it quickly surrendered. The Athenian fleet of twenty triremes would have easily outnumbered the small defending force from a town the size of Mylae even with its Messenian allies. These probably had fewer than 2000 soldiers altogether while the Athenians would have carried six hundred hoplites aboard their ships and the rowers, 170 to each trireme, would also be armed as peltasts, giving a total number of combat troops of at least 4000 (600 + 3400) since Thucydides does not mention whether or not the Rhegians also provided ships and troops on this occasion. The victors immediately marched on Messene and forced the Mylaeans and Messenians they had just captured to accompany them. Messene surrendered without a fight and became an Athenian ally (Thuc. 3.90). Laches had very quickly and with few casualties accomplished an initial but highly strategic objective: the command of the Straits and a secure foothold in Sicily.

From there Athenian attention moved much closer to Leontinoi with an attack on the town of Inessa, also known as Etna, on the southern slopes of the towering volcano a few kilometres inland from Catane (Thuc. 3.103). The inhabitants of this strongly fortified centre were probably a mix of mercenaries employed by the former Syracusan tyrant Hieron I (480–467 BC) and local Sicels, while a contingent of Syracusan troops was also present.[6] The town was also situated in the main north–south route to Leontinoi and hence its acquisition would mark another important tactical advance by the Athenians not only in their relief of their Ionian allies but in establishing a viable and important presence in eastern Sicily. However, although Laches was quite clearly following a very sensible and sound plan the lack of manpower and siege equipment became fully apparent. The Athenians were simply unable to take Inessa and Laches decided to withdraw by land. As they did so the garrison inside Inessa burst out and attacked the Athenians who were posted in the rear of the column as it moved north and after suffering heavy losses they arrived back in Messene. This was a setback for Athenian ambitions and Leontinoi remained isolated. Still the Athenians late in the summer took their fleet to Locri where they had some minor successes against this stalwart ally of Syracuse perhaps as a diversionary tactic. They withdrew to Messene where the arrival of winter far from reducing activity prompted the Athenians into a new venture against Himera, which was situated further along the north coast of the island and to the west of Mylae. This was clearly aimed at removing the Syracusan presence from the north of Sicily and was an operation carried out with the support of some Sicel communities from the interior.[7] Although the Athenians had some successes and carried off some plunder they were not able to take the city and maintain a permanent presence here. At the end of 426 there was a major eruption of Etna, the first in fifty years says Thucydides (3.116), which may have been witnessed by the Athenians on this expedition, but it may also have been extracted from the history of Antiochus.

During the winter the Athenians sent out a new general with reinforcements (Thuc. 3.115). Pythodorus took command and Laches after a mostly competent spell was relieved. The citizens of Leontinoi and perhaps some of the Sicels, possibly prompted by Laches, had travelled to Athens to request an increase in aid.[8] The Athenians, beset with the after effects of the plague which had destroyed the population responded cautiously but positively voting for an extra forty triremes to join the twenty already in Rhegium. Instead of sending out another 10,000 men who represented a substantial proportion of the total Athenian naval arm, an exploratory force that Thucydidies describes as a 'few ships' accompanied the new *strategos* to Rhegium with a view to reinforcing him if the circumstances were considered favourable.

Unfortunately, the main event of the next year (425 BC) was the surrender of 120 Spartiate hoplites on the island of Sphacteria near Pylos to the Athenian forces led by Cleon and Demosthenes. It was such a momentous occasion that it overshadows all other events for that year, including the continuing hostilities in Sicily and southern Italy to which Thucydides gives little coverage and much less coherence than he does to other episodes in his work (3.115–116, 4.24–25). What is clear is that the expedition to aid Leontinoi did not go according to plan mainly because the fleet decreed for that sector of the war was diverted to help the Athenian efforts against the Spartans in the Peloponnese. It shows that in the early years of the war while the strategic importance of Sicily and Sycause may have been recognized in Athens it was other areas: the Peloponnese, Ambracia, Boeotia and the Hellespont which called for more immediate attention.

Pythodorus was either a commander with less ability or plainly more reckless than Laches for his immediate action, an attack on Locri, ended in defeat. Since the winter was setting in he returned to Rhegium (3.115) having suffered some losses, although Thucydides suggests that these were not of major concern. For the following campaigning season Thucydides provides only a précis. The Messenians seems again to have allied themselves with the Syracusans,[9] and the latter were also equipping a fleet of warships and intended to launch an attack on the Athenians and Rhegians. At the same time the Locrians in response to the attack made on them in the previous autumn now invaded the territory of Rhegium. The Syracusans were keen to engage their enemy as soon as possible because they knew that the Athenians currently had fewer ships but that they would soon be reinforced. A successful outcome for Syracuse would be a blockade of Rhegium and control of the Straits and would almost certainly mean that the Athenian involvement in the region would be ended or put on hold seeing they had many pressing concerns elsewhere. The Syracusans had roughly thirty ships against a combined Athenian–Rhegian fleet of twenty-four. It was late in the afternoon and the unpredictable currents of the Straits evidently played a role in the fight, which began as a result of one of the Syracusan vessels running into difficulties trying to force a passage through the Straits.[10] At dusk the two sides separated to their respective harbours, Messene and Rhegium, with a single Syracusan ship lost. Soon after this skirmish the Locrians retreated presumably having first plundered and looted as much as they could. The Athenians appear to have still held Mylae since when the Syracusans moved north around Cape Pelorus with both naval and land forces they were intercepted by the Athenians along the coast. The Athenians lost one ship and withdrew. The Syracusans probably followed them back into the Straits where they sank another Athenian trireme. The Syracusans therefore came away a little better off in this fighting, although they actually had more ships but the Athenian fleet had far more experience. The Athenian fleet is next placed at Camarina in the far south where it had been summoned because there were fears that a coup was to be staged in the city, which would result in it being handed over to Syracuse. Thucydides does not discuss the outcome of this expedition and the subversive elements to which he refers were probably suppressed. In the meantime the Messenians had invaded the territory of Ionian Naxos and besieged the city. Some Sicels came to the support of the Naxians who made a sudden sortie from their walls and routed the Messenians who withdrew with heavy losses. The Athenian fleet made a timely appearance at the harbour of Messina on its return from Camarina. The defeat of the Messenian infantry was followed by a counterattack in which the citizens of Leontinoi played a major role – Thucydides (4.25) does not mention whether the Naxians also participated in this move – but the Athenian fleet took control of the famous harbour of Messene.[11] The Messenians aided by some Locrian troops, which had been sent in support, now made a sortie of their own and took the Ionian Greeks and their Sicel allies by surprise and caused heavy loss of life but the Athenians beached their fleet and came up quickly to join the fracas and the Messenians had to retreat into the city also receiving heavy losses. And so says Thucydides (4.25) the Greeks of Magna Graceia and Sicily continued to fight with one another but the Athenians played no further role in this strife. The historian does not say why the Athenians seemed disinclined to fight but it should be assumed that the forty warships promised for this theatre of the war never arrived and the attrition caused by several engagements meant that that Pythodorus did not see any useful motive in continuing. However, the Athenian fleet at Rhegium was not yet recalled to Greece.

Thucydides only returns to event in Sicily (4.58) when he relates the events of 424 and after the Athenian triumph at Sphacteria and elsewhere in Greece. The towns of Gela (Dorian) and Camarina (Ionian) are situated about fifty kilometres (30 miles) from one another on Sicily's south coast. Thucydides relates that envoys from these towns met and decided on a peace treaty. This news resonated across the island because its people had become weary of the incessant warfare, which had reached a stalemate. Therefore, a call went out for a more general congress of the Sicilian Greeks and this convened at Gela where representatives had free rein to complain about their treatment by other states. Thucydides gives what he says is a speech (Thuc. 4.59–64) delivered by a Syracusan envoy named Hermocrates,[12] a figure who came to play a major role in the political and military life of the city in the following two decades, especially during its conflict with Athens.[13] The speech is full of the sorts of themes to be expected in such a context, the rights and wrongs of going to war with one's neighbours and the uncertainty of how future times would treat each city, but the overriding message is the threat to the independence of the Sicilian states from the ambitions of the powerful Athenians. If Athens was allowed to achieve domination in that region it would remove the individual freedoms of the communities there with the result that to go to war for whatever the reason would depend on the judgement of an outsider. And that is perhaps most remarkable of the speech with its emphasis on a Sicilian identity and freedom outside the control of essentially a foreign power. What is disguised of course is that Syracuse wanted to have the role to which Athens aspired, but at least Syracuse was a Greek Sicilian city, as no doubt the envoys would have reflected upon. Hermocrates also made the point that Athenian intervention in the region had nothing to do with ethnicity but blatant imperialism and that Ionian and Dorian communities would be equally suppressed by the new dominant power. Therefore, the Sicilians should unite in resistance and circumvent such an event occurring by making a general peace between them. This was agreed and all the cities retained what they possessed so that none lost or gained by this new treaty. The Athenian commanders were summoned and told that this had happened and that the treaty also applied to them so that they had nothing more to do in southern Italy or Sicily. The Athenians agreed and their fleet left Rhegium and returned to Athens where the *strategoi* Pythodorus and Sophocles were subsequently prosecuted for collusion and corruption and exiled while the third general Eurymedon was fined.[14] The Athenian *demos* had not given permission for the expedition to cease and it was evidently believed that the generals had been bribed to leave the area. Once the expedition was back in Athens, however, Sicilian affairs were forgotten.

The defeat and death of the Athenian commander Cleon and his opposite number the Spartan general Brasidas at Amphipolis brought about another stalemate in the more general warfare around Greece, which resulted in the peace of Nicias in 421. This could never have been a permanent state of affairs since so little was solved but it allowed both sides in the conflict a breathing space before war inevitably broke out again. In the interim the Athenians again began to look in earnest at Sicilian affairs. In 415, again at the request of allies in Sicily, this time the Elymian community at Segesta, the question of intervention in Sicily was discussed openly. At the time Segesta was at loggerheads with its close neighbour the Greek city of Selinous over a disputed frontier. Selinous, although originally an Ionian foundation, was allied with Syracuse. Segesta had no obvious allies in the region since the Carthaginians who had a number of trading posts around the coast of western Sicily appear to have been disinterested in further involvement on the island after their disastrous reverse at Himera in 480.[15] The Segestaeans sent envoys to Athens to plead for aid not because they had before possessed any alliance between them, but rather drawing on recent events in Sicily, they wanted to warn of the dangers of the growth in Syracusan power.[16] These envoys emphasized the point that the Athenians had sent aid to Leontinoi because of ethnic links but since then that city had fallen to the Syracusans and Segesta, it was claimed, through its quarrel with Selinous (modern Selinunte), would be the next city to be added to the list of Sicilian communities brought under the control of Syracuse. The Athenians were not particularly interested in Segesta, which was small and relatively insignificant, but going to its aid appealed to their sensitivities and wishing to appear to be the defender of the weak against the strong. More important, however, was the possibility of defeating Syracuse and subjugating the Syracusans to the rule of the Athenian Empire, and if Syracuse then the whole of Sicily would follow.

The plan was hugely audacious and ill–conceived, says Thucydides at the start of his coverage of this latest episode in the Peloponnesian War.

In the winter of the same year the Athenians decided to sail once more to Sicily with greater forces than those Laches and Eurymedon had commanded and if at all possible to conquer the island. The Athenians were unaware of the island's size and its population either Hellenic or native and they did not understand that they were about to undertake a war which was almost on the same scale as their recent war with Sparta. (Thuc. 6.1)

As he had done before in his previous introduction to affairs in the west, the historian, again making extensive use of Antiochus of Syracuse, gives a quite detailed account of the foundation and early history of many of the Greek Sicilian cities and their neighbours. The extent of this information (Thuc. 6.2–6) should alert the reader to the enormous nature and status of the venture that was about to take place. First, however, Thucydides tells his reader that there were as many critics as supporters of this new proposal, which had to be voted upon by the citizen assembly. This much becomes clear from Thucydides' discussion of the public debate which followed. The Athenians had initially sent out a legation to explore the possibility of an alliance with Segesta and its members had been lavishly entertained on their arrival so much so that they left under the impression that the Segesteans were wealthy and would be able to pay for any military support they might receive. The Segestaeans had hoped that this would help allay the fears of any doubters although Thucydides makes it quite plain that the scale of the entertainment provided for the Athenians did not at all represent fairly the financial state of Segesta, which was really quite impoverished as events later showed.[17] The Athenian legates reported what they had seen while certain

Segestaeans who had accompanied them brought sixty talents of silver bullion, which once coined would be enough to outfit a fleet of sixty triremes for one month (Thuc. 6.8).[18] This was enough to impress the citizen assembly, which voted to send help, providing the people of Segesta paid for the upkeep of the fleet, which was to be a sizeable contingent with three commanders. The generals or *strategoi* elected for the expedition were all well experienced with many years' command between them: Nicias, the architect of the recent peace agreement with Sparta,[19] Alcibiades, son of Cleinias and a nephew of Pericles, and Lamachus.[20] They were instructed by the citizen assembly – the *ecclesia* – to bring help to Segesta, to free Leontinoi from Syracusan domination and to see to any other business that might be to the advantage of Athens.

Nevertheless, objections were raised by Nicias at the next meeting of the assembly, which Thucydides says took place just five days later and was meant to assign supplies for the fleet and agree a timetable for its departure. But Nicias who was unhappy about being made general of an expedition that he considered had a highly doubtful outcome chose this moment to try and persuade the citizen body to reverse its decision. Thucydides (6. 9–14) gives Nicias a speech in which the general outlined his objections to lending such substantial support for Segesta, although it was not quite appropriate for him to do so at that stage. At once, the position of the speech alone highlights Nicias' reserved and cautious disposition, which made him slow to act. He appears rather passive by nature, and this may account for his delay in declaring his pessimism about the people's decision for five days before finally deciding to speak against it when in fact he should have spoken up when the project was first mooted. Thucydides is laying the foundation for the vacillating leadership, which became so exposed and so vulnerable later in the expedition and especially towards the climax of the long siege at Syracuse.

Nicias' approach was partly humble, the personal honour was great, but he considered that it was to the advantage of the people that the question of an expedition to Sicily should be revisited. He fully understood the enthusiasm for the venture since there was no immediate threat to Athens in Greece but the absence of such a significant military element might just provoke an attack from unexpected quarters. Moreover, the Athenians were indulging in a high risk strategy to send so large a force so far from its home. And even if they were entirely successful and they established their rule throughout Sicily it would nonetheless involve immense energy and resources to maintain this new addition to their empire, and he doubted whether Syracuse was quite such a potential enemy as the Segestaeans made out. Then perhaps the real motive for the speech emerges as Nicias launched an attack on one of the other elected generals, Alcibiades, whom he suggested sought this command in order to make profits from any victories, but that his advice was rash and to the detriment of the Athenian state. In fact, Thucydides also suggests the relatively young Alcibiades was surrounded by youthful supporters while Nicias' friends were all older and possessed more experience in public and military affairs.[21] His advice is that the Sicilians should take care of their own affairs and that Segesta, which had begun a war without consulting Athens, should also make its own peace with the Selinuntines. He ended his speech by calling for a debate on the issue.

The debate, which probably took place in the open on the Pnyx beneath the Acropolis, was evidently allowed for Thucydides (6.16–18) says that most citizens remained in favour of the expedition and he gives the response of Alcibiades who had been both Nicias's target and had obviously been one of the most enthusiastic movers of this expedition. Alcibiades had achieved fame at an early age, although he could not attain the position of general beneath the age of thirty, partly because of his family connections with Pericles, who was held in high esteem, partly by his own charisma, and partly through his wealth which he certainly employed to accelerate his public career.[22] Thucydides says that while he spoke to deflect the invective delivered against him by Nicias whom he disliked, he was also concerned that the expedition should proceed because he cherished the idea of conquering not only Sicily but also Carthage and by extending the Athenian Empire would also enhance his own position. This ambition and the conspicuous consumption in which he indulged and which was easily observed in him proved to be his own undoing says Thucydides because the people came to distrust him and believed he intended making himself tyrant.[23] Therefore, although he was a talented and vigorous general, he was so feared especially after his flight to Sparta in 414 that commands were rather granted to others less able than him after his return from exile. And so, Thucydides maintains, Athens lost the war with Sparta. There is more than a grain of truth in this assertion, although the picture is much more complex, but the expedition to Sicily which he strongly favoured was a part of the undoing of Athens.

Thucydides has Alcibiades arguing that he was capable of the command to which he had been elected and that the citizen body should not change its mind about the undertaking and that he was confident that a victory could be achieved over the Sicilian Greeks. Alcibiades argued that the states in Sicily were unstable with heterogeneous populations that made them weak and lacking in purpose. Furthermore, this disunity of purpose meant that they were also unlikely to act together in the face of a foreign attack – quite contrary to the peace agreement of 424 between the Sicilian states it should however be noted – and that individual cities would make treaties with the Athenians when they arrived on the island.[24] Alcibiades went on to argue that the status and number of their hoplites was far less than the Sicilian Greeks claimed, while the Sicilians who were not of Greek origin would almost certainly join forces with the Athenians. Moreover, the Athenians need not have any fear of attack by the Spartans and their allies since there would still be more than sufficient forces to address such threats while this expedition was absent. He ended his speech by reiterating that there was no valid reason to overturn the previous decision to send out a fleet and armed forces to Sicily and that the Athenians were not looking to have new allies in communities such as Segesta but, by interfering in the food supply which was shipped to the Peloponnese from cities such as Syracuse, their presence on the island would be a source of constant concern for their enemies. Finally, Alcibiades stressed the point that success overseas would strengthen their position in Greece.

Alicibiades was supported also by the envoys from Segesta and certain exiles from Leontinoi. Nicias, sensing that his cause stood no chance of winning over the votes of the assembly, made a second speech in which he tried a different tack. He knew that the Athenian citizens were often quite cautious when it came to using public funds for financing even state business so he argued that from his personal knowledge of the Sicilian Greeks – he was known, and had guest friends, at Syracuse – their resources far exceeded those claimed by Alcibiades and if they wished to make a victory more certain they would need to allow the financing of a much stronger force. The outcome was actually the opposite of what Nicias expected, however, for the citizen assembly now fired up with even greater enthusiasm for this venture and says Thucydides the prospect of great wealth from the plunder voted for even more ships and troops for the command. It is very likely that Nicias was nonplussed by this result but being a skilled politician did not show his feelings. Yet his misgivings and the fact that he simply did not wish to have this command were personal weaknesses, which became pervasive, resurfaced time and time again, and contributed to an absence of bold leadership when it was desperately needed to retrieve some positive conclusion from the expedition.[25]

The Athenians now in a frenzy of patriotic fervour took Nicias at his word and recommendation and voted a hundred triremes, a minimum of 5000 Athenian and allied hoplites, plus as required lightly armed troops from as far afield as Crete (Thuc. 6.25). Indeed the *demos* gave the three generals almost *carte blanche* to arrange matters as they considered best. There was certainly a buzz in the city, which was suddenly interrupted by a scandal that nearly rocked the community to its foundations. The 'Mutilation of the Herms' duly described by (Thuc. 6.27–29) has become one of the most sensational incidents in all of Greek history. The Herms (*Hermai*) were rather simple rectangular blocks of stone topped with a bust of the god Hermes, often with the male genitals at roughly halfway down the length. These were commonly found at crossroads, most public and private buildings, including temple complexes, since Hermes was the god of highways and boundaries and his statue brought good luck to those who paid it due respect. To mistreat a Herm was to invite bad luck. Therefore, for the citizens of a city to wake up one morning to find many of its Herms defaced was to cause profound offence and much anxiety not least since it would quickly have been voiced that this profanation might predict a disastrous end to the plan to attack Syracuse. There were several suspects, and it should be noted here that the extent of the damage was probably less than is sometimes portrayed simply because so few individuals were regarded as being responsible for what is presented as a vast outrage. The affair certainly grew in magnitude because it occurred just before the Athenian forces were about to depart for Sicily, and mainly because one of those accused was Alcibiades. Various fifth columnists acting for Syracuse or Sparta were considered potential culprits but it was informers who declared that Alcibiades and a group of his friends were seen out late on the night in question in high spirits and possibly up to mischief.

Alcibiades naturally denied the accusation in the strongest possible terms and offered to stand trial on any charges immediately arguing that he could not undertake so important a command with such a cloud hanging over him. The charge regarding the Herms was obviously vague at best and politically motivated. So-called eye-witnesses whom Thucydides describes as either slaves or foreign residents (metics) could not place Alcibiades at the scene, but they did describe riotous and sacrilegious behaviour by young men said to be friends of the general who may have aided and abetted this mischief. The political opponents of Alcibiades who wanted to exploit the affair and wished to see him eclipsed as a force in Athenian public life knew that he would be acquitted of any serious offence if brought to trial immediately worked hard to see Alcibiades depart with the expedition. It was decided that if he had charges to answer he could be recalled.

The allies who were sending detachments to join the fleet were instructed to meet at Corcyra (Corfu), but the main Athenian component sailed together (Thuc. 6.30) from the Piraeus in front of much of the city's population, which had come down to the harbour to bid it well. After the usual sacrifices were made, the departure was announced on horns by the heralds and the entire fleet rowed out of the Piraeus together. There were sixty warships and forty transport triremes and the warships raced one another across the stretch of sea to the island of Aegina intent on making good time to meet the rest of the fleet.[26] Thucydides says that this display, the most expensive recorded to that time, was regarded as a true indication of the might of Greece and of Athens in particular, but that it was not much greater in terms of numbers than other expeditions that had left the Piraeus in recent years.[27] However, the fleet and armed forces collected to sail for Sicily, if not the furthest expedition in terms of distance from Athens, was certainly in terms of financial burden and commitment, the heaviest.[28] This was unique and is worth bearing in mind as the events unfolded later. The problem of communications and logistics over such a long distance in the ancient world meant that overall strategies in a state such as Athens, which were determined by the decision-making bodies of the democracy, took time to reach the front. This caused delays and confusion that added to what became an unimaginative leadership.

Syracuse was also governed by a democracy at this time so there were regular assemblies of citizens in which no doubt the news was first heard. But, says Thucydides, it was some time because any credence was placed on these reports, which is surprising perhaps since rumours of an impending invasion would have travelled quickly even if the event itself was much slower to happen. Merchant shipping between Sicily and mainland Greece would have taken as little as three days in fine weather and a favourable breeze by the direct crossing of the Ionian Sea, and perhaps only a week, or ten days at most, if a more cautious captain kept his vessel hugging the Sicilian coast to Messene, then called at the harbours along the Italian coast as far as Tarentum before crossing to Greece by the shortest route via the southernmost point of the Adriatic Sea to Epirus. The Athenians voted the funds for the expedition several weeks if not some months before its departure. Rumours would have been followed by concrete information just as quickly as the trade allowed. However, it should be noted that a literary device is probably intended by the historian here for just as the thought of an invasion was at first disbelieved in Syracuse, so too at the conclusion of the account of the siege the disaster that befell the Athenians was initially equally dismissed at Athens.[29] Thucydides says that numerous meetings were held until one in which Hermocrates, already a leading citizen in the previous hostilities with Athens and by now certainly highly influential in the community, came forward to give his opinion about the situation. Thucydides (6.33–35) again gives the speaker material appropriate for the occasion and incorporates the sorts of sentiments likely to have been aired aloud but obviously what we have here is a highly stylized composition that reflects public discussions occurring over a longer time and which involved many more speakers than Hermocrates in this supposedly single session. Notwithstanding the creativity of writer and his text, here Hermocrates advised his fellow citizens not to treat the news of Athenian ambitions as idle nonsense and to sit back nonchalantly but that they must instead prepare themselves for a possible invasion. They should at once seek allies in Sicily, Italy, Sparta and Corinth, and send representatives even to Carthage, and he also urged the Syracusans to launch all available warships and to sail to meet the Athenians at Tarentum and force them to return to Greece even before they have set sight on the island.[30] He suggested that if the Syracusans took the fight to the Athenians they would probably not venture further than Corcyra and that such a bold strategy would make their enemy rethink theirs and perhaps lose interest in the idea of attacking Sicily. Whatever decision the citizens of Syracuse decided, declared Hermocrates as he concluded his speech, they should be fully aware that 'the Athenians are coming to attack us, they are already en route, they will soon be at our door!' (Thuc. 6.34).

Many did not believe Hermocrates and considered him a scaremonger, while others thought that he had an ulterior motive that disguised a desire to become still more influential in the city. A favourite of the citizen body, a certain Athenagoras, spoke against the plans put forward by Hermocrates saying that the Athenians were unlikely to leave Greece because they would find attacking so strong a city as Syracuse a daunting prospect. He pointed out quite rightly that the Athenians would not be able to field as strong a force as they might in Greece for they could not transport a sufficient number of horses for their cavalry, and therefore would be outnumbered greatly by the strong Syracusan cavalry. Moreover, since they came by sea they would possess fewer heavily armed infantry than was available to the Syracusans.[31] The speech concentrates on whipping up the fear of the socio–political elite to which Hermocrates evidently belonged. Athenagoras was suggesting that if Hermocrates or any among his circle of friends or allies were granted wider military powers by the people he or they might be tempted to stage a coup and install an oligarchic government. When this speaker had finished delivering his harangue and more speakers came forward to join in the debate one of the generals who seems to have been acting as president of the meeting or its convenor intervened and brought the proceedings to a close. He stated that such arguments would not easily reach a sensible conclusion and it was better if suitable preparations were made and that it would be sensible for the Syracusans to take reasonable precautions in case the rumours of the Athenian approach proved to be correct.

The Athenians rendezvoused with their allies at Corcyra and the fleet was divided into three squadrons each commanded by one of the three generals (Thuc. 6.42). This allowed some independence of action and meant that they need not always sail together in one convoy, which would impose unnecessary restrictions on where they might land for supplies, especially water. An advance flotilla was sent out with instructions to ascertain which cities on their route would prove friendly and ordered to return as soon as possible with the information. The summer will have been well advanced by the time the Athenian fleet left Corcyra. Thucydides gives the complement as 134 triremes and two Rhodian pentekonters. The total number of rowers, some of whom would have fought as lightly armed troops is not given by the historian, but would have been nearly 23,000 men, with 5,100 hoplites.[32] In the transports there were just thirty horses for the cavalry, far too few for them to be an effective force in battle conditions and must mean that most of the cavalrymen – the *hippeis* – probably in total between 500 and 750 had no mounts and would have intended purchasing these in Italy or in Sicily. The Athenians relied heavily on their naval arm but if drawn inland or if their ability to employ the fleet was impaired they could be at a serious disadvantage. In addition to the fleet were thirty merchant vessels carrying food supplies but also the men to bake bread, stone masons and carpenters needed for constructing camps, siege works and repairing the ships. Numerous smaller boats accompanied the warships; a hundred of these had been assigned to the fleet but many others were there to do trade with the troops.[33]

This immense armada touched land at the Iapygian Pensinula (modern Seluntine Peninsula) and probably saluted the temple of Artemis at the spot today occupied by the church of Santa Maria di Leuca *de finibus terrae*, and the nearby lighthouse, then hugged the coast up to Taras (Tarentum). The Tarentines having been founded by the Spartans and as Dorian by descent having maintained links with their metropolis refused the Athenians entry to their great harbour. The invaders probably beached wherever water was available; the Iapygian Pensinsula has no easily accessible fresh water but the extensive beaches at Metapontum and the rivers Bradanus and Basento (Casuentus) that flow either side of this town will have been a likely stopping place. The Metapontines do not, however, appear to have offered aid either because they too considered themselves Dorian having been founded by Achaeans or since they possessed a powerful neighbour in Taras preferred to follow its lead. The following year under pressure from Athens they changed their policy and became an ally, although ultimately this was not an advantageous connection for Metapontum. From there the Athenians progressed down the coast passing Heracleia (Siris), Croton, the temple of Hera on the promontory west of Croton (today's Capo Colonna), Caulonia and Locri. None of these cities was keen to become involved in this affair and indeed Locri with its strong Syracusan association would have been as hostile as Taras. And when the fleet arrived outside Rhegium it was the same story and this from a city that had been the base of the previous Athenian operations between 426 and 424, and which considered that it had ties of friendship with Athens. The citizens of Rhegium refused admission to their city but allowed the Athenians and their allies some land nearby on which to make a camp and to hold a market for procuring supplies. In response to appeals to join this expedition they replied that they would consult with the other cities of Magna Graecia and would follow any single course agreed by all these communities. This must have been quite a shock for the generals who could have expected a more positive attitude towards them, but worse was to follow when the flotilla sent to Segesta now rejoined the main fleet. On board the ships they carried thirty talents of silver bullion, which was all the Segestaeans possessed towards the cost of the fleet's upkeep, barely enough for a fortnight! Thucydides says that this came as no surprise to Nicias but Alcibiades and Lamachus were taken aback at the incredible guile of the Segestaeans. Having lured the Athenians to within sight of Sicily they were unlikely to want to return to Greece empty-handed and so would remain whether or not further funds from Segesta would be available. It is now that the historian tells the tale about the cunning of the people of Segesta and their communal silverware (Thuc. 6.46).[34]

It was either an ignominious retreat or to carry on without Segestaean money and the Athenians would have to find the finances themselves. Nicias argued that they should proceed to Segesta bring about a peace settlement between the Segestaeans and the Selinuntines and demand payment of the outstanding instalment for the fleet's upkeep. This payment should be collected even with force and then the Athenians should proceed along the south coast of Sicily to Syracuse where demands should be made to allow the people of Leontinoi their freedom and then with much of their brief accomplished they should sail to Athens. Alcibiades disagreed and thought that they should investigate whether Messene would become an ally since it possessed such a good harbour, which would provide the Athenians with a secure base. They should also despatch heralds to all the Greek cities, except Selinous and Syracuse, and to the Sicels to see which would join them. When they knew where they stood for allies on the island they would then be in a position to attack Syracuse unless Selinous came to terms with Segesta and the Syracusans freed Leontinoi from their control. Lamachus gave a third opinion that they should attack Syracuse immediately while the people there were not only unprepared for such a major assault but that there would be the fear of the unknown, which would give the Athenians a clear advantage. If they delayed the uncertainty about the size of the Athenian force might well turn to contempt and the fight could turn into one of attrition. However, having given this advice, which included making the deserted site of Megara

Hyblaia a base, as events turned out this would probably have been the most successful option, Lamachus threw his weight behind the suggestion of Alcibiades.

Alcibiades crossed the Straits in his own trireme in order to seek an alliance with the Messenians but they too offered only a place for trading with the Athenians and neither access to the city nor commitment to the invaders' war effort. Next Alcibiades took command of sixty warships, presumably those assigned to him at Corcyra, and sailed down the Sicilian coast to Naxos (Thuc. 6.50), where the Athenians at last found a community pleased to see them. From there the Athenians proceeded to Catane, but here they were initially refused admittance and so the fleet camped near the mouth of the Terias River.[35] Alcibiades then ordered the fleet to sail for Syracuse, with fifty of the triremes in single file says Thucydides, and ten despatched as a forward party, which was instructed to enter the Great Harbour and through heralds announce that they had arrived to restore the freedom of Leontinoi. Any citizen of Leontinoi who could leave Syracuse was free to join the Athenians – although we are not told if this produced any useful results. The Syracusans simply manned their walls, their fleet safely inside the smaller of their two harbours, after some reconnaissance of the land and the harbours the Athenians left again for Catane. Here Alcibiades was admitted to present his case before an assembly of the citizen body.[36] A pro-Syracusan group of citizens had taken control of Catane and Alcibiades hoped that by appealing to a wider sentiment the majority of citizens would opt rather for an alliance with the Athenians. However, he was plainly not leaving this outcome to chance for while he was speaking some Athenian troops entered the city through a poorly constructed gate. As soon as it became known that armed Athenians were inside, the supporters of Syracuse fled. The citizens of Catane then voted to become allies of Athens and offered them the city as a base for future operations against Syracuse.

The fleet now returned to Rhegium with Alcibiades' plan seemingly well on the way to fruition since the entire force now relocated to Catane. There a message arrived from Camarina urging rapid action and that the city might be won over for the Athenian cause. The fleet sailed down the coast ignoring Syracuse but noting that no obvious measures were being taken against them put in at the beach at Camarina. Camarina was situated between much stronger neighbours Gela and Syracuse. It often suffered from the territorial ambitions of these states so might have been thought a possible ally. On this occasion the Athenians were met with a refusal, and so they sailed north and made an attack along the Syracusan coast where they lost some lightly armed troops who were killed by Syracusan cavalry. The effective use of the cavalry by the Syracusans should have alerted the Athenians to correct a dismal shortage in their own mounted troops. They were given no time to ponder on this problem because they were all taken by surprise from an unexpected quarter.

What they found when they arrived in Catane was the state galley the *Salaminia*. The Athenians kept two ships for public duty which they employed for delivering messages by the *demos* or magistrates to its army commanders in the field or to allied and foreign states. On board the *Salaminia* were officials sent to order Alcibiades to return with a view to him standing trial in the city, the charge being sacrilege. Added to the charge of malicious damage to the Herms was a more serious accusation of holding parties in which the Eleusinian mystery religion – a cult of Demeter the Earth goddess – had been parodied. There had already been a considerable witch-hunt at Athens after Alcibiades' departure where says Thucydides (6.53) numerous individuals had been arrested on rather flimsy evidence from dubious informers. Nonetheless, there was a general feeling that the whole affair needed to be cleared up and that Alcibiades was in some way heavily involved. There was a continual great fear of tyranny at Athens and anyone who might have aspirations in that direction was inevitably to be the subject of inquiry and Alcibiades with his wealth and flamboyant life was clearly to be identified as one who could have such ambitions. A charge of sacrilege could then have been politically motivated but also generally believed of the man accused.[37] Thucydides recounts that a particular informer who was believed by most citizens provided a list of names of those responsible for mutilating the Herms and profaning the mysteries. Those in custody were tried and executed and those who escaped were sentenced to death in their absence. Alcibiades was considered to be the ringleader and in the current public hysteria it was decided to summon him home.[38] Because he was not placed under arrest he was allowed to leave Catane in his own ship with his friends, some of whom were also accused. Together with the state's galley they beached near Thurii (Sybaris) where Alcibiades and his friends fled – either because they knew their lives were forfeit because of public opinion or guilt. Since they could not be discovered the *Salaminia* sailed on without them and the Athenians in due course handed down the death penalty to him and his friends.[39]

This episode resulted in the leadership of the Athenian expedition in Sicily being reduced to two generals since no replacement was sent for Alcibiades. The army was divided into two equal parts and the leadership of each was decided by lot. Nicias and Lamachus decided to go north from Catane through the Straits and then sail along the north coast to Segesta. While on the way they beached at Himera, which refused cooperation, but then the Athenians stormed a small Sicanian town named Hyccara and sold its inhabitants, who were at war with Segesta, as slaves. They handed over the town to Segesta, which had sent some cavalry to join the attackers. At Segesta Nicias managed to raise another thirty talents for continued payment of the fleet, while the sale of the Sicanians fetched another 120 talents.[40] Much of the heavy infantry remained on land at Hycarra and in a show of strength marched overland to Catane, a route that was in regular use with an identifiable road or track and not in any sense a forced marched through unchartered territory and probably via the Sicel community at Enna and then south of Mount Etna to the island's east coast. The fleet continued on its circumnavigation and Thucydides (6. 62) claims that the Athenians called on other Sicel communities to join them, although there were none along the south coast. Somewhere along the coast, however, they must have put in long enough to launch an attack on the Sicels of Hybla, a community that was in the mountains inland between Gela and Camarina, but the attack failed, probably because of lack of heavy infantry.[41] The Athenian fleet returned to its base at Catane as the summer of 415 came to a close.

Winter may have been approaching but probably sometime in November the Athenians were reluctant to allow the Syracusans any more time in which to prepare for future hostilities. It was also very plain says Thucydides that the confidence of the Syracusans had greatly increased because of the delays in attacking their city and may well have been especially bolstered by the Athenian failure to enlist the help of Messene and the failed assault on Hybla. In fact, the Syracusan cavalry was out in force throughout the region and came close to the fortifications of Catane. The Athenians were distinctly at a disadvantage against so formidable a cavalry force because they all but lacked any, and so although they wanted to engage their enemy it had to be done in such a way as to neutralize their opponents' supremacy against troops on foot. Nicias and Lamachus came up with a ruse to tempt the Syracusan army out to Catane. They sent a citizen of Catane to act as an informer with instructions to tell the Syracusans that they still had many supporters in that city and that the Athenians spent the night in the city some distance from their main armoury. If the Syracusans attacked before dawn there were citizens of Catane who would fire the Athenian ships, close the gates to prevent the Athenians from easily reaching their supplies and generally cause mayhem. In fact, the Athenians wanted to draw the main Syracusan army and its cavalry away while at the same time they would sail down the coast at night and, as advised by local guides, make a landing inside the Great Harbour near the temple of Zeus Uranios at Polichne. The temple complex (the Olympieion) with its archaic temple dating back to the early sixth century is situated at Daskon roughly at the mid-point around the bay that forms the Great Harbour.[42] The area, although fertile with good farming land, was also crisscrossed by drainage channels since it was and remains very wet and marshy, probably because it is in places below the level of the sea. In such a location the use of cavalry against a mostly infantry force would be less effective, while the highest point at Daskon would provide an easily defendable camp. Thucydides is not specific in his information but it is essentially accurate and indicates that he probably consulted an eyewitness or someone who knew the terrain. The one flaw in his description is that the plan he presents went rather too smoothly into operation. The Athenians intended sailing by night, not unprecedented certainly but also a strategy that might come to grief since the triremes had to follow each other and even with a full moon and clear skies probably also need some lanterns. The noise from over one hundred triremes moving just beyond the surf would also have been considerable. On the other hand their opponents had to march their army up from Syracuse to Catane, also overnight, which was also fraught with difficulty since the rugged landscape typical of limestone country is not easily negotiated, although some road or track must have existed by which they might navigate their way through the countryside. Again a considerable noise must have accompanied the marching army and some light must have indicated their whereabouts. They may well have departed during daytime and arrived near Catane before night and the Athenian fleet may also have sailed earlier than dusk. The question necessarily must be why they missed one another for the coastal plain is narrow and the lights of a fleet passing an army marching north must have been plainly visible. Had the Athenians seen the Syracusans they would know that the plan was working – which it did – yet the Syracusans were either very sloppy in their use of scouts or incredibly trusting of the information they had received. Thucydides, with his lack of personal knowledge of the area, therefore fell back on writing a very rough guide to what actually happened for he well understood that had the Athenians marched to Syracuse they would have been at the mercy of the Syracusan cavalry, but he did not know why the area around Polichne should be the most appealing landing spot other than his informant said so.

As it was, the Syracusans going overland northwards and the Athenian fleet moving southwards passed one another. It is remarkable that the Athenians were not spotted at Megara Hyblaia, which although devoid of a civilian population did have a Syracusan garrison. The Athenians also passed by the peninsula of Thapsos and the seaward fortifications of Syracuse again without it seems detection from a very lax foe. The Syracusans had in the meantime summoned their allies the Selinuntines and says Thucydides (6.65) made their camp at the Symaethus River not far from Leontinoi. When the Athenians heard that the Syracusans were on the move they set sail. At dawn the Athenian fleet beached at Daskon at more or less the same time that the Syracusan cavalry arrived at Catane to find that they had been well and truly hoodwinked. These rejoined the army which turned about and raced back to defend their city. The Athenians says Thucydides had the time on their hands to take up a strong defensive position where the enemy cavalry would be least effective since they would be protected by walls (probably boundaries between farms) farm buildings and trees (especially around Polichne) with the marsh of Lysimeleia in front of them and some hilly land to the other side. The Athenians also constructed a wooden palisade as a defensive wall for their beached ships, and built a fort at Daskon from local rubble. They also destroyed a bridge over the Anapos River on the road that led to Elorus to the south just to make communications even more difficult for the Syracusans. Since the major part of the citizen body was absent in the army there was no intervention in these preparations by the Syracusan troops remaining in the city, and it certainly seems likely that the Athenians probably had the best part of a day and possibly longer to accomplish everything described by Thucydides and that some of these activities have been compressed into a shorter period for dramatic purposes. The Syracusan cavalry were the first to appear seemingly having ridden back the fifty kilometres (30 miles) from Catane followed soon after by the infantry. These marched directly towards the Athenian position but when the attackers refused battle they broke off contact and retreated across the road to Eloros and made a camp, probably near the temple of Zeus.

The next morning the Athenians and their allies drew up for battle and Thucydides gives the line as consisting of the Athenian hoplites in the centre with Argive and Mantineans on the right, and other Aegean Sea allies on the left. The hoplites were drawn up in lines eight deep, but half the force formed a hollow square in the rear acting as a protective screen, also eight deep, both for the encampment and the triremes and their rowers, many of whom would have been unarmed. The Syracusans drew their hoplites up sixteen deep and occupied the centre of the army, with at least 1200 cavalry on their right supported by javelin throwers. Thucydides (6.67) also mentions the presence of troops from their allies including Selinous, and specifically two hundred cavalry from Gela, twenty horsemen and fifty archers from Camarina, but he does not stipulate that these occupied the left wing. Before battle commenced Nicias, as was usual practice among commanders, went along the lines encouraging the troops, and Thucydides gives some suitable sentiments, including the important point, which recurs, that the Athenians and most of their allies were far from home and unlike their enemy if they lost they would have great difficulty in saving themselves. This negative comment betrays an innate pessimism in Nicias' character and was out of place in what should have been a rousing message to his troops. Yet Nicias immediately led his troops into battle and took the Syracusans by surprise who were not expecting to be engaged so soon. Indeed some had apparently gone off into the city probably via the Akradina Gate, which was close by. Thucydides wants to give the impression of Syracusan inefficiency and lack of discipline, a theme that recurs and which is eventually corrected. It seems rather unlikely that with two battle lines drawn up that one side should decide to take time out, unless there was a delay caused by the essential process of making sacrifices before action. Nicias, later exposed as highly religious and superstitious, would not have neglected such an aspect yet here seems to have begun the fighting without even a perfunctory taking of the omens for success. Thucydides has clearly omitted some material here, which would explain just why some of the Syracusan hoplites were not yet drawn up in order. It could be that the battle took place late in the day and a deliberate tactic of Nicias in order that the untried Syracusan troops would be restless and less disciplined and more inclined to wander off to the families and homes, while the Athenians infantry had been put through their paces already during the march from Hycarra.

It seems as if the lightly armed troops – slingers, archers and javelin-throwers – on both sides were engaged while the priests were still engaged in the sacrifices, and the *carnyces* or horns were sounded for the advance and the hoplites clashed with little ground being given either way. A thunder shower broke the resolve of the Syracusans and brought on a surge by the Athenian infantry, although it was the Argives on the right wing who caused the Syracusan left to buckle and retreat. The Athenian hoplites in the centre then pushed back their opposite numbers and the whole Syracusan army broken into two halves retreated in disorder, their right wing into the city, the left wing towards Polichne. The Athenians were unable to ensure a rout however, since the Syracusan cavalry shadowed the retreating infantry. The Syracusans made a camp at the Olympieion at Polichne and the Athenians withdrew into their camp having first collected their dead. On the next morning heralds came from the city asking for permission to collect their dead, numbering about 260 (Thuc. 6.71), which was granted. The Athenians lost just fifty men. Soon after the cremation of the bodies had taken place the Athenians withdrew from the Great Harbour and returned to Catane and Naxos intending to use one or both as their base for the remainder of the winter.

But the winter months were not ones of inactivity for either side in this conflict. At Syracuse at a citizen assembly Hermocrates again gave advice about how to correct deficiencies in the organization of the army arguing that the recent defeat had nothing to do with the calibre of the troops but rather in the command structure and in the training of the individual soldiers. He recommended that the current system of electing fifteen generals to joint command of the army, which he said was inefficient and led to confusion, should be replaced with the election of fewer commanders. The citizens voted to elect just three generals with extensive powers to carry out any reforms in the training of the troops and in matters related to strategy and tactics. Hermocrates was one of three generals immediately elected by the people. The Athenians meanwhile transferred their main force north to Naxos and promptly attacked Messene. A pro-Athenian faction in the city had been expected to turn over the city to the invaders but Alcibiades at some point during the start of his exile after he had absconded from Thurii had warned the pro-Syracusan party.[43] These rounded up and executed the Messenian supporters of Athens and prepared for a siege. However, a combination of winter weather and a shortage of supplies prompted the Athenians to break off the siege and return to Naxos. There they despatched a trireme to Athens requesting supplies and either more mounts for their cavalry or money to purchase horses. The Syracusans spent their time in strengthening their fortifications in expectation of a lengthy siege, and threw up walls around the Temenos or sacred complex of Apollo, which lay adjacent to the theatre in Neapolis. They also constructed a wall 'facing towards Epipolai so that they could not be so easily blockaded which was more likely with the city limits as they were'.[44] They built or repaired forts at Megara Hyblaia and at Polichne in the hope that these could be maintained even if the city was invested. And when they heard that the main Athenian army had withdrawn from Catane to Naxos they put their own army on the march and raided their neighbour's territory and burned the Athenian camp there and so gained some useful preparation for future fighting. The Syracusans also heard that the Athenians were trying to reactivate their friendship with Camarina, which had been extremely lukewarm in its support of Syracuse in the recent hostilities. Hermocrates was sent as envoy to Camarina to put forward the Syracusan point of view and to try and keep them to their current alliance. The Athenians sent a number of envoys, including a certain Euphemus. Hermocrates argued before an assembly of citizens at Camarina that as Dorians they should be cautious in joining forces with the Athenians who were mainly concerned about extending their empire and that the Greek cities of Sicily should all look to preserving their freedom. Hermocrates claimed that far from living in dread of a strong Syracuse they should rather not welcome that it be weakened or defeated since the Athenians would surely be far sterner masters of the island. The people of Camarina should also note he said that the Rhegians who had ethnic ties with Athens had refused an alliance, although he preferred evidently to brush aside the fact that both Catane and Naxos had opted for the Athenian camp. The Athenians responded by defending their right to empire and that their achievement in bringing peace to the Aegean was hardly an odious event. Euphemus rejected the accusation that the Athenians were to be feared and instead argued that domination by Syracuse would be more exacting because it was so close whereas friendship with Athens would allow them greater independence because it was so far away. The listeners were well aware of their situation and history of oppression by Syracuse and the possible attraction of an alliance with Athens was tempting but in the end they voted to stay neutral in the war and the envoys of all states went away empty-handed.

The Syracusan envoys sent to the Peloponnese also tried to whip up support among the south Italian cities and later in the winter were in Corinth where the appeal for aid was immediately approved. In Sparta these envoys were present at the same time as Alcibiades and both made representations to the ephors, the Syracusans for military assistance, the Athenians for asylum and to give advice on future action against his own city (Thuc. 6.89–92). The Spartans recognized their responsibility towards fellow Dorians, but were probably dismissive of Alcibiades' claims that the Athenians had a grand strategy in place for conquering Sicily and Carthage before an invasion of the Peloponnese. However, they may have been most affected by Alcibiades' dramatic declaration that: 'if Syracuse falls then with it the whole of Sicily and Italy soon afterwards' (Thuc. 6.91).[45] Therefore, they decided to send Gylippus, one of the Spartiates,[46] to Syracuse with a small force of helots to take command of the defence of the city, while the Corinthians would supply some triremes and expertise on naval matters. The Athenians, as if responding to the moves in a game of chess, now switched their base from Naxos back to Catane and rebuilt the camp that had been torched by the Syracusans. They sent out envoys to both Carthage and the Etrurian cities in the hope of securing allies or mercenaries, and indeed they were joined by some Etruscan fighters. Requests for horses were sent to Segesta and to any of the Sicels who had become their allies, while the authorities in Athens promised more reinforcements and supplies. And so the timetable was set for an acceleration of the hostilities with the arrival of the spring in 414 BC.

The Athenians first began their summer campaigning with an attack on Megara Hyblaia which had a garrison of Syracusan troops. The fort was attacked but not, it seems, taken and the Athenians were content to raid and destroy nearby farmland. Some Syracusan cavalry were driven off with casualties near the River Terias. On returning to Catane the army moved inland to attack the Sicels at Centuripa who surrendered and came to terms with the attackers, and the Athenians also burned crops belonging to the communities of Inessa and Hybla. When they arrived at their base camp, waiting for them there were 250 cavalrymen and thirty mounted archers with their supplies, but not a single horse. Nonetheless the Athenians had also been supplied with 300 talents of silver to purchase mounts.[47] The Syracusans realized that the intention was to gradually encroach on their territory and win over as allies any communities who had grievances against them. Moreover, they believed that the most likely direction of attack, since the enemy army was to the north, lay via the ridge of Epipolai. If an invader held Epipolai they would command the heights over the city and the main route into the interior. If the Syracusans lost Epipolai it would place them in a very serious and weak position. And so, although Thucydides does not give a date it was most probably early May of 414, the Syracusan generals decided to hold a general assembly of all military forces outside the city walls near Akradina. Hermocrates and his two colleagues had also decided to post a force of 600 infantry under the command of a mercenary name Diomilos of Andros on Epipolai as a guard. As the Syracusan forces were gathering they suddenly became aware that Athenian forces were already in possession of Epipolai and that their plans for the defence of their city had been completely undermined. How can this have happened?

The Athenian fleet carrying the infantry must have sailed down the coast the day before. Somehow this convoy, which was well in excess of one hundred warships, at least fifty transports and numerous smaller vessels, eluded the notice of the Syracusan garrison at Megara. This is a striking instance of incompetence by the Syracusans for the weather must have been calm and clear. The garrison may perhaps have been bribed to ignore the passage of such a large fleet or were extremely careless in their duties. Early in the morning the Athenians landed near the bottom of a hill now known as the Scala Greca, which Thucydides calls Leon, and marched their hoplites, probably 5000 in all, at the double for the five to six kilometres (less than 4 miles) along the edge of the north facing escarpment up to Eurialos at the most westerly edge of Epipolai. They effectively and rapidly cut the route from the interior to the city. The fleet in the meantime put some fortifications across the Isthmus leading to Thapsos and anchored their triremes on the northern shore out of sight of any Syracusan guards watching the northern approaches to the city. Again there were clearly and inexplicably none! And so in a matter or two to three hours the Athenians went from being an enemy some distance away to being in sight of the city's western defences.

The Syracusan command was taken completely by surprise and there was considerable disorder. Diomilos with his 600 troops was ordered at once to rush Epipolai but these had five kilometres (about 3 miles) uphill to charge. It must have been approaching the middle of the morning with the heat becoming intense and the enemy already in position and able to defend the summit of the ridge. The Syracusans were badly defeated with Diomilos and half his detachment lost and on the next day the Athenians marched down to the city walls in a show of strength but retired when no opposition came out to meet them, Instead they returned to Eurialos and began to build a fort that Thucydides says (6.97) was at Labdalum, which is probably more or less where the Eurialos Gate stands today on the edge of the escarpment looking north to Megara. This fort was intended as a supply depot in the forthcoming siege operations. As work started here cavalry reinforcements began to arrive from Segesta, which supplied 300 men, while another hundred came from Naxos and some of the Sicel allies. Together with their own 250, which had now been provided with mounts bought from Segesta and Catane, the Athenians could now field a reasonable 650 cavalry, although that still left them inferior in numbers to their opponents.

The Athenians now decided to advance to a line closer to the city walls, a site named by Thucydides (6.98) as Syra, somewhere in the vicinity of the Temenos of Apollo in Neapolis, where they constructed a circular fort. The Syracusan generals were rightly alarmed at the speed with which the Athenians were now moving and clearly intent on a close investment of the city. They ordered the army to draw up somewhere along Epipolai near the city's northern walls to face the enemy, which was also drawn up in battle order. However, the Syracusans were in some disorder again and rather than risk another defeat the generals ordered a retreat leaving some cavalry to disrupt the Athenian construction work, although these were also beaten off with some losses on their side. The Athenians then started to build a stockade along the northern wall of Syracuse heading in the direction of a place named as Troigilos, which seems to have been at the sea. There is considerable doubt about its whereabouts, some scholars placing it near the Scala Greca on the northern edge of the escarpment and hence close to Leon,[48] others placing it on the coast immediately to the north of Akradina. The first would mean that the wall was being extended in a northerly direction, the second in an easterly direction and rather shorter. Whichever is the correct hypothesis, and there is no archaeological evidence to support either view, the intention was to isolate Syracuse from any supplies coming in by land. The Syracusans were advised by their generals and in particular Hermocrates not to take the risk of another full engagement with the enemy but rather they should disrupt the Athenians in their attempt at investing the city. Therefore it was decided to prevent a complete circumvallation by extending a wall of their own at right angles to that of the Athenians and which could be accomplished easily enough since the attackers would not be able to use their full forces against the Syracusans unless they stopped their own activity and had to be on their guard against attack from those inside the city. This counter wall must have been about two metres in width (6 feet) and Thucydides explicitly states that it was to contain towers and hence was intended to be a structure equal in height – perhaps five metres (15 feet) to the city's permanent fortifications. Assuming that this wall was meant to intersect the Athenian line close to the fort at Syra, which cannot have been no more than 200 metres (600 feet) away the construction was not that ambitious but will still have involved several hundred labourers and guards. The Athenians' much longer stockade on the other hand would have needed almost all available manpower since it was clearly being built at various points simultaneously and when finished was intended to cover several kilometres. The Syracusan wall was close to the Temenos of Apollo since sacred olive trees were cut down for building the towers (Thuc. 6.100), and although it was soon obvious what the intention was a lull in the fighting also occurred. After a day or so, however, the Athenian response was decisive. A troop of three hundred Athenian hoplites with some lightly armed troops in attendance were ordered to attack the Syracusans while many of the labourers and guards were having food, probably the ancient equivalent of the siesta. At the same time the rest of the army was divided in two sections under one of the generals, one half to move towards the city the other apparently as a reserve to lend aid where needed (Thuc. 6.100).[49] The Syracusans retreated in disorder to the city at the Temenos of Apollo hotly pursued by the Athenians who succeeded in gaining an entrance into the city but were then pushed back out suffering some casualties. Meanwhile the Syracusan wall was dismantled and much of the building material taken away for the Athenian stockade. Thucydides says that on the next day (6.101), it was decided to extend the wall from opposite Neapolis down to the Great Harbour. Orders were also given for the fleet, which had remained at Thapsos for probably about a week, to sail into the Great Harbour and join the land forces. When the Syracusans saw that the stockade was being advanced down the steep slope to the marshy ground at Lysimeleia they decided to build a counter wall with a ditch beside it out from Akradina and so prevent the Athenians from access to the sea.[50] At dawn the Athenians launched an attack on the Syracusan wall and when confronted with the marshy ground of this low-lying area used the wood from doors and buildings to cross the mud.[51] The Syracusans scattered leaving the latest counter wall in Athenian hands, but the Athenians led on this occasion by Lamachus were keen to deliver a stunning blow. They pursued the fleeing Syracusans especially those who had formed up on the left to receive the Athenian attack and who were heading south towards Polichne, while their right wing retreated inside the city at Akradina. The way was difficult for both the pursued and the pursuers since the land was criss-crossed with ditches and thick undergrowth and long reeds much as it is today. Lamachus and some of his troops got ahead and were caught by some Syracusan cavalry that was covering the retreating infantry. Lamachus and the five or six with him were killed and their bodies carried back to the city (Thuc. 6.101). This coup appears to have given the defenders in the city new heart since they regrouped and raced out again with the aim of breaking down some of the Athenian stockade higher up on Epipolai opposite Neapolis and even to capture the circular fort at Syra. The fort was saved by Nicias who was there in person and who organized its defence, including setting fire to some of the wood that had been cut for the stockade, but a three hundred metre section (900 feet) of the Athenian wall was destroyed. The Athenians down in the marsh now returned to lend aid to Nicias while at this point (Thuc. 6.102) the fleet sailed into Great Harbour apparently only then just spotted by the Syracusans who immediately withdrew again into the city.

The usual truce was declared for collecting the dead and the bodies of Lamachus and his men were handed back to the Athenians for burial. And as Thucydides notes, now the entire fleet and the infantry were re-united and a camp was constructed along the beach at Lysimeleia, the siege wall was carried down from Syra to the sea and a second wall was built behind it within which all the besiegers could bivouac.[52] The future seemed rather bleak for the Syracusans since the recent victories of the Athenians and the rapidity with which the siege was being pressed brought them new allies both in Sicily and in Magna Graecia. Indeed, three pentekonters arrived from Etruria manned by mercenaries keen to join the Athenians with a view to some rich pickings from the siege. Inside the city the generals were relieved of their duties and three new *strategoi* were elected, but these seem to have been keener to reach a settlement with the besiegers rather than taking the field against them. Negotiations were opened with Nicias, who was now in sole command of the expedition, and a peace agreement was openly discussed among the citizen body. Gylippus sailing with just four triremes from the Peloponnese heard of the dramatic decline in Syracusan fortunes and seems to have given up the idea of attempting to reach Sicily. Instead he crossed to Taras because he wanted to ensure that the Italian Greek cities did not pursue a policy of rapprochement with the Athenians. There he heard that the situation in Syracuse was not quite as desperate as previous reports had stated and that forces could still gain entry to the city, which was not yet fully encircled. He decided that rather than sail down the east coast where he might be intercepted by Athenian patrols he would go to Himera and go by the overland route.

Gylippus put in at Himera where he found support and from Selinous and Gela and some of the Sicel communities in the west. With his own force of about 600 armed rowers and 100 hoplites, together with 1100 mostly infantry from Himera, plus some Selinuntines and Geloans, and about 1000 Sicels, Gylippus set out overland and rapidly approached Syracuse. As he did so the Syracusans were discussing how best to finalize the surrender to the Athenians, but before they reach a formal decision, a Corinthian trireme captained by a certain Gongylus, one of the fourteen warships sent by his city, evaded the watching Athenians and entered the Small Harbour. This Gongylus appealed to the Syracusans to delay their decision and informed them of the imminent arrival of the reinforcements in the other ships they had requested from Sparta. The Syracusans immediately changed their minds and ordered their land forces to go out and meet Gylippus. The Spartan had reached Eurialos and was apparently unchallenged gaining access to Epipolai, although there was an Athenian garrison nearby at Labdalum. This lack in Athenian action suggests that Gylippus may have arrived either at dawn or late in the evening and so, although a small force numbering barely 3000, he went undetected. The Athenians must later have come to rue their chances of dealing with Gylippus at his most vulnerable. Whenever the precise moment of his arrival we again have evidence of inefficiency and carelessness by any guards posted on duty.[53] The Syracusans turned out in force and must have occupied an area on the northern side of Epipolai, which they would have reached from a gate in the Neapolis district of the city. Thucydides says that the Athenian siege wall was intermittent in this sector and in places still under construction but that there were large gaps and clearly no besiegers on duty to prevent a sortie. The Athenians were clearly taken unawares but also advanced to meet their enemy. Before they engaged, Gylippus sent a herald to the Athenian line demanding as a condition for peace an instant withdrawal by the attackers.

The Athenians did not deign to reply to this request and sent the herald packing. However no battle took place since the Athenians took up a defensive position beside their wall while the Syracusans did not form their line to Gylippus' liking with the result that Thucydides says (7.3) he first ordered a withdrawal to a more level area and then to higher ground near the Temenos of Apollo. The text here is confusing since Gylippus was met on Epipolai by Syracusan forces and so must have been north of the fort at Syra. Yet the action has now moved to Lysimeleia near the Athenian camp if Thucydides is correct in asserting that the Syracusans moved to higher rather than lower ground. It is at least possible that events have been telescoped but again easily shows the historian's lack of secure knowledge of the geographical context of his subject. On the next day Gylippus drew up the Syracusan force again in front of the Athenian wall and while his enemy was distracted by this move he sent a detachment to attack the Labdalum fort. The defenders were taken by surprise and killed and the fort destroyed all of which took place out of sight of the Athenians below in Lysimeleia. At the same time an Athenian trireme was captured by the Syracusans, an ominous event that should have made the beisiegers more alert to the fact that the besieged had recovered some of their confidence.

The Syracusans then decided to construct a new counter wall somewhere above Neapolis to prevent the Athenians from completing their encircling wall but also to ensure access to the interior via Eurialos and which would confine the besiegers to the low-lying land near the Great Harbour. Gylippus ordered a night sortie against the northern end of the Athenian wall but unluckily for him found a strong Athenian force in position there. The Syracusans withdrew and the Athenians took measures to strengthen this sector of their siege wall. Moreover, Nicias in a very thoughtful strategy, decided on placing a garrison in three forts on Plemmyrion, the spur of land that forms the southern entrance to the Great Harbour. He quite rightly considered that it was essential to control this entrance to allow the Athenian ships to come and go at will and also that this point would be a useful place to store munitions. Still, this also resulted in the northern escarpment on Epipolai being abandoned, and with that decision, also any easy overland communication with Catane and Naxos. Thucydides also comments (7.4) that this was the beginning of a deterioration in the fortunes of the Athenians, mainly because for those troops who were garrisoned on Plemmyrion there was a problem in obtaining water and wood for fuel, and that foragers were frequently caught and killed by Syracusan cavalry that operated in this area from the camp they possessed at Polichne.[54] News had also reached Nicias that a fleet of Corinthian triremes had left the Peloponnese and so he sent a flotilla of twenty warships across to the coast of southern Italy to intercept these. The Syracusan counter wall on Epipolai was proceeding very well and so Gylippus decided to draw the Athenians out for another engagement. The Syracusans formed up in the narrow space between their own walls and the Athenian stockade. The two sides do not appear to have wasted any time in coming to blows in this confined space and the Syracusans unable to exploit their greater cavalry power were defeated. Gylippus summoned an assembly of the troops and made an apology for this failure, which he said was the result of his own poor leadership and not from any lack of bravery by the soldiers. Nicias knew that the counter wall which had nearly reached the end of the Athenian wall had to be stopped so when Gylippus led out the Syracusan army again, the besiegers were keen for a further engagement. The Syracusans formed their line of battle on more open ground and when the fighting began their cavalry easily put the Athenian left wing to flight and the rest of the besieging force was driven back within its wall.[55] By the following evening the Syracusans had achieved their objective of building their counter wall beyond the northern point of the Athenian stockade. This meant that the Athenians would need to throw greater resources and effort to try and complete the encirclement of the city, which, in fact, they never accomplished.

Soon after this triumph the reinforcements from Corinth, which Gongylus had said were on their way, and which had clearly been detained arrived. One of the triremes must have been lost since just twelve triremes beached safely in the Small Harbour having eluded the Athenian warships stationed along the coast. The crews of these vessels lent a hand in completing the Syracusan cross-wall, while Gylippus slipped away from the city to visit potential allies on the island and raise further troops. He also intended to increase the Syracusan naval arm in order to tackle head on the problem of the powerful Athenian fleet. Envoys were sent to Sparta and Corinth requesting further aid especially for troops, which the Syracusans felt they lacked, in order to tilt the balance of the war in their favour. They also manned their fleet and began to put the crews into a period of training before they attempted to fight their more experienced adversaries.

Nicias, on the other hand, seems to have been quite shaken by the recent reverses on Epipolai and immediately adopted a much more defensive policy. He also wanted further reinforcements and to stress to the authorities at home the worsening situation of the expedition. Instead of entrusting the task of appealing to the citizen assembly for more help to heralds whom he considered not entirely to be trusted to be accurate he decided to write a letter. Nicias' letter (Thuc. 7.10–15) is a remarkable composition, obviously not an authentic document, but the rather plausible thoughts and arguments attributed to the general by the historian.[56] Nicias was keen to stress the seriousness of the Athenian position. It was delivered to the *ecclesia* or citizen assembly by the *epistates* or 'chairman of the meeting' and Nicias' main argument emerged as follows. The besiegers once more formidable in numbers and experience had become the besieged because of the arrival of reinforcements for the Syracusans. The Athenians had been defeated in battle, could no longer finish their encircling wall and had to defend their own camp while the Syracusans were daily growing in power. Nicias had been informed that the Syracusans had also requested further aid from Sparta and that Gylippus had gone in search of new allies in Sicily. He further details many of the recent events outside Syracuse, stresses – perhaps untruly – the loss of superiority of the Athenian land forces and the threat that was now emerging from the manning of a large Syracusan fleet. Considering that Nicias had only lost Labdalum and the fight by the cross wall, his message is unduly pessimistic while the Athenians still commanded the sea lanes. He also places considerable emphasis on his own state of health, which was so poor that he evidently believed he should be relieved of his duty. The citizen assembly would have nothing to do with this excuse however, and not only made two of his senior officers, Menander and Euthydemus, co-generals to alleviate his burden but they also voted to finance the despatch of an additional army and navy to reinforce Nicias. The generals elected were Demosthenes and Eurymedon, both of whom possessed a great deal of experience and were able commanders. Eurymedon was ordered to leave for Syracuse immediately, although it was by then the second half of December, with a fleet of ten warships carrying 120 talents (Thuc. 7.16).[57] Demosthenes was given instructions to collect the new force and lead it to Sicily in the following spring.

By that spring of 413 the siege of Syracuse was beginning to consume the energies of all main participants in the struggle. The Spartans authorized the sending of a considerable force to Syracuse composed, states Thucydides (7.19), of 600 hoplites under the command of the Spartiate Eccritus, but also 300 hoplites from Boeotia, 500 from Corinth including mercenaries and two hundred from Sicyon.[58] A heavy infantry force of 1600 was a major injection of manpower to bolster the Syracusan army. A large number of merchant vessels will also have been needed to transport these troops. To avoid interception by Athenian warships stationed off the coast of the western Peloponnese, a Corinthian fleet of twenty-five ships (Thuc. 7.19) was ordered to sail to Naupactus at entrance to the Gulf of Corinth to distract their enemy.[59] The Athenians meanwhile fulfilled their promise to Nicias by instructing Demosthenes to proceed to Sicily with a fleet of sixty-five triremes, sixty of them Athenian, five Chian, with a further complement of 1200 Athenian hoplites, as well as allied troops (Thuc. 7.20).

Thucydides reports that Gylippus returned to Syracuse in the spring of 413 and also brought fresh troops from communities willing to supply them. He was intent, however, on increasing the strength of the Syracusan fleet and in this aim he was strongly supported by Hermocrates. They argued that the Athenians, although appearing to be formidable and natural seafarers, had learned their skills only when threatened by the Persians. The citizens of

Syracuse could in a similar way acquire the same skills in order to defeat their enemy. They added that if the Syracusans were prepared to direct their energies towards becoming a powerful naval state they would stun the Athenians who hitherto had comprehensively dominated this theatre of war. The Syracusan fleet, augmented with the ships of their Corinthian allies, numbered eighty and fully manned they went onto the offensive in conjunction with an assault directed on land by Gylippus against the Athenian forts on Plemmyrion (Thuc. 7.22). It was obviously crucial that the Syracusans gain control of Plemmyrion if they wished to really pile the pressure on the Athenians, and a naval victory would be a spectacular blow and would result in the besiegers themselves becoming blockaded. Gylippus moved his troops, especially cavalry, to Polichne and the fort near the Olympieion overnight. At dawn the Syracusan fleet made their initial moves with forty-five triremes sailing out of the Small Harbour, probably around Ortygia and into the Great Harbour through the gap between the island and Plemmyrion. Thirty-five triremes put out from their berths in the Great Harbour. The intention was to cause confusion and to have in effect a two-pronged attack. The Athenians from their camp in Lysimeleia, a short distance from the Syracusan fleet which would have been beached beside the agora, put out sixty triremes. Twenty-five Athenian warships engaged the thirty-five Syracusan triremes from the Great Harbour, the remainder made for the entrance to meet the other enemy ships sailing in via Ortygia. This was the first great naval engagement of the campaign and indeed of the general hostilities between the Greeks to date in the entire war.

The number of warships engaging in such a confined space must have been an amazing sight and probably unprecedented for it brought a huge audience of onlookers onto the beaches around the Harbour. The Athenian soldiers on Plemmyrion were naturally drawn to the events unfolding before their eyes and to get the best views went down to the water's edge. Gylippus' troops attacked without warning and took the Athenians unawares; and again we see the extreme carelessness in the matter of keeping sentries on duty and the unbelievable naivety regarding the possibility of a joint land-naval attack. The largest of the Athenian forts fell to Gylippus almost immediately and the other two soon after when they were abandoned by their few defenders. Their only means of escape was by sea and any available vessel either beached or at anchor nearby. Those who did indeed clamber into a nearby merchant ship or small boats were initially pursued by a Syracusan trireme, but as the Athenian warships got the upper hand in the sea battle the soldiers stationed at Plemmyrion made their escape. The Syracusan fleet at the entrance to the Great Harbour lost formation and was routed falling back with at least eleven triremes and their crews destroyed.[60] However, the Athenians also lost three triremes and although they set up a trophy on a small island at the entrance to the Great Harbour celebrating their victory, the besiegers had lost control of Plemmyrion and with that unfettered access to the open sea. There may have been some celebration among the crews that evening, but the Athenian commanders by then must have been very worried about the future.

The Syracusans now demolished one of the Athenian forts on Plemmyrion and garrisoned the other two. The biggest coup in this victory was not the loss of Athenian soldiers, although there were heavy casualties but rather the loss of the supplies. The forts contained food supplies for the army and a great deal of equipment enough, says Thucydides, for forty warships and he also notes ominously that from then on the siege of Syracuse increasingly became the siege of the Athenian camp in Lysimeleia. The authorities in Syracuse may have been a little concerned about the failure of their ships, in battle but undeterred they sent out twelve ships, one of which carried messengers to the Peloponnese to carry news of the Athenian reverses and to urge the Spartans to increase their efforts against Athens so that the latter would not be able to send further aid to its own troops. The other eleven triremes crossed to Italy where they destroyed some Athenian supplies at Caulonia, and at Locri they met some of the Boeotian hoplites from Thespiae whom they carried down the coast. They were intercepted by twenty Athenian triremes at Megara Hyblaia and lost one ship but the rest arrived safely in their home port.[61] Frequent skirmishing between the two sides continued and the Athenians attempted to take possession of Syracuse's main dockyard in the Great Harbour, next to its agora, which was separated from the camp of the attackers only by a series of stakes driven into the sea. The Athenians managed to extract many of the stakes but these were replaced by the defenders. It is interesting to note that there was no Athenian attempt to win back Plemmyrion, which could easily have been accomplished while the besiegers could move freely around the Great Harbour. This is yet another indication of the timidity of Nicias' leadership.

Help was, nonetheless, on its way to Sicily from Athens. After carrying out some raiding operations along the coast of the Peloponnese (Thuc. 7.26) Demosthenes rendezvoused with allied contingents at Corcyra and crossed the Ionian Sea to southern Italy. Eurymedon joined him returning from Syracuse with the news of the loss of Plemmyrion and that there was now considerable urgency regarding the relief of the Athenians. The Syracusan success brought a positive reaction from various cities in Sicily and the Peloponnese, and about 1500 troops were brought to the city from the Greek mainland by a Corinthian commander,[62] while Camarina, once uncertain about where its loyalty should lie, now also sent 500 hoplites and 600 lightly armed troops, while Gela provided the crews for 5 warships (nearly 1000 rowers), 200 cavalry and 400 lightly armed troops. The focus of the fight was at Syracuse but the participants in the struggle were quickly coming to be representative of the entire Greek world in a way that is highly reminiscent of the Trojan War, as it is told by Homer.[63] The Greeks of southern Italy were similarly caught up in this gargantuan struggle. Demosthenes arrived at Thurii, the former Sybaris, and the citizens here provided, perhaps under pressure, a sizeable additional force of 700 hoplites and 300 lightly armed troops. The Athenian fleet sailed along the coast to Croton while there was a review at the Sybaris River of the Athenian land forces. This army marched south to the Hylias River where it was met by Crotoniate heralds who denied them access to their *chorē*. Rather than risk losses fighting against Croton the Athenians camped at the River and rejoined their fleet which transported the infantry to Rhegium.

The Syracusans were well informed about the Athenian relief column and were also very keen to try and inflict a further defeat on the besiegers, if at all possible, before their reinforcements could arrive.[64] Before they ventured out to engage their opponents however, they were advised by their Corinthian allies to make structural changes to their triremes. Athenian triremes had a forward battering ram or prow, which was long and hollow and designed for ramming amidships when a trireme conducted the periplous or encircling manoeuvre.[65] Corinthian triremes had a shorter but solid prow ideal for frontal ramming, which was better suited for the limited manoeuvring space in the Great Harbour (Thuc. 7.36). These changes to the Syracusan triremes must have occupied builders for some weeks before they felt they were able to go into battle a second time with a greater chance of success. Gylippus' tactic was again to use both land and naval forces in tandem to drain the Athenians of their manpower and supplies. He ordered the Syracusan army to form up outside the walls at Akradina, and also instructed the garrison at Polichne to march out against the Athenian encampment facing the Olympieion. The Athenians were therefore faced with hostile forces on either side of their camp. Moreover, the Syracusan fleet also put out knowing that the Athenians had land behind them while they had the open sea to retreat to, and the Athenians were limited to a forwards and backwards movement only. The appearance of their enemy's fleet threw the Athenians off balance and they were slow to launch their own ships probably because a good number of the rowers had been armed to fight as light armed troops. The Athenians finally manned seventy-five triremes against about eighty from Syracuse (Thuc. 7.37).

The two navies seem to have spent their time skirmishing but no engagement occurred and the sides broke off contact late in the afternoon, although Thucydides (7.38) states that two Athenian triremes were sunk. The land forces are not mentioned but presumably there was also no fighting to speak of. The next day was quiet but Nicias appears to have been sufficiently perturbed to order his trierarchs to repair any warships which could then be launched. His concern is also evident in that he instructed stronger defences of the anchorage along the beach beside the Athenian camp. At this stage it, like the Syracusan harbour further along the beach beside the agora, had been protected by stakes driven into the sand and which projected out of the water. Now Nicias also commanded merchant vessels to be anchored outside this stockade, at intervals claims Thucydides (7.38) of about sixty metres (200 feet) and that these acted as entrances and exits to an enclosed space into which the Athenians triremes might retreat if so needed.[66] These gaps in the stockade were also protected by metal dolphins which if lowered could entangle the rigging of any enemy ship in pursuit. This strengthening of defences occupied a whole day.

After a day's respite from fighting, the Syracusan fleet moved out in the Great Harbour again and the two sides spent another day sparring without any particular outcome. Then Ariston, one of the Corinthian commanders, suggested that the entire Syracusan fleet should retreat into its anchorage as if terminating the day's proceedings. In the meantime merchants and other retailers were instructed to set up their market beside the beached ships so that the crews could take their food beside their ships rather than in the agora or in their homes. The strategy proposed was that they should have their food and then immediately re-launch their ships for an attack on the Athenian naval base. The Athenians on the other hand assumed that the fighting was finished for the day and went about their business in a much more leisurely fashion. It is possibly by now unremarkable to report that they were taken in by the ruse when the Syracusan fleet suddenly re-emerged into the Great Harbour. There was confusion in the ranks of the Athenians, many of whom had not eaten since the morning, but they took to their ships to tackle the Syracusans. A stand-off immediately began but the Athenian commanders decided that with tired crews they could delay no longer and went on the offensive. The Syracusan triremes with their stronger beaks met the frontal attack easily and the confusion on the Athenian side was compounded by the enemy's use of small boats which sailed between the warships with crews of javelin throwers and archers. The Athenians reversed oars and backed off, which became a retreat in haste to find safety. Two Syracusan warships that attempted to enter the Athenian anchorage were caught and disabled by use of the metal dolphins. However, altogether the Athenians suffered the more serious loss of seven triremes and the crews of these ships who were mostly killed. The Syracusans were exultant believing that they had obtained superiority on sea and were also confident that they could now get the better of the besiegers on land as well.

It was within a day or so of this victory that Demosthenes and Eurymedon arrived at Syracuse (Thuc. 7.42) in front of the defenders who allowed them to beach at the Athenian camp in Lysimeleia without hindrance. It became immediately apparent once the generals met that there was a great divergence in opinion of how to take the siege forward to a successful result. Nicias still firmly believed that Syracuse could be forced into an outright surrender since friends in the city informed him that there was a severe shortage of funds for continuing the war. He asserted that the Syracusans had already spent 2000 talents and they could not maintain such a massive expenditure indefinitely. The Syracusans had also received a severe shock at the sight of the number of enemy reinforcements, which were almost equal in size to the current besieging force in Lysimeleia.[67] Being again heavily outnumbered they were obviously not keen to engage immediately in battle, and this is precisely what Demosthenes advocated believing that a rapid and unexpected offensive which took advantage of the Athenian superiority in manpower would cause despondency to grow in Syracuse. Therefore, a plan was hatched whereby Demosthenes and the other two generals, Eurymedon and Menander, would lead a night attack on Epipolai, while Nicias was to remain in reserve in the camp.[68] The object was to regain command of the heights and deprive their opponents of contact with the interior of the island. The generals surely also contemplated that such an assault might bring about an entry into the city and that would certainly force a rapid conclusion to the conflict. The new arrivals set about ransacking the land around the Anapos River and met no resistance from the Syracusans other than those stationed out at the fort at Polichne,[69] but an attempt to break up the latest Syracusan cross-wall failed when the Athenian siege equipment was set alight. The Athenian infantry mustered in the camp and each man provided with rations for five days. In order to maximize the surprise the forces were to depart at about midnight since it would be impossible to mount an attack on Epipolai by day without the element of surprise (Thuc. 7.43). The troops had to march more or less the same distance – six kilometres (3–4 miles) – that the Syracusans were obliged to when Nicias and Lamachus made their landing at Leon and went up to Eurialos at the western edge of Epipolai. The acquisition of Eurialos, almost certainly where the Athenian fort of Labdalum had been situated and where there was now a Syracusan garrison, was crucial since this place could not only block any supplies entering the city from the west but also reopened for the Athenians the overland connection with Catane.

At first, the plan went smoothly and the Athenians scattered the Syracusan garrison at Eurialos. However, there were three other forts on the plateau to which the majority of the defenders of the first fort escaped and they alerted the others to this attack. Yet how this army of probably at least ten thousand hoplites was able to charge Eurialos without detection seems far-fetched, but it is again an indication of lax sentry duty and the expectation that war would be fought along accepted practice and hence would not occur at night. Indeed Thucydides states that this was the sole night battle of the entire Peloponnesian War.[70] Having taken the fort at Eurialos, which was probably where the attackers should have paused and waited for dawn, the impetuous Demosthenes who wanted a major victory by storming the Syracusan cross–wall at Neapolis at once allowed his troops to proceed in the darkness with the moon behind them into unfamiliar terrain. Initially impetus carried them forward so that Syracusan reserves numbering about 600 who came out to face this assault were routed after heavy fighting.[71] Gylippus was informed of the attack and ordered out extra troops from the city, while some Athenians occupied the cross–wall, probably those closest to the wall from Lysimeleia and not those moving across Epipolai from the west. These are said to have started dismantling the Syracusan fortifications while the main force of the Athenian infantry moved forwards against the defenders who had just come out of the city. The attackers seemed to be having the best of it when some of the hoplites who had recently come to Syracuse from Boeotia suddenly turned the tide and the Athenians began to fall back. The result was a disaster, and Thucydides gives us a glimpse of the unfolding drama.

It was difficult to discover from either side what exactly happened. During the day those engaged in the fighting have a clear idea of the action they are involved in even if they cannot see everything. At night however no one can be sure of what precisely occurred. The moon was full but this allowed only the visibility available during such light. Those fighting could see the outlines of figures but were unsure whether these were friends or enemies. There were large numbers of heavy infantry from both sides moving around in the confined space. Some of the Athenians had been defeated but others had yet to fight and were coming up on the offensive. A great part of the army had only just arrived on the summit while still more troops were still making their way up, and were unsure in which direction to go. (Thuc. 7.44)

Not only was there a complete lack of order but there was also now absolute mayhem since in the darkness the only way to identify friend or foe was by shouting out the watchword. The Syracusans were cheering at their turning back of the attack and were also shouting out the Athenian watchword to catch out the enemy. Added to this was the singing of the paeans of various contingents in the opposing armies, which because of their similarities caused further confusion.[72] This resulted in the Athenians killing their own troops in error, but mostly in widespread panic from the desire to escape. The troops who had recently arrived were completely at a loss with their bearings and among these there must have been heavy casualties. The veterans of the siege at least had some knowledge of Epipolai and how either to retrace their steps to the west or, as Thucydides claims, to throw away their armour and to plunge down the steep southern side of the plateau for the safety of the camp near the harbour. By daybreak the scale of the defeat became evident. Wandering Athenians were rounded up and killed by the Syracusan cavalry. The Athenians received back their dead under a truce while the victors set up trophies on Epipolai. There were fewer dead, Thucydides says, than the quantity of arms lost by the defeated side.

After this tremendous if unexpected victory, the Syracusans sent envoys to Akragas in the hope of securing an alliance while Gylippus went off again into the interior to search for more troops (Thuc. 7.46). In the Athenian camp the generals are said to have held discussions about the way forward following this major reverse especially since disease was starting to take a toll among the troops.[73] Demosthenes wanted an immediate withdrawal while the Athenians still held command of the sea and could easily transport the troops out through the entrance to the Great Harbour. Nicias remained opposed to this move but gave only vague reasons for remaining in the camp. The others believed he might have been relying on informants in the city, although by this time surrender by Syracuse appeared extremely remote. The arguments persisted but Nicias refused to budge in his assessment of their future prospects and since he retained seniority in the command the others did not over-rule him. Akragas did not form an alliance with Syracuse but Gylippus returned with a substantial force including those troops recently despatched from the Peloponnese who had been blown off course and had spent some time in Africa (Thuc. 7.50).

The Athenian command belatedly appreciated the fact that, with these further forces at the disposal of the Syracusans and because nothing new had been attempted following the defeat on Epipolai, either a new scheme had become vital or they were faced with a withdrawal the timing of which was no longer of their choice. Demosthenes again was the most strenuous advocate of abandoning the siege completely while their infantry and naval forces were intact, and Nicias no longer opposed the idea of a retreat but that it should be done without a vote among the Athenians, which would have quickly alerted their enemy. It was decided therefore to give orders as secretly as possible and depart quickly and by taking the Syracusans by surprise allow them no time to cause further damaging losses to the Athenians, expeditionary force. No sooner had this been decided than an eclipse of the moon took place. The date was in the late evening of 27 August and was a celestial phenomenon, which was not only unexpected than also disconcerting to those present especially, it appears, to the Athenians.[74] Thucydides (7.50) says little except that the Athenians saw this as somehow connected in a negative way with their decision to retreat. There was therefore a general feeling among the rank and file that they should delay their departure, which was supported by Nicias, who was, says Thucydides: 'rather drawn to superstitious practices and predicting omens of this sort and so on the advice of seers refused absolutely to contemplate any further action of any kind until the lunar cycle of twenty-seven days had run its course.' A lunar eclipse observed in Lysimeleia must have been a dramatic sight. The moon rises from the east out of the Ionian Sea and there are no natural obstacles to obscure its course from its rise to its decline. The sky in antiquity was obviously far less polluted and much less affected by modern artificial lighting, which today detracts from the splendour of such celestial movements especially when the moon is at its greatest extent as it was on the night of 27 August 413 BC. Plutarch in his *Life of Nicias* (23–24) dwells at some length on the episode and goes some way to explaining why there was such dismay. While the eclipse of the sun, although perhaps the more dramatic event in the heavens, was already understood by the fifth century BC the reason for the eclipse of the moon was not and hence the great uncertainty about its meaning and the fear of whether or not the moon would return in its next cycle. This must in part explain Nicias' action and why he was not challenged by the other generals; and yet no consternation is evident among those inside Syracuse about the same event. Plutarch also states that the seer Stilbides, on whose judgement Nicias usually relied, had recently died and those who gave the advice to delay were of much inferior calibre to this man. Plutarch states that the opposite for what was advised should have been the correct solution: that the moon's disappearance would hide the withdrawal of the Athenians. Nicias' anxiety to follow the seers' deliberations illustrates his own fears, but may also cloak his growing alarm at leading a failed venture for which he stood to be blamed and probably convicted for mismanagement.[75] In the event, the Athenians were not to be idle during this spell, whether they wanted to be or not.

The Syracusans regarded the eclipse as a heaven-sent bonus and were galvanized into further action when they heard of the Athenian decision to stay put. They perceived that there was now a real opportunity not just to inflict further defeats but to destroy the besiegers utterly. They no longer wanted the Athenians to withdraw in strength nor indeed to retreat to another base in Sicily from which to continue to be a threat. The crews of the warships were put into immediate training and after some days it was decided to combine a land and sea attack against the harassed Athenians (Thuc. 7.51). The date was probably very early in September when at first a small attack was made on the Athenian fortifications with a sortie from Akradina in which the besiegers lost about seventy of their cavalry, a severe loss when the opposition had such superiority in this quarter, and a few hoplites and the Syracusans understandably withdrew, probably exultant.[76] On the next day the Syracusans launched seventy-six triremes into the Great harbour and made another land sortie from Akradina (Thuc. 7.52). The Athenians responded by launching eighty-six warships, far from the total entire number they possessed, but which probably represents what was realistic to man in the light of so much illness in the camp. The fleet on this occasion was under the command of Eurymedon who took up the accustomed position of a commander on the right wing. As usual the right wing moved forward on the offensive to carry out the periplous and ram the Syracusan warship amidships. However, the Syracusan triremes were far quicker off the mark and smashed into the Athenian centre with their smaller and more effective beaks. Eurymedon was either slow in making his manoeuvre or his attention was somehow diverted because he now found himself isolated from the rest of the fleet. His squadron now found itself the object of a vigorous attack and no longer the attacker and when cornered Eurymedon was killed and his trireme destroyed along with the others that had formed the right wing. Thucydides (7.52) again gives little detail here perhaps because he viewed this episode as one of a sequence in the declining fortunes of the Athenians. However, Diodorus (13.13.3) provides a fuller account of Eurymedon's end, which is probably derived from the Syracusan historian Philistus who may well have been an eyewitness of the events. Diodorus confirms that Eurymedon commanded the Athenian right wing and that his opposite number was the Syracusan Agatharchus and that the Athenian left wing was under Euthydemus with Sicanus commanding the Syracusan right wing. Python from Corinth was in command of the Syracusan centre opposite Menander, the other Athenian *strategos*. The Athenian line was longer than that of its opposition and should therefore have not come into difficulties but Eurymedon in attempting the periplous detached the Athenian right wing from its centre and the Syracusans turned to face him having greater space to manoeuvre their triremes. He was forced back into the small bay at Daskon, which was held by the Syracusans operating out of their fort at Polichne. His entire squadron of eight triremes beached and all were destroyed together with their crews (Diod. 13.13.4). The casualties here alone would have totalled more than 1500 men since the Syracusans had no need for prisoners. This dramatic turn of events affected the Athenian line, which gave way from the right says Diodorus and their whole fleet fell back in some disorder to their fortified anchorage. Most of the Athenian warships made it inside their makeshift gateways but some were grounded along the beach outside their camp and the Syracusans tried to destroy them using a derelict merchant ship as a fire-ship, although this was ineffective. When the Athenian reverse became apparent Gylippus ordered his infantry along the beach from Akradina to intercept any ships that were beached to the north of the besiegers' compound. The distance from the walls of the city to the Athenian camp were barely a kilometre and so any movement on the ground was easily to be seen. On duty at the Athenian fortifications facing the city were some Etruscan mercenaries and these charged out and attacked the Syracusan infantry forcing them into the marshy ground of Lysimeleia. The Syracusans commanders ordered in more infantry but the Athenians responded in equal measure mainly because they knew the problems that would be caused by the loss of further vessels. Most it seems were carried or dragged to the safety of the stockade. Diodorus (13.13.8) agrees with Thucydides (7.53) in stating that eighteen triremes were lost and 2000 men from their crews were killed. Although Diodorus is not specific this probably means that the Athenian total losses were twenty-five or twenty-six triremes and about 3500 killed. Thucydides gives no casualty figures for this engagement because it was unnecessary: the mighty Athenian fleet had been defeated in a sea battle and that was momentous enough for his account.

The effect of this naval defeat on Athenian spirits was so alarming that Thucydides (7.55) gives the impression that it produced intense inertia and lethargy. Nicias was still firmly against doing anything until the lunar cycle resumed and was probably supported by many in the ranks. The loss of the general Eurymedon was also keenly felt and there seems to have been a widespread disbelief that was almost a state of denial that they should suddenly find themselves in such a dangerous predicament. The Syracusans, on the other hand, were elated and maintained a frenetic activity in the widespread hope that just a little more effort on their part would result in the complete destruction of their attackers, an idea that would have been beyond anyone's thoughts a few months earlier. They also began to make plans for blockading the entrance to the Great Harbour, which would result in the

Athenians either having to force their way into the open sea or retreating overland.[77] Thucydides states that the entrance to the Great Harbour was 'eight stadia' (1600 kilometres or a little under a mile) and that this was sealed by bringing up a large number of, presumably, derelict triremes and other vessels and lining these up end to end or broadside on so forming a barrier. Diodorus (13.14.2) adds the detail that moored at anchor were 'triremes, merchant ships and smaller vessels joined together with chains of iron and between these ships they nailed down boards as bridges, completing the task in three days'. In effect not only was the Great Harbour sealed but it now acted as a fortified wall on the water over which the Athenians would have to scale to escape.

It is an extraordinary reflection on the low psychological state of the Athenians that they observed the construction of this boom in the harbour and did nothing about it. Instead there was a meeting of the generals and all the senior officers to formulate the next objective. They were running short of supplies since it had been thought that a withdrawal would have taken place some three weeks beforehand. No one had thought to send messengers to Catane, the nearest Athenian ally, for additional supplies when the delay because of the lunar eclipse became effective. Therefore, it was decided to attempt to storm the barrier in the harbour with all available triremes and manpower, leave a garrison in the camp at Lysimeleia with all the sick and wounded, but make this fortified zone more compact and easily defendable by abandoning the circular fort at Syra at Neapolis on Epipolai. This was hardly a positive move except that Nicias was to remain in the camp until such time as he could be reinforced by the Athenians when they had regrouped at Catane. If they were unable to take the barrier of ships then they would burn their triremes to prevent them falling into the hands of their opponents and march out from Syracuse to a safe haven overland.

The date was by now the end of September for the lunar cycle had concluded and plans for the attack on the barrier were put into effect. Thucydides (7.60) says that the Athenians launched 110 warships, which were also packed with javelin throwers and slingers, while the Syracusan fleet was much as it had been before.[78] Before the Athenians and Syracusans engaged each side was addressed by its commander. Gylippus urged crews of the triremes and the garrison on the harbour barrier to find that additional energy to repulse the impending attack so that they would free themselves and the whole of Sicily from oppression and that victory was in their grasp. Nicias addressed the infantry, which he drew up along the beach in order to give help where it might be needed for any warship in trouble, and encouraged them in this latest endeavour and said that although they had suffered defeats not to be downhearted. He then went from trireme to trireme offering words of support to the captains and the crews but significantly he is said to have felt that he had not said enough and that he was in a highly anxious state of mind (Thuc. 7.69).[79] That said the Athenians sailed out into the Great Harbour from their camp commanded by Demosthenes, Euthydemus and Menander; the wings of the Syracusan fleet as before were commanded by Sicanus and Agatharchus with Python in the centre. The Syracusans wanted to engage the Athenians as quickly as possible; the Athenians meanwhile wanted to avoid contact with the opposing fleet since their objective was to punch a hole in the boom and reach the open sea, and therefore all manpower had to be focussed in that sector of the battlefield. The Athenian rowers set off at a sprint for the barrier using all their energy to reach this goal as quickly as possible and Thucydides (7.70) certainly gives the impression that the barrier was stormed by the crews of some of their warships and that fighting was intense here. The attack was hampered however by the presence of the Syracusan triremes, which attacked the Athenians mostly from the rear. There was no room for tactics or manoeuvres and therefore the fighting spread from ship to ship as one after another was rammed and the space in front of the barrier became packed with stationary triremes. This must explain the huge losses to the Athenian fleet compared to those suffered by the Syracusans. Thucydides states that some Syracusan triremes were positioned in front of the barrier and these were probably destroyed in the Athenian charge. Thereafter the Athenians lost ships which were rammed by the Syracusan triremes in their rear. Thucydides makes it clear that a hole was made in the barrier probably by loosening one or more of the ships in the chain and some Athenian triremes may have made it to the sea, but there they would have faced more enemy warships placed precisely to prevent any getaway.[80] The battle's course is described in dramatic terms, the aspirations of both sides in the conflict, and the cheers and sighs of dismay from each side when they were winning or losing. The graphic scenes of death and mayhem are worthy of any Greek tragedy (Thuc. 7.70–71; Diod. 14.15.4–17.5).[81]

In the end the Athenians broke probably from sheer fatigue and bolted back to the beach near their camp since many were unable to enter the anchorage. Athenian losses are said to have been as many as sixty triremes and crews lost, a staggering figure if accurate (Diod. 13.17.5) and the heaviest loss to any Athenian-led force since the defeat in Egypt in 454 BC.[82] The Syracusan losses are put by Diodorus at a much more modest eight lost and sixteen severely damaged. The Athenian crews struggled ashore having abandoned their ships on the beach and then they besieged the tents of the generals demanding an immediate withdrawal by land. Thucydides (7.71) observes darkly that the Athenians now stood little chance of extricating themselves from the trap that was mostly of their own making. Demosthenes urged the ranks to attack the barrier again since even with sixty losses the Athenians still had superiority in numbers to their enemy. The men would have nothing to do with this suggestion and refused even to man the ships, a situation tantamount to mutiny. What is more shocking is that the Athenians were altogether so dispirited that no truce was arranged to collect the dead; and even Nicias does not appear to have insisted on the completion of funeral rites. This omission from custom and practice highlights the despondency among the ranks but that there was also widespread panic and anxiety about the future. The Athenians were quick to decide that they must depart on foot as soon as they could and head north into the allied territory of Leontinoi or Catane. In the meantime, Hermocrates got wind of their imminent departure, although it cannot have come as much of a surprise, but he was also faced with a dilemma. Like the authorities in the city, Hermocrates wanted to destroy the Athenian besieging force if possible and he did not want them to escape that same night, but just at that moment most of the population of the city were understandably enjoying the victory and since it coincided with a festival to Heracles, the majority were drunk in the double celebration. Therefore, Hermocrates decided on a ruse to fool the Athenians into a further delay in order to allow the Syracusan troops to recover. He sent messengers on horseback to within earshot of the Athenian stockade and these shouted out that as friends of the Athenians they wanted to warn them not to leave their camp at night since the Syracusans were guarding the roads and that they should rather leave by daylight. This message was relayed to the generals who believed the information and ordered the troops to spend greater time in their preparations. It may seem incredible but it was not until a further two days after the final battle in the harbour that the Athenians were ready to march out, by which time the Syracusan troops were of course on full alert and guarding all available routes out of Lysimeleia.

The sick and the wounded were left behind, a sure sign of immense panic, and these faced certain death soon after the Syracusans entered the camp after the departing Athenian army. Thucydides gives a glimpse of the harrowing last moments as those who were physically able formed up to depart. Family members and friends were left behind by the able-bodied in the rush to escape. Some are said to have struggled to follow but were quickly left behind to their fate. At least fifty triremes in battle-readiness were left behind as well as many smaller craft. Without another battle the Syracusans doubled their naval strength (Diod. 13.19.1; cf. Thuc. 7.72; 'nearly sixty'). The Athenians and their allies made their departure in two roughly equal groups of 20,000 each. The heavy infantry formed a square and within this protected cordon were the horses, the pack animals and the non-combatants. The vanguard was commanded by Nicias, the rearguard by Demosthenes. Thucydides gives a brief speech to Nicias as his group was about to march with an exhortation to persevere in a time of great adversity the main ingredient, but the pathos of the message cannot have been lost on the audience who knew the result of the expedition. Demosthenes is said to have gone about his troops with a similar message of encouragement. The Athenians set off moving up the Anapos Valley. One can but surmise what the Syracusans must have thought as they witnessed this movement of 40,000 men from the vantage point of their walls. Although the plan was to march in two defensive squares this is actually an impossible task to accomplish unless the landscape is a perfectly flat desert. The valley of the Anapos River was hardly that since it possessed cultivated fields, walls and drainage ditches and further inland the landscape changed into one of an uneven limestone terrain. It is therefore not surprising that by nightfall of 1 October the Athenians had marched just about ten kilometres (6 miles) close to where the modern town of Floridia stands some height above the valley and they bivouacked here since it was easily defendable. Earlier in the day they had fought to cross the Anapos River and put a small Syracusan force to flight (Thuc. 7.78), but at least they were moving in the direction where safety lay. On the next morning (2 October) they descended from their first camp and intended to continue their march using the mostly dry Anapos River as a track that would lead them up into the Hybla Mountains behind the limestone mass of Mount Climiti and thence towards Leontinoi, a distance of two or three days' march.[83] The river bed at this point runs through a low gully or ravine, which is steep sided and flat topped, before opening out again towards the mountains. Since the land around is very uneven this was the obvious route for an army trying to maintain a square formation to march. However, Syracusan forces were present in large numbers too and had barricaded the exit or northern end of the ravine and positioned archers and javelin throwers on the cliffs above. The Athenians made an assault to force their way through what Thucydides (7.78) calls the ἀκραῖον λέπας or 'high cliff'. The Syracusan troops on the top of gully threw missiles down onto their enemy while the stockade in front of the Athenians proved to be too strongly defended to overthrow. The Athenians withdrew and made a makeshift camp at the southern end of the gully. Next day (3 October) they tried again but while they were attacking the barrier Gylippus sent further troops to the south end of the ravine to erect another barricade in the rear of the Athenians, but they countered this tactic and drove off the Syracusans. By late in the afternoon there was still no breakthrough and having taken heavy losses the Athenians regrouped where they began in the morning. Supplies were short and there was little water and it was clear that forcing this route through the gully was impracticable. The alternative was to attempt the direct route to the north, which lay between Mount Climiti and Eurialos. Although this was route was relatively easy for infantry to proceed it also made them an easy target for the Syracusan cavalry and the archers who were shadowing the retreat. The next morning (4 October) the Athenians advanced barely a kilometre up this slope suffering heavy casualties and finally retreating to the previous evening's place of encampment. The way forward was impossible. The troops were exhausted and there were few supplies left to them and all hope of retreating to the north was quickly receding. Nicias and Demosthenes therefore decided on an act of desperation by changing course to the south, but there were no allied cities along the south coast of the island. The Geloans and Camarinaeans had both sent troops to Syracuse and would be unlikely to offer help unless compelled and the Athenians lacked the means to force alliances on these states. Thucydides suggests that messages had been sent to some of the Sicel communities who were sympathetic towards the Athenians and that they were expected to bring aid but he does not specify who these were. These possible allies were certainly not the Sicels of Hybla whom the Athenians had only just recently attacked and these Sicels occupied much of the mountainous areas to the south of Syracuse. It could be that Nicias thought it was possible to go inland from the coast via one of the river valleys to the south of the Anapos – there were several to choose from – and that one of these would eventually bring the Athenians to safety. If they moved quickly enough they would also place a sufficiently long distance between them and the Syracusans, which might deter any pursuit out of Syracusan territory. Thus they might still escape to Leontinoi. It was a gamble but the Athenians had left themselves no alternative. What the Athenians had not anticipated was that the Syracusans would pursue them to the bitter end.

Leaving camp fires alight to confuse the enemy Nicias and Demosthenes set off in a south westerly direction that same night. The distance to the coast was not that great but any march overnight in unfamiliar terrain was going to be difficult for any military force. The Athenians were also hampered by their recent setbacks, their lack of rest and numerous injured personnel, yet by daybreak (5 October) Nicias in the vanguard had reached and crossed the Cacyparis River (the modern River Cassibile) a little less than twenty kilometres (12 miles) south of the Anapos Valley and close to the sea.[84] Here they again scattered a small Syracusan detachment, which was in the process of blocking the coast road, and the Athenians continued south (Thuc. 7.80). At the same time the Syracusans further north woke up to the fact that the Athenians had disappeared. At first there was some suspicion that Gylippus had connived in this attempt to escape since he was believed to have no particular grudge to bear against these adversaries. However, once tempers had cooled the order went out to pursue the enemy at any cost. Nicias' force was moving at a better pace than those of Demosthenes mainly because, according to Thucydides (7.80), his troops were leading the way and the general although not in a good physical state himself, set a fine example believing that the further they went from Syracuse the greater the chances of salvation. The rearguard under Demosthenes was in a poor way by comparison, in greater disorder and moving much more slowly, but managed to keep up until it reached the Cacyparis, after which it lost contact with the vanguard. Soon after crossing the river the Syracusans caught up with the Athenian rearguard and instead of maintaining their march Demosthenes decided to draw up his troops for battle by which time they became surrounded. The Athenians then took up a defensive position in an olive grove, which was walled but gave little protection from javelins or volleys of arrows.[85] There was no escape and by the afternoon terms had been discussed, and a surrender of an army took place, not unprecedented except in scale. Six thousand are said to have surrendered with only the promise that they would not be killed and were taken as state captives.[86] Demosthenes is said to have tried to commit suicide but was foiled in the attempt and was taken as a prisoner to Syracuse. Of the other 14,000 in the rearguard many had been killed or been left to die from their wounds, others were wandering the countryside and were rounded up as prisoners to end their days as slaves to private individuals

Nicias and his half of the army had meanwhile reached and crossed the Erineos River (Thuc. 7. 82) and since he was some distance ahead of the rearguard and found no opposition in the vicinity he made camp. Nicias must have imagined that safety was very nearly in sight for the Erineos Valley led into the interior and could bring the Athenians to Leontinoi, but also they were now beyond the *chorē* or traditional territory of Syracuse.[87] The Athenians probably believed that they would now be allowed to leave without further attacks. On the next morning (6 October) the Syracusans caught up with the Athenians and through heralds informed them of the surrender of the rearguard. Showing for the first time a glimmer of scepticism, a trait that would have better served his cause earlier in the expedition, Nicias refused to believe them and demanded a truce in which to send one of his own cavalrymen to discover firsthand whether or not this was the truth. This scout soon returned with the news that Demosthenes had surrendered to the Syracusans, so Nicias sent a herald to Gylippus and the Syracusan commanders with an extraordinary offer.

He said that Athens would repay whatever costs the Syracusans had incurred on account of this war if his army was allowed a free passage. He offered to give an Athenian citizen as a hostage for each talent Syracuse had spent on the war.[88] (Thuc. 7.83)

The offer was rejected and the Syracusans launched an immediate attack on the weary Athenians who were again surrounded. The fighting ended with the dusk but as the Athenians had no supplies to speak of it was decided to try and continue their march by night. Unfortunately for the Athenians the Syracusans were not to be fooled a second time and were vigilant in their night watch, which was alerted to such an attempt. The Athenians seeing that they were discovered instead of attempting what they had planned decided to sit out the night and move on in daylight. With the sun (7 October) the Athenian force moved forward again in some disorder since the Syracusan cavalry and archers were everywhere attacking from all sides against an enemy which was virtually at its wits' end. Sometime during the late morning the Athenians reached the Assinaros River (modern Tellaro) probably close to the modern village of San Paulo. Nicias may have still entertained hopes that if they crossed this stream the Syracusan might pause long enough to let the survivors escape from what was little better than a rout. The Tellaro today is hardly more than a muddy stream in the summer months and the water that is flowing does so across a wide plain towards the sea. The Athenian troops desperate for water plunged towards this source of sustenance and Thucydides (7.84) remarks that the mere sight of water brought an end to all order and discipline. There was a frenzied rush to drink and cross the stream while at the same time the Syracusans maintained their relentless attacks especially since the land was very suitable for the unhampered use of cavalry. The death toll here was especially high since killing enemy infantry who had thrown away their arms and armour to get at the water or to get away was an easy exercise for those on horseback. It is said that men drank the water beside their dead comrades whose blood mingled with the mud such was the insanity of the end of this saga. There was simply no further fight left in the Athenians but Nicias managed to find his way to Gylippus to whom he surrendered and asked that the killing be stopped.[89] Gylippus seems to have possessed sufficient authority to be able to rein in the blood lust of his troops and those who were still alive were taken as private possessions for sale or to be kept as house slaves. Thudydides suggests that few Athenians were taken as official prisoners of Syracuse from the catastrophe on the Assinaros because, unlike the fight at the estate of Polyzelos two days before, there had been no formal surrender of the army. Nicias with his immediate staff was however taken back to Syracuse. The generals – we are not told if Menander was still alive – were relieved of their arms and armour and two trophies were erected; one *tropaion* was erected at the Assinaros River, the other at the place where Demosthenes had been captured.[90] The Syracusans could have set up several so total was their victory. The two generals were either executed or murdered soon afterwards. The Syracusans feared that Gylippus might allow them their freedom if they were transported to the Peloponnese. It was also believed that Nicias in particular might be forced to divulge the names of his friends in the city and that these were keen to see his end. Their bodies were exposed to the elements and never buried, a sad conclusion to a tragedy of immense scale and human cost. The Athenian casualties will have numbered well in excess of 50,000 hoplite infantry, lightly armed troops and rowers from the triremes.[91]

The extent of the detailed background to the siege, almost the whole of Book 6, gives some indication of Thucydides' conviction that this single event held a central point in his narrative. Given that his account of the war ended in 411 with Book 8 and that hostilities continued until 404, it is likely that the siege of Syracuse would have occupied a point more or less mid-way through the history and was both the temporal and narrative climax in the description of Athenian power. After Syracuse only a steady decline and fall could be anticipated.[92] Nicias is surprisingly spared much if any criticism by ancient writers from Thucydides to Plutarch who judged him to have been a relatively good and honest individual who made mistakes but was unlucky to fail as he did. Plutarch does accuse him of being timid and a coward and that when forced to take the command against Syracuse he showed a lack of spirit. Yet there is also praise for a man who evidently disliked the war but was consistently elected to senior positions because his fellow citizens considered him a trusted and good commander. He also notes that Nicias had a good record and came close to winning the siege at Syracuse but that his illness and the jealousy of the Athenians contributed to his failure (Plut. *Comparison of Nicias and Crassus*, 2.3–5.1). This is interesting if a little misleading for Nicias did not possess the leadership qualities necessary to bring this unique expedition to a successful conclusion. He was much too conservative, uncertain and pessimistic and completely lacking in any flair or imagination. Throughout the twenty-one months or so of the expedition's life he constantly reacted against the temerity of his fellow commanders yet gained nothing by his own over-cautious approach. His delay in leaving Syracuse brought about the annihilation of his fleet and army and for that he was solely responsible. His fear of facing his fellow citizens having failed in his task actually hastened that disaster to the army over which he had command.

It is obvious that it was only after the final sea battle in the Great Harbour that a full retreat became an acceptable plan to Nicias, but by then the trap had been sealed. The overland route was fraught with danger and Syracusan superiority in cavalry meant that the Athenians embarked on what was virtually a suicidal plan. There was hardly any chance of extricating themselves at such a late stage. The loss of Plemmyrion should have brought about an Athenian withdrawal. A strategic retreat even if only as far north as Megara Hyblaia would have prevented the successful sealing of the harbour mouth and, if a division of forces had not been made then, certainly when the Syracusans began to contemplate this objective and when a strenuous Athenian counterattack should have been launched. The loss of Labdalum was also a major setback, which ought to have been rectified, and which was clearly in Demosthenes' mind when he advocated the night attack on Epipolai. The failure to complete the circumvallation of Syracuse is also indicative of very poor leadership. Nicias clearly hoped that by leaving the city with a land-link it would encourage an armistice but had quite the reverse affect. And once Gylippus arrived the psychological state of the besieged so improved and continued to become so much more positive than the besiegers that the denouement could almost be predicted from then on. Thucydides was right in his assessment of the scale of the Syracusan victory and its wide-ranging effect on the politics of the Greek city states. His estimation of Nicias is, however, unnecessarily kind possibly from a familiarity with that individual's personality but in not attributing just blame to the commander of the expedition he has left an indelible flaw in his account of this most famous of military events in antiquity.

Chronology

427   Summer: Athenian fleet of twenty triremes under Laches despatched to Rhegium

425   Early in the year: Pythodorus replaces Laches as general in charge of Athenian operations in Sicily

424   Summer: peace in Sicily

415   Late spring: the debate in Athens about aid for Segesta
July: Athenian expedition leaves Athens for Corcyra

414   April/May: Athenians land at Leon and occupy Epipolai

413   April/May: Spartans invade Attica and fortify Decelea
Middle of August: Athenian defeat on Epipolai 'The Night Battle'
27 August 8.00 p.m.: lunar eclipse begins

28 August – 27 September: Athenians delay departure on the advice of the seers

Early September: battle in the harbour and death of Eurymedon at Daskon

Second half of September: the entrance to the Great Harbour blocked in three days

Late September: the final battle in the harbour

28– 30 September: further Athenian delay in the camp

1 October: Athenians march as far as Floridia

2–3 October: battle in the ravine of the Anapos River

4 October: morning – Athenians attempt to cross into the Megarian Plain

night – Athenians change their route by marching to the south

5 October: Demosthenes surrenders with 6000 of his rearguard

6 October: Athenians attempt another night march but fail

7 October: final destruction of the Athenian expeditionary force at the Assinaros River

The family of Alcibiades

Megacles m. Agariste (daughter of Cleisthenes of Sicyon)

Hippocrates   Agariste m. Xanthippus   Cleisthenes

Megacles   Pericles († 429)   Ariphron   Deinomache m. Cleinias
(exiled 486)

Pericles († 405)   Hippocrates († 424)   Alcibiades († 404)

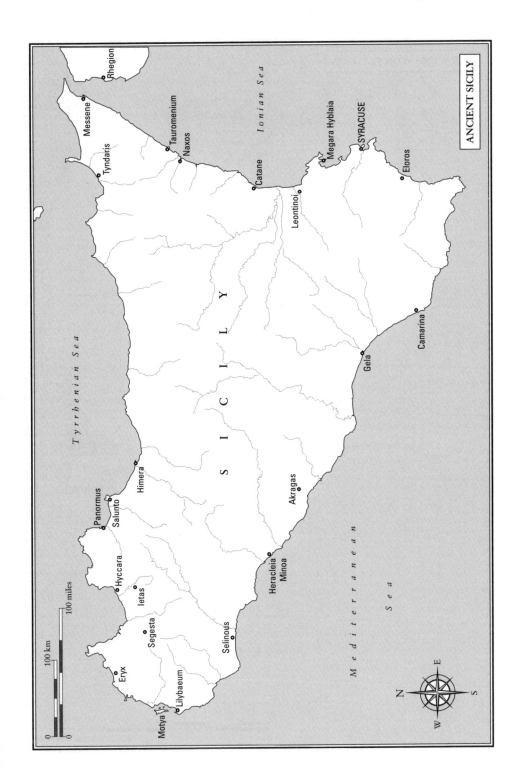

ANCIENT SICILY

Rhegion

Messene

Tyndaris

Tauromenium

Naxos

Catane

Ionian Sea

Megara Hyblaia

SYRACUSE

Eloros

Leontinoi

Tyrrhenian Sea

Panormus

Salunto

Himera

Hycara

Ietas

Segesta

Eryx

Lilybaeum

Motya

Selinous

Heracleia

Minoa

Akragas

S I C I L Y

Gela

Camarina

Mediterranean Sea

100 miles

100 km

N
W   E
S

SYRACUSE: MAIN FEATURES

N
W E
S

Leon

EPIPOLAI

Troigilos?

NEAPOLIS

AKRADINA

Little
Harbour

Lysimeleia

ORTYGIA

Anapos River

Great

Harbour

Daskon

POLICHNE

0   2 km
0   2 miles

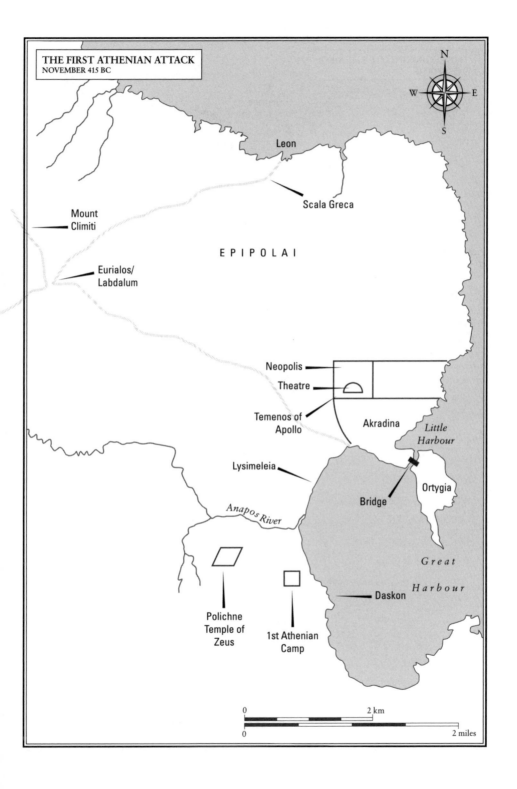

THE FIRST ATHENIAN ATTACK
NOVEMBER 415 BC

N
W E
S

Leon

Scala Greca

Mount
Climiti

E P I P O L A I

Eurialos/
Labdalum

Neopolis

Theatre

Temenos of
Apollo

Akradina

Little
Harbour

Lysimeleia

Bridge

Ortygia

Anapos River

Great

Harbour

Daskon

Polichne
Temple of
Zeus

1st Athenian
Camp

0   2 km

0   2 miles

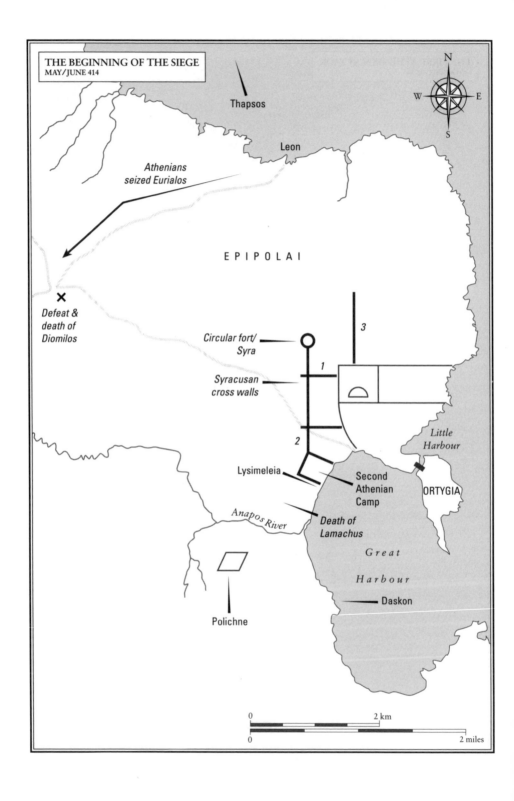

THE BEGINNING OF THE SIEGE
MAY/JUNE 414

N
W E
S

Thapsos

Leon

Athenians
seized Eurialos

EPIPOLAI

✕
Defeat &
death of
Diomilos

3

Circular fort/
Syra

1

Syracusan
cross walls

2

Little
Harbour

Lysimeleia

Second
Athenian
Camp

ORTYGIA

Anapos River

Death of
Lamachus

Great

Harbour

Daskon

Polichne

0   2 km

0   2 miles

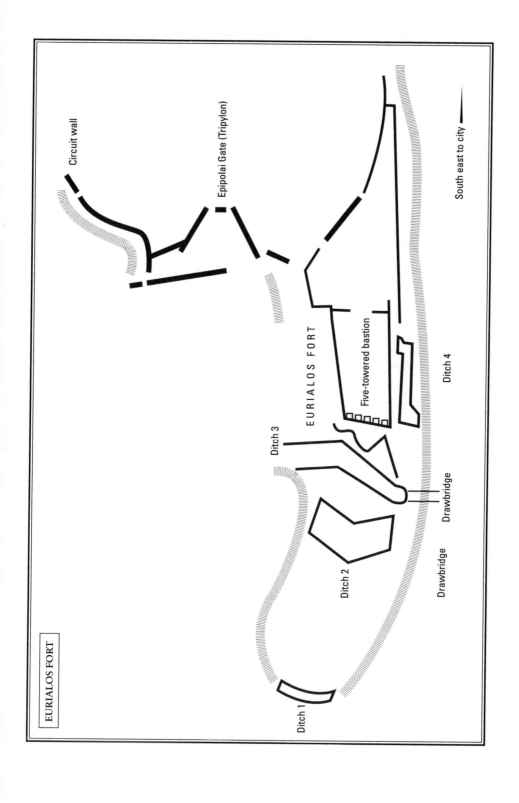

EURIALOS FORT

Circuit wall

Epipolai Gate (Tripylon)

EURIALOS FORT

Five-towered bastion

Ditch 4

Ditch 3

Drawbridge

Ditch 2

Drawbridge

Ditch 1

South east to city

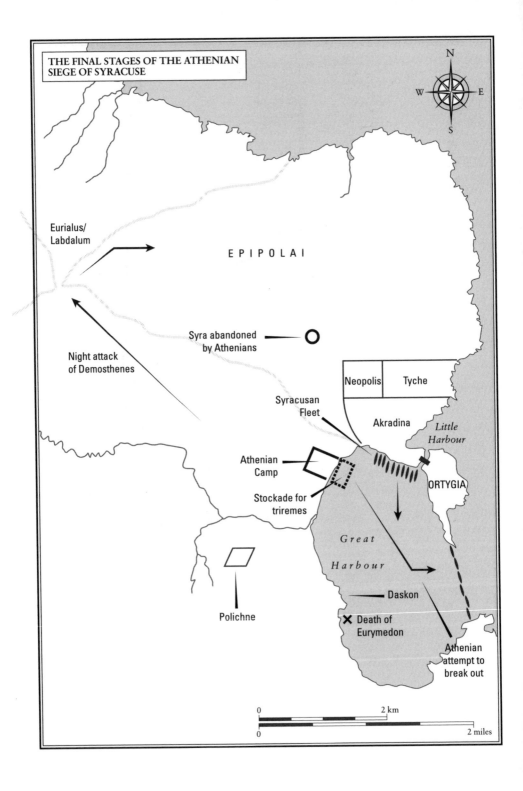

THE FINAL STAGES OF THE ATHENIAN
SIEGE OF SYRACUSE

N
W E
S

Eurialus/
Labdalum

EPIPOLAI

Syra abandoned
by Athenians

Night attack
of Demosthenes

Neopolis   Tyche

Syracusan
Fleet

Akradina   Little
Harbour

Athenian
Camp

ORTYGIA

Stockade for
triremes

Great
Harbour

Daskon

Polichne

✕ Death of
Eurymedon

Athenian
attempt to
break out

0   2 km

0   2 miles

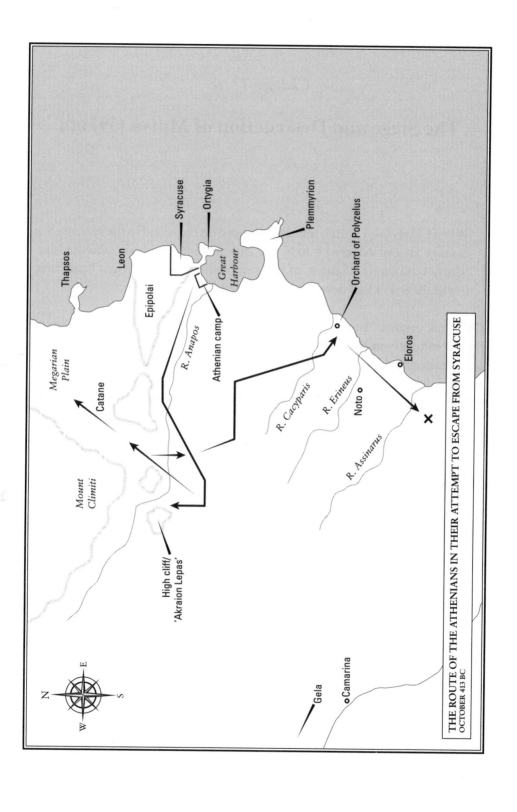

THE ROUTE OF THE ATHENIANS IN THEIR ATTEMPT TO ESCAPE FROM SYRACUSE
OCTOBER 413 BC

Chapter Three

The Siege and Destruction of Motya (397 BC)

When Cluverius, a Dutch traveller, stopped on the island in the seventeenth century AD and declared it to be the ancient Motya, nobody believed him. Motya was merely a figment of the imagination of some ancient historians, it was alleged; it had never actually existed.[1]

It has become quite clear from discussion hitherto that sieges figure prominently in the history of Sicily and Magna Graecia throughout the Classical and Hellenistic periods of antiquity. This is particularly so from about 510 BC and the siege of Sybaris (see above Chapter 1) down to 212 when, during the Second Punic War (218–201 BC), Syracuse was sacked by the Romans after enduring its fourth major siege in two hundred years, but which was the only one to end successfully for the besiegers.[2] The battlefield to be retraced in this chapter is situated on one of a small archipelago of islands lying off the west coast of Sicily known today as San Pantaleo or Mozia. The island is situated no more than 1500 metres (slightly less than 1 mile) from the mainland between the modern towns of Trapani (Drapana) and Marsala (Lilybaeum), and forms part of the rim of a bay in which there is a shallow lagoon.[3] A visit to Mozia today can only be accomplished by taking a small motor boat from an equally small but modern harbour. The water in the lagoon is shallow and roughly a metre to a metre and a half in depth (3 to 4½ feet), yet this is considerably deeper than it was in antiquity or even a century ago when the area around the island was probably more like tidal flats and marshland. Access to the island was by means of a manmade causeway that linked its northern end to the mainland today known as Birgi, which contained the main cemetery of the community. A hundred years ago it was possible to cross the causeway by carts that had extremely large wheels, a mode of transport no longer available since the sea level has risen along this coastline by as much as a metre. On the island itself, which is barely more than five kilometres (3 miles) in circumference, and never more than five metres in height (20 feet) above sea level, there was a trading settlement named Motya, which was founded by the Carthaginians, probably towards the end of the seventh century BC.

In the summer of 397 BC this emporium, it hardly deserves to be described as a city so confined is its urban space, was besieged and then destroyed by an army of Sicilian Greeks and their Sicel allies commanded by Dionysius, who eight years before had made himself the tyrant of Syracuse. Conflict in Sicily between its various inhabitants was endemic and largely based on ethnic differences not only between the earliest settlers the Sicels, Sicanians and Elymians, but also between the later arrivals the Carthaginians and Greeks, and even between Ionian and Dorian Greeks.[4] The literary sources which are Greek dwell on the hostilities between the people who had settled in Sicily from Greece and those from North Africa, and the people also known as Punic whose origins were in Phoenicia. The first attested warfare between the Sicilian Greek cities and Carthage is noted by Herodotus (7.157–162) towards the start of the fifth century when the latter attacked Himera on the north coast of the island,[5] but this may simply be the earliest recorded instance of strife between these two communities. However, it seems plain enough that after a tremendous Greek victory outside Himera, where the Carthaginian general Hamilcar was defeated and killed (Diod. 11.22.4) during a battle that saw the Greeks commanded by Gelon tyrant of Syracuse, Carthage is not known to have intervened in Sicily for over seventy years. Indeed, there appears to have been no attempt by Carthage to regain lost ground even at a time when the Sicilian Greeks were divided among themselves and lacked strong leadership following the death of Hieron I, successor of Gelon, in 467 down to the invasion of Sicily by the Athenians in 415. Internal weakness in Carthage or military adventures closer to home may explain this apparent lack of interest but it is a curious one for such a powerful and usually imperialist state. The awakening of new interest in Sicilian affairs may in part be put down to personal motives for the revenge of the death of Hamilcar, but equally perhaps on account of very visible friction throughout Sicily towards the end of the fifth century brought on because of a resurgence in border disputes between Segesta and Selinous. It was this antagonism between Elymians living in the former and Greeks in the latter that had provided the Athenians with the pretence to intervene in Sicilian affairs in 415. Segesta on that occasion had requested Athenian aid, but following the disaster of the Athenian expedition against Syracuse, which was an ally of Selinous, the Segestaeans had been left vulnerable to attack from their neighbours. To counter this, and since they had nowhere else to turn, Segesta now appealed to Carthage for protection. The Carthaginian senate is said to have debated the issue and accepted this request and appointed a certain Hannibal as commander of their forces. His appointment may well have been deliberate since Diodorus notes:

> Hannibal was by nature a hater of the Greeks and wished to make amends for the disgrace of his ancestors. (Diod. 13.43.6)

Hannibal was the grandson of Hamilcar and is considered to have been keen to exact retribution on the Greeks, especially the Himeraeans, for the Carthaginian defeat in 480, but also for the subsequent mistreatment of his father, Giscon.[6] We are told that Giscon and his family, which presumably included Hannibal, lived in Selinous where he had died (Diod. 13.43.5). Giscon and his family may well have been exiled because of his father's defeat (Diod. 13.59.5) and although only conjecture it is possible that the Selinuntines had also treated Giscon with a lack of respect while he was a resident there. The connection between this family and the city at the very least indicates that Hannibal knew Selinous well, but why should he have singled it out as his primary objective and not Himera? Selinous was an ally of Syracuse whose growing power in Sicily must have caused some disquiet in Carthage. Selinous was also at war with Segesta, now in an alliance with Carthage, which made it an obvious target. However, Selinous had also been an ally of Carthage (Diod. 13.55.1) when Hamilcar had fought against Gelon therefore there was a history of cooperation between the two states. Perhaps inactivity by Carthage in the intervening years had made Selinous seeks allies elsewhere. It was a settlement of Megara Hyblaia, which was an Ionian Greek city, and it was therefore not a natural ally of Syracuse, but self preservation and an eye on future prosperity could easily have been enough for former enemies to become allies.[7] Whatever the reason for the alienation of Selinous from Carthage, an initial attack here would relieve at a single blow the pressure on Segesta and remove any possibility of an attack from the west against Carthaginian forces advancing on Himera. Hannibal landed at Lilybaeum and proceeded along the coast via the River Mazarus towards Selinous scattering any opposition before him (Diod. 13.54.6). Hannibal's next actions clearly show a good acquaintance with Selinous and any problems he might face with its fortifications. As it turned out these did not delay him for long. Diodorus gives this siege full coverage (13.54.6–58.3), and it is worth examining it in detail for it has clear relevance for any further discussion about Motya's destruction.

Hannibal is described as having effective siege equipment at the ready, including, it is said, six wheeled towers and the same number of battering rams, which he ordered to be drawn against the walls of the city as soon as his army had invested the city. Interestingly enough Diodorus states that the fortifications of Selinous were in a state of disrepair since they had never before been threatened with attack, and that the Carthaginian siege towers were taller than the city's walls. A Carthaginian fleet, although not mentioned, must also have been accompanying Hannibal and surely must have blockaded the city, which is not attested as possessing any warships, while messengers sent to request immediate aid from Syracuse, Gela and Akragas left by horseback just before all means of communication by land were cut by the enemy. No Selinuntines are reported to have made their escape by sea.

The siege was relatively brief, lasting about nine days (Diod. 13.56.5),[8] and was concentrated on the landward defences, which suffered considerable damage from the siege engines of the attackers. An initial incursion by Campanian mercenaries was repulsed with heavy losses on each side, but the defenders had fewer resources to call on while the besiegers were able to bring up fresh troops and maintain constant pressure on the citizens of Selinous who had no respite from the continuous assault. The breach, which had to some extent been repaired by the defenders, again became the main focus for the attack and the besieged were driven from the walls by the ferocity of the Carthaginian assault. The end for Selinous was not far in sight. Citizens and their families and neighbours appear to have prolonged the fall of the city by barricading the narrow streets to prevent easy access but as weapons and missiles were exhausted they were eventually overcome and the looting and murder began in earnest, since Hannibal had promised the city as a prize to his army. Those Selinuntines who congregated in the agora were massacred, and the city was soon stripped of its treasures and burned, but not totally destroyed for Diodorus states (13.59.3) that Hannibal allowed any survivors who had not been enslaved to return to the city and farm the districts around on payment of a tithe to the Carthaginians.[9]

The narrative appears to be detailed but on reflection contains nothing specific about a city which the writer ought to have at least been acquainted.[10] There is no mention of the acropolis, or the sector of the city containing some of the largest temples to be found in Sicily. His reference to the agora is vague when it must surely have been close to the more eastern of the harbours in the broad valley, which separates the temple quarter from the acropolis.[11] Taken altogether this looks suspiciously as if Diodorus has written about a generic situation employing the usual siege *topoi* rather than relating his account to a historical episode. The siege took place when the historian said it did but the details he gives are not about this particular episode. Just at the end there is suddenly a note about Selinuntine casualties, which seems plausible: 16,000 killed, 5000 taken captive (Diod. 13.57.6) and 2600 who escaped to Akragas (Diod. 13.58.3). Selinous is likely to have contained a population something in excess of 20,000 inhabitants but not much more since it was not a city comparable in size to Syracuse, but even this is perhaps untrustworthy. If scepticism ranks high here it is because the aim is to trace the battlefield and little can be done with this general and it must be said superficial text of Diodorus. Can the physical remains of Selinous be more of a help in understanding this event?

The extant remains of Selinous are impressive and extensive covering a large area, but it is as well to remember that what appears to be the main habitation zone is actually the acropolis of the city before its destruction by Hannibal's army. It was re-occupied by the Carthaginians who refortified this sector and seem to have abandoned the rest. The fact that so little is to be seen from the original settlement suggests either that the destruction in 409 was total in that area, or that the debris was thoroughly reused in later rebuilding or, probably most likely, that there was less population density here than appears to be indicated in Diodorus' dramatic image of the besieged city. This is important and can be related later to the analysis of the situation at Motya a decade or so after this siege.

From his victory at Selinous Hannibal advanced quickly on Himera (Diod. 13.59.4), which was his particular objective. Indeed on the face of it Hannibal's entire expedition is recounted as one motivated by a personal vendetta and barely connected with the threat posed to the security of Segesta by the Sicilian Greeks. Moreover, Himera detained the Carthaginians for much less time than Selinous, even though its defenders were reinforced by perhaps as many as 4000 troops, primarily from Syracuse and the other Greeks (Diod. 13.59.9),[12] while Hannibal is reported as having now augmented his army with 20,000 Sicel and Sicanian allied troops (Diod. 13.59.6).[13] He immediately put his siege engines to good use battering and undermining the city's walls. A breach was made early on but the defenders managed to push back the attackers and repair the stretch of wall that had collapsed. The Himeraeans then decided to march out the next morning to face the enemy, a move which took them by surprise and the Greeks had some initial successes in scattering mostly barbarian mercenaries. However, Hannibal ordered more troops into battle and these swung the fight against the Greeks who lost 3000 men (Diod. 13.60.7). As this battle was coming to an end with a withdrawal of the Himeraeans into their city, a fleet arrived in their harbour which, Diodorus states, had originally been sent by the Syracusans commanded by Hermocrates to help the Spartan war effort against the Athenians. This fleet was now returning to Syracuse but had been diverted to offer aid against the Carthaginians. With the fight clearly going against them, Diocles, the commander of the Syracusan troops, recommended the entire evacuation of the city using the twenty-five triremes in this fleet. The citizens of Himera were unhappy with this suggestion but there seemed no other viable course of action. Diocles advised that as many as could be carried should leave at once and be left further along the north coast beyond the borders of Himera and while that was taking place the city should be defended until the fleet could return to provide further assistance.[14] The triremes that were available, if truly warships and not transports, would not have been able to carry much additional weight so those who made their escape in the first round of evacuation were probably not that many and lucky indeed to have got away. The defenders maintained a vigilant watch over the next night while Diocles and his Syracusan troops, accompanied by numerous Himeraean refugees, broke out from the city and made their way by land to safety.[15] The following day the assault resumed, and continued into the next with the defenders determined in hang on until the ships arrived. As the fleet approached, the walls were again breached and this time the enemy began to pour into the city, which after being burned was completely destroyed. The Syracusan fleet does not appear to have either engaged or made any attempt to pick up survivors, although Diodorus may have missed this point. He is more interested in dwelling on the fact that 3000 prisoners were slaughtered in revenge for the death of Hannibal's ancestor and women and children enslaved. Still, it is plain that far from being a generic re-enactment of a siege the details provided by Diodorus are much more specific with geographical factors such as mountains close by to the city, the arrival and participation of the Sicilian Greek squadron and the ferrying of survivors to Messene point to a more detailed and knowledgeable source than that which was available for Selinous. It is also possible that Diodorus had visited Therma, the Roman successor to Himera, whereas it is surely certain that he had never travelled to Selinous.

The availability of a fleet to rescue or partly rescue the Himeraeans is also worthy of some comment. A similar expedition to Selinous could surely have been organized considering that Syracuse had possessed a war fleet of roughly a hundred triremes in 413 and must have captured at least the same number from the Athenians who had abandoned their ships when they retreated from the city. Yet no attempt was made.[16] This option was not only considered by the Carthaginian general Himilcon when he attempted to relieve Motya a decade later but one that he put into motion. That the Greeks were unable to mount this sort of action speaks volumes about the lack of unity among the Sicilian Greeks except when there was a supreme leader on the island.

After the sack of Himera and the removal of still more plunder Hannibal set sail for Africa.[17] Still, it should also be noted that the Carthaginian position in western Sicily had been much strengthened and in fact Hannibal had accomplished his task to the letter. The two westernmost Sicilian Greek city-states (*poleis*) had been destroyed and the security of Segesta was vastly improved. Selinous had probably been left with a Punic garrison, if not then its fortifications must have been substantially reduced while Himera was never re-established and a new Carthaginian settlement called Therma was built situated in close proximity to the former Greek foundation (Diod. 13. 79.8).[18] The Greek reaction to the disasters in the west of the island was not entirely one of inactivity but there are clear signs of confusion and amateur management of a military campaign. There was certainly not indifference since troops had been raised from Gela, Syracuse and Akragas to march to the relief of Selinous. Although these had not proceeded beyond Akragas before the few Selinuntine aurvivors arrived there, these same troops, or at least the Syracusans, did march overland in an attempt, futile it so happened, to attempt to turn back the Carthaginian tide.

The sole counterattack, if it may be called that, was a certain amount of military activity that the Syracusan Hermocrates launched on his own initiative (Diod. 13.63.2–6). He occupied a section of Selinous, probably the acropolis, with some of his supporters and rallied survivors from that catastrophe and even some citizens from Himera. He had then attacked Panormus and Motya and gained some notable successes against the citizens of both, although, on account of lack of numbers, he did not succeed in seizing either of these cities.[19] His main concern was to return to Syracuse, which he did early in 408, but he went first from Selinous to Himera where he collected the bones of his fellow citizens and ordered these to be transported back by wagon to their home.[20] However, Hermocrates remained on the road, according to Diodorus (13.75.3), and did not accompany the dead into the city since it was forbidden for exiles to join in burial rites, but in fact because he wanted to bring dishonour on Diocles who was a political opponent. The arrival of the dead had the required effect and Diocles was exiled but Hermocrates was also not invited to return since the majority of citizens were suspicious of his motives. So he set out at night in an attempt to seize power, although he did not have large forces at his disposal. He arrived at Akradina and since the gate here had been secured by his allies he entered the city. The disturbance alerted the citizens who gathered in large numbers in the agora where Hermocrates and many of his supporters were killed. One of these supporters was a certain Dionysius son of Hermocrates (Diod. 13.91.3) who was wounded in the fighting but was hidden by his family to avoid capture and certain execution (Diod. 13.75.9).[21]

In 407 envoys from Syracuse made complaints about the destruction of the Greek cities in western Sicily to which they received ambiguous answers from the Carthaginian senate, which at the same time safeguarded its recent territorial expansion by ordering the foundation of Therma in the former territory of Himera (Diod. 13.79.8). In fact, the Carthaginian response, in comparison to its recent inactivity in Sicily was prompt and belligerent.[22] There was an immediate levy of a new army, preparation of warships and a fleet of transports and the appointment of new commanders. Unsurprisingly, Hannibal was chosen to command a new and much more ambitious campaign, which was for total control over Sicily. Equally unremarkable is Hannibal's reluctance to take sole responsibility and so Himilcon, son of Hanno, a relative, was appointed as joint commander. These organized the hiring of mercenaries from as far afield as Iberia, Campania and Cyrene and gathered all these at Carthage. Diodorus (13.80.5) says that Timaeus reckoned the troops collected numbered 120,000 while Ephorus claimed that there were 300,000 in this latest Punic army. The numbers of transports available to ship these troops is given as 1000, which is much the same as Hannibal had employed in this earlier expedition but forty triremes, which had been sent in advance to ensure a safe arrival of the army, were caught by a Syracusan squadron near Eryx and fifteen were sunk. Hannibal responded by sending a further fifty warships in order to make sure that he had control of the sea in what was always a perilous procedure, that of transporting an entire army prior to making a seaborne invasion. Hannibal's planning had so far been meticulous particularly in taking as many precautions as he could to prevent any disaster before he was on Sicilian soil.[23] The details provided by Diodorus seem realistic enough, although it is worthwhile bearing in mind that these were the actions of any good and competent general before going on a military adventure: and so, topical elements may well become embedded in this account too.

The Sicilian Greeks were obviously aware of these preparations for war and Syracuse is said to have made proposals for joint action (Diod. 13.81.2). The city closest to the Carthaginian possessions in western Sicily was now Akragas and its citizens realized that they were likely to be the primary target in any forthcoming war. Diodorus says that the Akragantines collected their grain into the city and all their moveable possessions in preparation of a possible siege.[24] He also states that there were 20,000 citizens and a total population of 200,000 (13.84.3) and that it was a place of great prosperity, although it is not compared to Syracuse. Having emphasized the great wealth and resources of this city it is plain that it was simply no match for a state such as Carthage and although the tangible remains of Akragas (Agrigento) are impressive it evidently did not possess the resources to meet the threat from an invading army. This becomes evident from the fact that the Akragantines hired a Spartan named Dexippus who was living in Gela to command 1500 mercenaries, and besides these 800 Campanian mercenaries who had previously fought under Hannibal in the previous campaign but who had fallen out with the Carthaginians whom they claimed had underpaid them for their services. These were garrisoned on the acropolis of the city on the summit of which stood a temple to Athena.[25]

The Carthaginians are said to have advanced quickly into the territory of Akragas (13.85.1) and made two camps, one on the hills near the city and one close to the walls. Heralds were sent into the city seeking a treaty between Carthage and Akragas but when this was rejected the siege began in earnest. Siege towers were immediately brought against the weakest sections of the city's fortifications, perhaps close to the temple of Zeus since the action appears to have been in this vicinity, always bearing in mind that specific topographical details can be mixed indiscriminately with quite unhistorical material by an ancient historian like Diodorus. The defence held on the first day and after the attackers had withdrawn in the evening a night sortie by the Akragantines resulted in the burning of the siege towers. This did not, however, dampen Hannibal's spirit; he instead ordered that ramps be constructed towards the walls in several places and that any material that came to hand, including tombs, should be used for this purpose.[26] When the tomb of the Theron former tyrant of Akragas was struck by lightning when it was in the process of being dismantled a plague broke out among the besiegers.[27] The prime casualty of this epidemic, probably cholera or dysentery, was Hannibal (Diod. 13.86.3), but many others died as well. No disease occurs with such rapidity and therefore the siege must have dragged out for a much longer time than Diodorus intimates. The construction of ramps against walls on an even surface might takes several days or even weeks.[28] If these ramps were being thrown up near the Olympieion then they would have involved a great deal of effort not to mention complicated construction work since the walls of Akragas at this point are situated on a steep-sided incline. Moreover from that point north to the acropolis the Hypsas River flows through a deep and narrow gorge and separates the city's fortifications from the attackers. There is no ease of access to the city's walls at any point except at the city's main gates on the eastern side, which appear to have been ignored by the besiegers, perhaps deliberately as we shall see. Thus it is probable that what we have again here is a topical siege element that has crept into Diodorus' text and that Hannibal actually died suddenly – he was not young – but in a situation that lent itself to the outbreak of epidemics associated with large numbers of human beings gathered together in high-density living conditions without even basic hygiene. His death could have caused a crisis in confidence among the Carthaginians, a point that is certainly implied (Diod. 13.86.3), but Himilcar (or Himilcon) took preventive action by making the appropriate sacrifices to the gods,[29] while at the same time maintaining the pressure on the defenders by filling in the gorge to the north of the Olympieion, in order to bring his siege engines closer to the walls.

Reinforcements totally 30,000 infantry, 5000 cavalry and 30 warships arrived from Syracuse commanded by Daphnaeus.[30] As they advanced probably along the coast from Gela, which is a mere sixty–five kilometres (40 miles) to the east, Himilcon sent out a column said to have been 40,000 in total to intercept them and a fierce battle took place on the western bank of River Himera (Diod. 13.87.1). The Syracusan-led army was victorious and the Carthaginians lost at least 6000 troops and in the rout that followed it seemed likely that they would suffer far more casualties and the siege would be lifted. But the pursuit of the Sicilian Greeks was far from organized and Daphnaeus was worried in case Himilcar (Himilcon) would appear with the rest of his army and take advantage of the lack of discipline among the pursuers as had happened recently at Himera. The Carthaginians were in full retreat heading apparently to the camp that was on the hills overlooking the city in the hope that this would provide a safe haven. Those troops inside Akragas also wished to take a full part in this likely victory but were ordered not to leave the positions on the walls in case Himilcar (Himilcon) saw some way of entering while they were in pursuit of the enemy. The Carthaginians therefore gave up the camp that was close to the city walls and this was occupied by the Greeks. Then the incriminations began since it was argued that the Greeks could have won an outright victory if the Akragantines had played a more active role in the rout of the enemy. The Akragantine generals and the Spartan mercenary Dexippus were all accused of incompetence and four of these senior officers were stoned to death when citizens meeting in an assembly turned violent.[31] The Carthaginians were now confined to their camp but Daphnaeus considered it to be too strongly fortified to be successfully assaulted and so instead decided to try and starve the enemy into surrender by attacking any of their foragers and cutting their communication links. The Carthaginians were soon suffering and some of the Campanian mercenaries mutinied and threatened to go over to the Greeks unless supplies were brought in. Himilcar (Himilcon) promised to solve this logistical problem within days. He had heard that supplies were being brought to Akragas from Syracuse by sea and so commanded that forty triremes from Panormus and Motya be launched to intercept this convoy, which as it turned out was not accompanied by warships since the Greeks believed that with winter coming on the Carthaginians would not risk putting out a fleet in risky weather conditions. Yet at the same time the Syracusans allowed transports to sail without a guard in a time of war or at least sufficient escorts and so this fleet was easily captured and completely reversed again the condition of the protagonists.[32] The Campanian mercenaries serving with the Greeks now deserted to the Carthaginians since they believed that the fate of Akragas was sealed since all the supplies they had collected for the siege were exhausted and no other source of relief seemed likely, although the city was not fully encircled and the road to Gela at least remained open. Dexippus seems to have been one of the first to voice the idea of quitting the city and his advice was followed by the Syracusans. Diodorus (13.88.7) claims that the Spartan had accepted a bribe of fifteen talents (a huge sum) from the Carthaginians. However, it is more likely that the loss of the supply fleet and the presence of so many additional troops in Akragas simply meant that the sources of food were running dangerously low and with the arrival of winter there was no way to replenish the granaries and warehouses. There was just one solution and it was quickly aired: that the city should be immediately abandoned.

This had not worked at Himera where fewer people were involved and where the evacuation occurred in daylight. At Akragas, the generals ordered an immediate evacuation at night, and this in a city in which there may have been 200,000 residents, a claim made and repeated by Diodorus (13.84.3, 90.3), although there were probably far fewer than this.[33] Still there was no prospect of escape by sea and so all refugees had to go by the single road to Gela. Panic and chaos became quickly apparent as the Akragantines fled from the city knowing they would be vulnerable to attack while trying to elude the enemy, although it is said that some attempt was made to organize the departure and guard those who were defenceless en route. Many, in fact, made it to safety and were later to make new homes for themselves in Leontinoi on land provided by the Syracusans (Diod. 13.89.4). By sunrise Himilcar (Himilcon) was leading his troops into the city where any remaining defenders were killed, but also those who were too infirm to have left. Those who thought that they would be safe by taking refuge in one of the numerous temples were sadly mistaken for the Carthaginians are said to have dragged them out and killed them too. Thus the temple of Athena on the acropolis was destroyed by those inside hoping for sanctuary, including a certain Tellias, one of the most prominent citizens of the city whose luxurious lifestyle and dramatic end is related by Diodorus (13.83.1–84.1, 13.90.1–2).[34] The city was thoroughly looted but since it was already the solstice (Diod. 13.91.1) Himilcar (Himilcon) did not give orders for the complete destruction of the city since he needed the standing buildings as billets for his troops for the rest of the winter. The fall of Akragas sent shock waves across the island where many Greeks moved to Syracuse seeking safety or transferred themselves and their families to one of the Greek cities in southern Italy.

The loss of Akragas had an immediate impact of public affairs in Syracuse where recriminations against their own generals were made by some of the refugees while complaints were also made against the Syracusans who had been supposed to lend aid. Still, in public assemblies there was a general reticence to attack the generals involved until Dionysius, former ally of Hermocrates, accused the military elite of conniving with the Carthaginians and receiving bribes to give up the defence of Akragas. This was greeted with general approval until the presiding officials imposed a fine on Dionysius 'according to the laws' for causing unruly behaviour, but a wealthy aristocrat named Philistus offered to pay the fine and any others the speaker might incur so that these opinions could not be suppressed.[35] Dionysius continued to harangue the crowds and caused such anger at the current board of generals whom he also accused of favouring oligarchic goverment that at his insistence they were dismissed and new military leaders more in sympathy with the ordinary citizen were elected.[36] Having stirred up a great deal of anger and frustration it is not remarkable that among the new generals was also Dionysius. Dionysius was a popular figure and had gained a reputation for heroism in battle especially in the recent confrontation with the Carthaginians. However, Diodorus (13.92.2) makes this election the first in a series of moves by which Dionysius gained supreme power at Syracuse and thus while isolating himself from the other generals and putting it about that they were in cahoots with the enemy he was actually preparing to seize power for himself. Although there were attempts by influential citizens, through their own speeches to stem the increasingly powerful position that Dionysius was acquiring, fear of a Carthaginian invasion by the overwhelming majority meant that his opinions were considered more vital for the survival of Syracuse. He advised the recall of all exiles, mainly former supporters of Hermocrates, because he argued that true citizens, whatever their political views, would fight more keenly for their city than mercenaries. No one dared to oppose this argument since it was strongly supported and any opposition might be taken to be unpatriotic. Dionysius, on the other hand, is said to have hoped that the returning exiles would be in his debt and support his bid for sole power.

Pleas for help were received from Gela,[37] now on the frontline of the war with Carthage, and Dionysius was sent out in command of 2000 infantry and 400 cavalry (Diod. 13.93.1). At the time Dexippus the Spartan mercenary was in command of a garrison there but among the general population *stasis* or civil unrest had broken out between certain sectors of the community. Dionysius restored order by ordering the execution of the wealthiest and confiscating their possessions; and from these he was able to pay the arrears owed to Dexippus' mercenaries and increase the payment to the troops under his own command so that he had by this time a solid base of military support. Nevertheless, Dionysius clearly did not regard this as sufficient to mount a real bid for power especially when he was unable to persuade Dexippus to join him as an ally. He decided to return with his forces to Syracuse, although the people of Gela were unhappy about losing military support when the Carthaginians advance might occur at any time. Dionysius promised to return. On his arrival in Syracuse he accused his fellow generals of conspiring with Himilcon to hand over the city to the Carthaginians. The result was that on the next day at a hastily convened public assembly, following the argument that it had been Gelon when similarly in sole control of affairs who had won a great victory over Carthage, Dionysius was elected *strategos autocrator*, or general with supreme powers (Diod. 13.94.1). With these powers he could be confident that he would be able to suppress any opposition that emerged against him. Thus far Dionysius had shown consummate skill in achieving his ambition without leaving himself vulnerable to counterattack. He realized that public opinion was extremely fickle and that he had to act quickly to safeguard his position for already some citizens were already having second thoughts about the appointment. Dionysius perceived a change of opinion and so ordered a general levy to be held at Leontinoi about thirty kilometres north of the city (25 miles). On his way to the town he made camp and during the night gave out that he had been the intended victim of an assassination attempt and immediately took himself off to the acropolis at Leontinoi. On the next morning he addressed a gathering and persuaded the people of the town to provide him with a personal guard of six hundred soldiers (Diod. 13.95.5).[38] And it seems that this was enough to consolidate his position as sole ruler, initially at least, but later on he also employed a thousand citizens from Syracuse and within a short time a large number of mercenaries. He also appointed to commands only those he could trust – Philistus was probably among these – while Dexippus about whose loyalty he had doubts he sent packing to the Peloponnese, while leading opponents were executed (Diod. 13.96.3).[39]

In the spring or early summer of 405 (Diod. 13.108.2) the Carthaginians advanced from Akragas intent on the capture of Gela. Before they went Himilcon ordered the destruction of Akragas, including its temples, and instead encamped outside Gela. Another damaging siege appeared to be about to begin, and Dionysius had yet to return from Syracuse. The Carthaginian camp is said to have been at a *temenos* of Apollo close to the city walls, which contained a great bronze statue of the god. This is the sole mention of any topographical feature at Gela. This statue was taken as loot and sent to Tyre, the metropolis of Carthage, where it was retrieved by Alexander after his successful siege of that city in 332. On that occasion great celebrations and sacrifices were made to the god for the victory over the Tyrians. This short digression by Diodorus, who refers to Timaeus as his source here, may not appear particularly important, but as we shall soon see this congruency between the siege of Tyre and these events in Sicily, especially those at Motya, is indeed highly significant.[40]

Unlike Akragas, Gela was a harbour town situated on a low spit of mostly sandy land just above the beach and it was therefore susceptible to any attack whether from the sea or by land. Nor indeed did the Geloans possess the human resources available to the Akragantines, having a much smaller population; and it is really quite surprising that they chose to stay and fight rather than flee.[41] Their initial defensive response to a sustained assault with siege engines was to launch sorties and attack foragers illustrating that they were confident of receiving the promised aid from Syracuse, but even so it was not immediately forthcoming. Diodorus' narrative here can be described as one containing trite generalizations about heroic activity and contains nothing specific, but he does indicate (13.109.1) that Dionysius apparently soon kept his word.[42] He also made camp but on the opposite side of the town and harassed the enemy by using his lightly armed troops to attack foragers. For twenty days there was a stalemate before Dionysius set in motion an ambitious strategy to defeat the Carthaginians,[43] and in describing this action Diodorus shows some appreciation of the geography around Gela (13.109.4– 5). He ordered his fleet to move along the coast and disembark troops near the enemy camp. These ships were also to shadow his left wing comprising Italian Greeks who were to advance along the beach with the town to their right. Meanwhile, the right wing comprising the Sicilian Greeks was to move forward keeping Gela to their left. Finally Dionysius leading his mercenaries was to attack the enemy head on by marching through Gela and then making a sortie from the gates or gates nearest to the enemy camp. The fleet carried out its instructions to the letter and the Carthaginians rushed troops to where these Syracusans had beached. In doing so they left a part of their fortifications undermanned and this was stormed by the Italian Greeks who had come along the beach. The main Carthaginian force now had to rush back to repel their attackers who were pushed back outside this camp with heavy losses but were able to make for the city and safety because they had cover from archers on the ships and some assistance from the Geloans, some of whom marched out in aid. On the other hand, the Sicilian Greeks on the right flank were not in place early enough and although they scattered a Libyan contingent when these were reinforced by the main Carthaginian force they also retreated within the walls of Gela. And since the city was cigar-shaped

– the old quarter of the modern town indicates this clearly enough as it lies along a low ridge beside the sea – and the streets were certainly narrow and crowded with onlookers and refugees, Dionysius made such slow progress that by the time he arrived at the end closest to the enemy he found the rest of his army had been defeated.[44] The entire army that had come to relieve Gela was now also inside the city.

At this point Dionysius discussed with his advisors what the best option might be and the unanimous opinion was that a withdrawal from Gela was the only course of action. An order was issued to send a herald to Himilcon requesting permission for the Greeks to collect their dead for burial. More importantly, that same evening Dionysius instructed the people to leave the city by its east gate and he himself left with the greater part of his troops. Left inside Gela were two thousand lightly armed troops ordered to keep the fires lit and make the sort of noises expected from a city at night. At dawn these were also told to vacate the city. The Carthaginians only became aware of what had happened when they realized that in front of them Gela was now deserted and they entered without opposition. In the meantime, Dionysius and his army had arrived at Camarina, a city even less easily defendable than Gela.[45] He delivered its citizens a stark choice: leave at once for Syracuse or suffer almost certain death at the hands of the Carthaginians who were not far behind. A further mass displacement of people therefore occurred in just a matter of months and all sought refuge in Syracuse.[46] There a great deal of resentment against and distrust of Dionysius surfaced mainly among his fellow citizens and especially the more wealthy members of the *polis*. They questioned his motives and his intentions. Why had he not arrived at Gela sooner than he had? Why had he ordered a retreat so quickly when he had only suffered a minor reverse? Why had Dionysius' mercenary soldiers hardly been employed in the battle against the Carthaginian camp whereas the Sicilian and Italian Greeks had borne the brunt of this fight? Had there been some subterfuge between Dionysius and Himilcon since the Carthaginians had not taken the trouble to pursue the retreating Greeks? All of these complaints can be answered in retrospect. Having encountered the strength of the Carthaginians at Akragas only months earlier Dionysius took the care to prepare a sufficiently strong relief column for Gela. Such preparations took time and this was during the winter months. The loss of 1600 troops from even as many as 50,000 is not an insignificant loss and no mention is made of wounded. The retreat seems to have been undertaken with care and there is mention by Diodorus of military escorts for the refugees (13. 111.5) while a second defeat might have resulted in wholesale slaughter. The mercenary troops had indeed not engaged with the enemy but from the strategy intended by Dionysius they were certainly meant to and only failed to do so because of the unexpected circumstances once they were inside Gela. Lastly the Carthaginian failure to follow up their victory is perhaps puzzling but not if the troops of Himilcon were intent on looting Gela. Many of his soldiers were employed for the campaign and discipline would have been better to maintain if they were happy. Moreover, it is clear that all was not well with his army. Many of the troops had suffered in an epidemic when outside Akragas and, although there is a lacuna in the text (13.114.1), Diodorus appears to indicate that another outbreak of disease had had a crippling effect on the Carthaginian morale and effectiveness to campaign further.

Such answers were probably not voiced or argued with conviction at the time, and it was rather Dionysius' perceived continued grip on the power he had just acquired that was the source of concern for many who were not his supporters. His power and position suffered a jolt when, on account of the severity of their losses, the Italian Greeks decided to return to their homes. More serious were the clandestine activities of the Syracusan cavalry, drawn from among elite families, who as a group decided to ambush Dionysius as he returned to the city from Camarina. When it was clear that his mercenaries were still loyal they went on ahead and after being admitted into the city they made for Dionysius' house, which was between the agora and the Great Harbour. His wife, daughter of Hermocrates, was attacked – she is said to have committed suicide later as a result of her ordeal – and the house ransacked. Dionysius either had some inkling that all was not well or had been informed of what was happening and to retrieve the situation made a desperate charge for the Syracuse. He arrived at Akradina with 100 cavalry and 600 infantry in the middle of the night and entered the city here only after destroying one of the gates by fire (Diod. 13.113.1). He was joined by more of his troops and then made for his home. On the way they encountered some of the cavalry and a fight took place in the agora in which, with superior numbers, Dionysius was easily successful. After this his troops went in search of all possible sympathizers while the majority of the cavalry withdrew from Syracuse and occupied a fort near Catane. The rest of the army arrived the next morning but significantly many among the citizens from Gela and Camarina preferred to wait out their exile in Leontinoi rather than remain in Syracuse. Soon after Himilcar (Himilcon) sent delegates to Dionysius to request a truce and this was quickly arranged. The citizens of all five Sicilian Greek cities that had been sacked by the Carthaginians were invited back to their homes on payment of taxes to Carthage. The Elymians and Sicani were to be allies of Carthage and Dionysius was confirmed as sole ruler of Syracuse.

Dionysius made a peace with the Carthaginians but it was never meant to be more than a breathing space or a pause before the next conflict since neither had achieved their aims: the Greeks to retake lost lands and the Carthaginians to occupy eastern Sicily. The truce seems to have lasted for about eight years, and Dionysius used the time to consolidate his power in Syracuse and remove possible competitors for power. He won over the citizen body by employing them to build new fortifications along the northern edge of Epipolai, and repaired the dockyards and ordered the construction of new warships.

The war had ended with a considerable Carthaginian advance across Sicily and had included the sack of Akragas and looting of its treasures, at that time without doubt the second most powerful of the Greek cities on the island. However, the Carthaginians were evidently in too weak a state to launch an attack on Syracuse itself and the subsequent peace was a compromise between the two states. Dionysius' authority was challenged during the retreat from Gela and although he quickly reasserted his position, for a time his rule was unsteady. He had to endure at least one major conspiracy against him while at the same time in order to enhance his reputation as a successful warrior he ordered some highly aggressive expansionism of Syracusan territory. He captured Catane, destroyed Naxos, and ordered the depopulation of Leontinoi (Diod. 14.15.1–4). By 401 his leadership seemed unassailable.[47] And with that security he was able to cast his eye on the west of Sicily where he recognized that the Carthaginian policy of light-touch hegemony was more appealing than his rather heavy-handed imperialism and he realized that if he wished to prolong his rule he needed future military triumphs. Territorial gains from the Carthaginians therefore become high on his agenda.[48] His decision to intervene in western Sicily was hastened by the apparent weakness in a possible Carthaginian response brought on says Diodorus (14.41.1) by the effects of particularly virulent epidemic. Nonetheless, precision when it came to strategic planning is again evident in that Dionysius ordered the building of new and extensive fortifications to protect the city (Diod. 14.18.1–8).[49] Having done this, and along the way also curried public favour by using the scheme as a means of employing large numbers of citizens who were well rewarded for their efforts, he next turned to the construction of warships. Syracuse already possessed a powerful war fleet of almost certainly more than one hundred triremes.[50] But Dionysius was not content with simply having a powerful fleet of warships; he wanted an exceptional number and he wanted larger and more powerful vessels. Diodorus claims (14.41.3) that the tyrant also ordered the construction of quadriremes and quinqueremes, and that this was the first occasion that the latter had been built. This claim has been treated with some scepticism since quinqueremes do not appear to have been in regular use for another fifty years or so.[51] This is an interesting point and relevant to the discussion here since it was in preparation for the campaign against Motya that such warships are particularly stated as being intended for use. These same vessels thereafter only feature in texts relating to the reign of Alexander (336–323 BC). Since there were far more vessels than could be manned by citizens alone Dionysius intended to hire mercenaries for at least half.[52] The forests on Mount Etna were a major source of timber but the mountains of Calabria also provided the vital natural resource for this undertaking. It is likely that the need for timber made an alliance with Locri a necessity and it is notable that at precisely this time Dionysius was married to the daughter of one of the most prominent Locrian citizens (Diod. 41.44.6).[53] The economic ties between Syracuse and Locri and the resultant advantages for both – for the former a constant supply of timber for the latter a part in Syrcausan imperial expansion – ensured an alliance that lasted the next fifty years.

Not simply content with new and more powerful warships, Dionysius' attention also turned to the mass production of armour and weaponry (Diod. 14.41.4–6). He was not prepared to rely on the personal arms of any individual citizen or soldier in his employment and wanted standardization and quality. In many ways in his ambitions can be seen the beginning of a state's professional army and navy. The description is extraordinary since Diodorus gives the impression that citizens were organized by their ruler into identified guilds overseen by a master craftsman and that groups then made the required items according to specified designs demanded of them by the state. This course was pursued in the belief that identical armour and weaponry would instil great fear into any enemy.[54] The project won universal approval and all suitable sites in Syracuse were a hive of activity. Indeed we are even given an exact figure for shields, daggers and helmets of 140,000 each, and 14,000 breastplates, which gives a good indication of the massive scale of this production (Diod. 14.43. 2). The invention of the catapult is claimed for Dionysius (Diod. 14.42.1, 42.3) and these are described later in use in engagements with the enemy, and probably also account for the building of decked vessels such as quinqueremes, which could accommodate siege engines not only as transport but also for use on the battlefield whenever that might be close to the sea.[55]

Moreover, an attack by Syracuse against Carthaginian territory had to be accompanied by diplomatic moves to ensure cooperation from the other Greek states and especially the Sicels through whose land any army must move when it headed to the west of the island. He also tried to elicit at least tacit approval from the citizens of Messene and Rhegium with promises of territory to be won from the enemy, but failed in this endeavour since both cities were natural allies of the Naxians and other communities ruined by Dionysius. Finally, in hiring mercenaries he cast his net wide enlisting soldiers from Greece and especially among the Spartans (Diod. 14.44.2).[56] And since he apparently offered good terms of service he was able to recruit large numbers of well motivated individuals. In fact, he had much success in implementing his new scheme because it was received enthusiastically in Syracuse (Diod. 14.45.4) and in other Greek cities because it was to be a war of revenge for the previous humiliation inflicted by the Carthaginians. All in all it would seem incredible that Dionysius could possibly fail in his grand designs. However, a word of caution may be raised here because, for all the preparation that was undertaken the result was actually a trifle since the result was largely a restoration of the *status quo* of a decade before. Dionysius and the Syracusans, in fact, gained very little from the hostilities and so the detail given by Diodorus may rather have been intended to illustrate the pride or *hubris* of the tyrant, which then caused him to fall, almost, from grace. The cost of launching an attack on Carthaginian possessions in southern and western Sicily far outweighed the benefits and it is a wonder that Dionysius survived what became little short of a catastrophe. The text tells of great exploits, its origins perhaps lies in the court of the Syracusan tyrant, or certainly from the stylus of a friendly historian.

His first action was to sanction attacks on individual Carthaginians living in the Greek cities as metics or foreign residents (Diod. 14.46.1). These were clearly merchants or involved in other areas of business and often wealthy. It provides perhaps a surprising image of ancient Sicily as a place where Punic and Hellenic cultures rubbed shoulders and for much of the time co–existed amicably enough. It is possible that where wealthy foreign residents lived close to native citizens this might have been a source of resentment and led to animosity, although it should be noted that the Greeks by and large do not seem to have mistreated this element in their cities even in time of war. The Greek action is clearly described as one of deliberate policy directed by Dionysius and hence a calculation in his plans. Such ethnic violence is not well attested outside military campaigns and may here have been designed to tie the Greek communities more closely to Dionysius, to direct anger at the perceived enemy and away from the ruler. The drawback was that such a policy was bound to result in revenge attacks of the same sort and this would inevitably lead to more polarized communities in Sicily. This initial move occurred in 398 and a savage purge of the Carthaginian communities living in the cities along the eastern seaboard of the island seems likely (Diod. 14.46.1) The rationale of such an action is not hard to find, both as a cause for war and the elimination of possible collaborators or fifth columnists but also through the confiscation of property and wealth to finance the war effort. What is surprising about this deliberate action is that, given the ferocity of the Carthaginian treatment of the Sicilian Greeks less than a decade before, and when there had been a peace treaty of barely half that time, it was against resident Carthaginians who had not hitherto attracted animosity. The Punic and Greek residents evidently lived in close proximity in all the coastal cities. On the east coast the Carthaginians were the metics, and on the west coast the Greeks; and this co-existence, which must have occurred over a very long time, is another crucial element for understanding the events as they unfolded in Motya. But not just in Motya but in other besieged cities in antiquity. The ethnic makeup of ancient cities is not often considered when analysing military campaigns especially in sieges and how these would have affected various segments of the communities affected.

The siege of Motya is described in a detailed account by Diodorus (14.47.1–14.53.5) and his coverage of this event has found its way into most modern studies of the period without much comment about the validity of its content and if it is questionable then the text's possible intent. Too often the work of Diodorus is taken at face value because his calibre as a historian is considered rather limited and that he lacked the talent to insert into any narrative he obtained from earlier writers his own perspective or message. In fact, as I shall suggest, his coverage of Dionysius' campaign against Motya, may be a little lacking in subtlety but it is nonetheless intriguing for what appears to be an underlying theme of pride and retribution (*hubris* and *nemesis*); moreover, that the siege and destruction of Motya has more to do with these opposing concepts than with a real historical event. The *hubris* is at once indicated by the next action in this episode. Dionysius sent a legation to the Carthaginians, which announced that the Greeks would wage a new war against them unless they gave back to the Greeks those cities they had taken by force (Diod. 14.46.5). Not only were his preparations complete but he was also aware that the disease that had run rampant among the troops of Hannibal and Himilcon during the campaign in 406 had later also badly affected Carthage and its hinterland. The result was real or perceived weakness brought on by this epidemic and therefore there was an ideal opportunity to launch an onslaught when the enemy would have concerns about raising troops and other vital supplies facing an imminent war.

Diodorus (14.47.4) does not give a detailed account of the direction Dionysius took from Syracuse to the west of the island in the late spring of 397. However, his route may be discerned prior to the arrival of the Greek army at the fortress of Eryx. The total given for Dionysius' forces at this stage is 80,000 infantry, 3000 cavalry, 200 warships and 500 transports (Diod. 14.47.7). The scale of Sicilian Greek involvement is difficult to gauge even if Diodorus speaks of great enthusiasm for the campaign and that Dionysius received contingents from Camarina, Gela, Akragas and even Himera and Selinous. The fact that these communities had all been devastated less than a decade before suggests perhaps more a token support and that it may not have been given so very willingly but rather under an obligation to the supreme leader of most of the Greeks in Sicily. The addition of troops from these cities does, nonetheless, indicate a line of advance across the south coast rather than through the interior and noticeably no specific mention is made of Sicel allies or their troops.[57] The prospect of plunder to recoup recent material losses and simply for revenge may have made the venture popular but Dionysius also aimed to strengthen his own position through a successful war. Hence some exaggeration about the support and participation seems highly likely.

Eryx, the modern town of Erice, situated on a virtually impregnable rock rising nearly thousand metres (3000 feet) above the sea next to Cape St Vito, was never a major power in antiquity and quickly sided with the Greeks (Diod. 14.48.1). It was an Elymian town and the Elymians were allies of Carthage but self preservation seems to have been the compelling reason for the citizens of this town. That was not the case of Segesta and Entella, which remained true to their allegiance with Carthage and were both besieged (Diod. 14.51.5).[58] The main object of Dionysius was not an Elymian town however, but the Punic settlement of Motya, which is described as being the greatest in Sicily which the Carthaginian possessed with which to wage war on the Greeks (Diod. 13.47.4). This statement is of interest since the physical remains of Motya are not at all or in any way comparable with any of the Greek *poleis*. This is why the discussion so far has noted the accounts of the various episodes affecting Selinous, Himera, Akragas, Gela and Camarina. Yet Diodorus portrays Motya as a prize worth the elaborate preparations he has described in his narrative. Further the citizens of this town were apparently not concerned that such a huge army should be approaching their territory.[59]

The Motyans appear to have been confident that relief from Carthage would arrive without delay. Diodorus does not comment on the town's fortifications but says only that the homes there indicated the individual wealth of its citizens (14.48.2). He notes that the island was six stadia from the mainland (3636 feet = 1200 metres) to which it was joined by a causeway. This mole was broken up by the Motyans to make access to the island more difficult but the low level of the surrounding sea in the bay at that time would surely not have caused too great a problem to any besieging force. As a result of the defensive measures taken by its inhabitants, Diodorus says that Dionysius ordered more moles be built (14.48.3) but since there is no archaeological evidence for any such measure what is meant here is some repair to the existing causeway. Dionysius also had his warships beached and made an encampment and then proceeded with the greater part of his army to attack the various towns in the area, including Panormus and Solus, and carry off any moveable goods from their territories. Leptines, brother of the tyrant, was appointed in command of the siege, although little appears to have taken place at this stage. It is worth noting, however, that if a siege even in its initial stages requires only a part of the invading force then the besieged town was not regarded as the most important prize of this campaign. Motya is indeed given as the aim of Dionysius but this could easily have been written with hindsight and this town may only have become the focus of attention later on. Indeed this certainly seems to be the case since the Greeks singularly failed to take any of the local urban centres with the exception of Eryx; and this after all the preparations and accompanying siege train.

We are told that there was a rapid Carthaginian counterattack, perhaps more aptly described as a diversionary episode. Himilcon who was now in sole command of the campaign had clearly not fully collected his forces so instead he despatched a squadron of ten triremes with orders to enter and attack the harbour at Syracuse after darkness had set in and to cause as much damage as possible. This order was carried out to the letter and ships and supplies were evidently destroyed before a successful withdrawal was accomplished. However, if it was meant to cause severe disruption or interfere with the logistics of Dionysius' army then it had only a limited effect and was not regarded as serious enough to warrant a recall of the Syracusans to their city. Indeed the opposite effect might be inferred since it seems to have focussed Dionysius' efforts at Motya. It is said that he considered a sack of this town might serve as an example to others and bring about a capitulation of the other local centres of resistance. This would arguably indicate that the destruction of Motya was a later objective than Diodorus claims.

At this stage Himilcon now possessed under his command a fleet of at least one hundred triremes and he crossed from Carthage to Selinous and then along the coast and into the bay that contained Motya, arriving early in the morning and taking his enemy by surprise (Diod. 14.50.2). He is said to have destroyed some of the Greeks ships that had not been brought ashore and brought his fleet – most than likely some part of the total since the bay is not large enough to accommodate so many large vessels – and prepared to attack those ships drawn up on the beach. Himilcon rightly reasoned that a major blow to Dionysius' naval arm would force a withdrawal of the Greeks. The text of Diodorus at this point is difficult to reconcile with the site of the battle as it is to be seen today (see plates).[60] Dionysius gathered his infantry at the mouth of the harbour but seeing that the enemy were on guard, preventing any ships from sailing, decided not to put his triremes into the harbour for he recognized that the narrow entrance would involve a small number of them having to come to grips with a much larger concentration of the enemy. Therefore he employed the additional manpower from the infantry to carry or drag the Greek ships over the spur of land separating the beach from the open sea and when launched these now had superior numbers to their opponents. Himilcon tried to engage those first put to sea but his ships were turned back by the sheer volume of missiles hurled from the land and from archers, slingers and catapults on board (Diod. 14.50.4). The catapult with its heavy dart is noted as having caused considerable damage. Himilcon broke off the engagement, now outnumbered, and sailed directly back to Carthage. And with his departure the fate of Motya was sealed.

Dionysius had also completed his landward approach to the island and therefore was able to advance his siege engines against the fortifications of the town, and especially wheeled towers, which are said to have been six stories in height and therefore equal to the height of the houses inside Motya. The Motyans put up a valiant and courageous fight and employed all manner of countermeasures to repel these attackers. For example, they used the masts of ships and placed men at the top of these who threw fire bombs which were made by covering lengths of hemp rope with pitch down onto the siege equipment of the Greeks (Diod. 14.51.2). The besiegers seem to have overcome this tactic by dowsing their battering rams and towers with water and at last made a breach in the walls. A terrific fight broke out at this spot says Diodorus since the besiegers now sensed that victory was close at hand and they could at last exact revenge on the enemy for all the brutality the Greeks had endured in recent years. On the other hand, the citizens of Motya battled with equal determination since they realized that there was now no hope of relief from Carthage and so they were faced with the grim alternative of either death or enslavement. And so just like the Selinuntines, the Motyans blocked off their narrow streets with all manner of debris and used the height of their houses as it they were inner walls and rained down missiles on the attackers. In response the Greeks brought their wooden siege towers inside the town and manned these with soldiers who used gangplanks from the tops of these towers to gain access to the houses. Relentlessly, the Greeks advanced while the citizens of Motya, urged on by their families, resisted as best they could, and inflicted heavy casualties on the besiegers.[61] This street by street fighting apparently went on for some days until Dionysius changed his tactics. It was usual for the Greeks to take a break in the fighting at dusk in order to eat their dinner. The Motyans began to rely on this interval to replenish their stocks of weapons and take some rest but one night Dionysius ordered a night assault and when his troops had gained possession of some vantage point these were able to admit more of their fellow besiegers into the town. The Motyans attempted to retrieve the situation but the end for them was by then in sight.

Diodorus also states the attackers began to pour into the town across the causeway, which probably indicates the main thrust of the assault was always from the north and through the north gate of the town and from there a few hundred metres to its agora.[62] No prisoners were taken and men, women and children were slaughtered wherever they were encountered. The savagery of this final episode can in part be explained by simple bloodlust, which often accompanied a rout, but Diodorus also suggests (14.53.1) that there was a common feeling among the besiegers that this was a payback for previous Carthaginian brutality. However, it should be noted that more often than not it was a lack of discipline among some sections of the opposing armies that caused the mayhem and not the policy of either Carthaginian or Greek commanders. Thus we are told that Dionysius did not want wholesale killing because of the loss of revenue there would be from a sale of prisoners as slaves and indeed when it became clear that his own soldiers were ignoring his orders he sent heralds into the town with instructions to urge the citizens to seek safety in temples respected by the Greeks. Some did indeed make for these sanctuaries and the killing was soon replaced with looting from the lavish personal belongings of the people of Motya. Dionysius was happy to allow his troops to plunder at will in the belief that this favour would be repaid with greater loyalty towards him in the future. He also rewarded individuals for conspicuous gallantry, but also sold off those Motyans who survived as slaves and executed any Greek mercenaries who were discovered to have been among the survivors.[63]

Once Motya was secured Dionysius installed a garrison under the command of a Syracusan named Biton.[64] Leptines, a brother of the tyrant, was made overall commander of operations in the region and left in charge of a fleet of 120 warships with which to intercept any Carthaginian counterattack. Leptines was also instructed to pursue the sieges of Entella and Segesta which, Diodorus claims (14.53.5) were to be sacked if taken. Since the summer was coming to an end Dionysius returned to Syracuse with most of his army, his objectives mostly accomplished and his reputation as a successful general much enhanced. News of the disaster at Motya quickly reached Carthage where measures for a response were put into place. Himilcon was again chosen as the sole commander for this expedition.[65] Over the winter of 397/6 BC he is said to have amassed huge numbers of men, equipment, ships and even chariots.[66] At the beginning of the next summer the Carthaginians returned to western Sicily intent on restoring their former prestige and position. The Carthaginian fleet headed to Panormus but some of the ships, fifty in total claims Diodorus (14.55.3), were intercepted and destroyed by a Syracusan squadron led by Leptines. The remainder made it to port and Himilcon advanced in an easterly direction, although the historian's account here betrays the fact that he did not know this region at all. Diodorus has Himilcon seize Eryx while Dionysius, having returned from Syracuse, was apparently close by continuing his siege of Segesta with the entire Greek army. It would be impossible for armies of such huge size, which are attributed to both sides in this conflict, to have avoided each other in the narrow valley that leads up to Segesta from the sea and which connects this town with Eryx. It is perhaps more likely that Dionysius was not even in western Sicily with his main army, which is why the Greeks retreated so rapidly. This occurred because once they had taken Eryx the Carthaginians made camp opposite Motya on the mainland and quickly regained the town. Dionysius appears not to have made any attempt to come to the aid of the garrison there and is reported to have withdrawn entirely into the interior of the island. Those Elymian or Sicanian communities that had made treaties with the Greeks were promised lands if they left the region and came to Syracuse, but the offer was mostly rejected and they returned to their former allegiance with Carthage. There may well have been Greek garrisons inside Motya and besieging Segesta but the ease with which the Carthaginians regained control of the area shows that the main Sicilian Greek army was not engaged in this round of fighting or at least at this stage. Himilcon's great invasion of Sicily in 396 is not strictly relevant here except that within a single campaigning season he reversed all of Dionysius' territorial gains. The final outcome, although involving a withdrawal of the Carthaginians from Syracuse, which they were attempting to besiege, brought about a reiteration of the status quo as it had stood in 409. Dionysius' grand designs therefore came virtually to nothing and it was several years before he was able to make further territorial gains, which he did rather at the expense of fellow Greeks in Sicily and southern Italy rather than of Carthage.

Our attention next turns to events over sixty years later when Alexander the Great besieged the Phoenician city of Tyre. Tyre was the metropolis of Carthage and the Carthaginians established Motya, a connection well worth bearing in mind. Alexander had already defeated Persian armies at the rivers Granicus and Issus in 334 and 333 and was now intent on removing from his enemy any harbours they possessed and so their ability to attack him from his rear or deny him communications with and supplies from Greece and Macedonia. Also a naval confrontation that might have occurred between the Greeks and the Phoenician–Egyptian led Persian fleet and which might have been lost would have been damaging to Alexander's prestige and slowed the pace of his advance. This clearly dominated his thinking when he sent home the Athenian contingent in his fleet and virtually abandoned his naval arm after he had captured Miletus and Halicarnassus in the winter of 334/3. After his defeat of Darius at Issus in the following year Alexander was clearly intent on seizing as many of the eastern Mediterranean seaports as possible in order to facilitate his advance into Mesopotamia. Sidon, Byblos and Marathus in the northern Levant quickly switched their alliances from Persia to Alexander (Arr. *Anab.* 2.16) but the Tyrians, at first welcoming suddenly changed their minds when Alexander stated a desire to pay reverence to the local cult of Heracles (Diod. 17.40.2–3).[67] The city barred its gates and when Alexander threatened force to gain entry the citizens prepared for a siege. Diodorus also states that they were prepared to take this course, surprisingly perhaps seeing Alexander's string of recent victories, out of loyalty to the Persian king whom they expected would reward them well if they delayed the Greeks long enough for Darius to launch the expected counterattack after his defeat at Issus. They confidently believed that they could outlast any attack launched against them, even by someone who had recently besieged and taken at least three cities.[68] Alexander was certainly no novice when it came to sieges. His preparations, like those of Dionysius at Motya, were elaborate and thorough. The city lay off the coast a distance of just four stadia (about 800 metres, 800 yards), but had two well fortified harbours and unlike the Motyans a strong fleet. Alexander's response was to order the construction of a mole about sixty metres in width (200 feet or two *plethra*, Diod. 17.40.5) out towards the island using demolished buildings from a section of the city that was on the mainland.[69] The Tyrians perhaps unwisely mocked this construction, which did indeed initially suffer when the citizens from the island launched their ships, took the men working on this mole by surprise and caused heavy casualties. Alexander took charge of his own fleet and the Tyrians rather than face this challenge immediately retreated. They only just managed to extricate themselves from what could have become a disaster since they narrowly avoided being blockaded by the Greeks outside and being faced with a battle to regain their own harbour.

A short time afterwards the mole sustained severe damage as the result of a storm and to counter future adverse weather conditions wooden stakes were driven into the sea on either side of the causeway as breakwaters to reduce the effects of waves and currents (Diod. 17.42.5–7). Alexander then completed the mole and ordered his siege engines to be brought across to batter the walls of the city. Diodorus goes into extraordinary detail (17.43.1–10) about the means by which the defenders tried to repel the attackers; and again the internal evidence from the text clearly shows the historian using two sources one after the other, the first containing rather less detail than the second, and although not giving identical information some points are incorporated twice by Diodorus. This extended use of his sources can create an effective and lively dramatic element in the scenes the historian describes and can contribute to the heightened tension even if the audience were well aware of the denouement. If well constructed it will work but here as in the description of exactly the same sorts of defensive actions at Motya it appears rather clumsy and poorly executed. It is also probably meant to appear technical in that Diodorus dwells on the inventive measures designed to intercept missiles from the attackers and either break these up or somehow catch them in soft surfaces, which reduced their efficacy.[70]

> The citizens of Tyre had workers of bronze and machines and they constructed curious countermeasures. To destroy some of the darts from the catapults, deflect them or reduce their force they made wheels with spokes which they made to rotate. From other siege engines balls were caught in fabric which was soft and gave way so that the force of the missiles was broken. (Diod. 17.43.1–2; cf. 17.45.3)

Most of the detail, however, is given to the use of broiled sand (cf. Curtius, 4.3.25–26), which was poured from the battlements onto attackers and which ran into their armour and thus caused such pain that these unfortunate soldiers died. Other Greek or Macedonian soldiers were seized and made defenceless by clever use of nets or were raised up by their shields, which had been seized by hooks, and then dropped from a great height. The ingenuity of the Tyrians is impressive until one remembers that similar techniques and machines are also attributed to Archimedes at the siege of Syracuse by the Romans between 214 and 212 BC. There is probably some projection of later techniques back into a more distant historical context. Finally, the incessant assault on the walls caused the fearful Tyrians to construct an inner wall five cubits (7½ feet or roughly 2 metres) inside the first and this new wall was ten cubits in width (15 feet or 5 metres). The gap between the two was filled with rubble in order to strengthen the fortifications against the constant battering. Nonetheless, a section of the wall about thirty metres in length collapsed (Diod. 17.43.3, one *plethron* or about 100 feet) and the Greeks made their first incursion, which was, however, repulsed, and overnight this stretch in Tyre's walls was

Chapter One

1. Sybaris: 'The city quickly grew because the land was so fertile.' (Diod. 12.9.1)

2. Sybaris with the Pollino Massif in the background.

3. The Via Decumana at Sybaris-Thurii Copia.

4. The Bay of Sybaris.

5. Temple of Hera outside Croton.

6. General view of Metapontum.

7. The Argive Heraion at Metapontum.

8. Bridge leading to the acropolis (right) at Taras (Taranto) with harbour entrance in background.

Chapter Two

1. View of Ortygia and the Great Harbour from the Eurialos Fort.

2. View from Epipolai towards the Megarian Plain with Leon and Thapsos in the foreground.

3. The Temple of Zeus at Polichne with Ortygia and Daskon in the background.

4. View from Lysimeleia to Mount Climiti: the initial route of the Athenian retreat.

5. The small harbour from Ortygia with Akradina in the background.

6. Entrance to the Great Harbour from Ortygia to Plemmyrion.

7. The theatre adjacent to the Temenos of Apollo in the Neapolis District of Syracuse.*
* The crane was used as a prop in a production of Euripides' *Medea* (May 2004). The Temenos lies beyond the crane next to the line of trees.

8. Entrance to the Great Harbour: the Athenians set up a trophy in front of Plemmyrion (right) (Thucydides, 7.23).

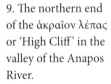

9. The northern end of the ἀκραῖον λέπας or 'High Cliff' in the valley of the Anapos River.

10. The gorge of the Erineos above Noto: a possible way of retreat for the Athenians.

11. Nature of the terrain above Noto, which contributed to the Athenian defeat.

12. The Tellaro River (Assinaros River) at San Paulo: the destruction of Nicias' vanguard.

Chapter Three

1. Motya: Approach from the mainland: salt pans in the foreground, Aegades islands in the right background.

2. The steps in the fortifications at Motya.

3. The cothon or ship repair yard at the south end of Motya with the entrance top centre.

4. Southern fortifications of Motya with Lilybaeum (Marsala) across the lagoon.

5. The acroplis at Selinous.

6. View of the temple precincts of Selinous from its acropolis.

7. The North Gate at Selinous.

8. A street inside the acropolis at Selinous: 'The Defenders gathered in bands at the entrances of the alleys and tried to fortify these streets holding off the enemy.' (Diod. 13.56.7)

9. The stepped fortifications facing the sea at Selinous.

10. The Temple of Heracles at Akragas (Agrigento), Temple of Zeus (Olympieion) in the foreground.

11. The Tomb of Theron at Akragas with the Temple of Heracles in the background. The attempt to destroy the tomb is said to have caused the sickness that infected the Carthaginian besiegers

12. The acropolis at Akragas viewed from the Temple of Zeus (Olympieion).

Chapter Four

1. The *Fossae Marianae* ('Marius' Canal') at Arelate (Arles).

2. Hispania Citerior: Emporion (Ampuries) with Rhodes (Roses) in the distance.

3. The landscape near Aquae Sextiae (Aix-en-Provence).

4. The limestone terrain characteristic of Provence near Aquae Sextiae.

5. The Roman amphitheatre at Tarraco (Tarragona), seat of the proconsul of Hispania Citerior.

Chapter Five

1. A view of the acropolis at Pergamum from the valley of the River Selinous.

2. The theatre and fortifications on the summit of the acropolis at Pergamum.

3. The theatre at Ephesus from the harbour road.

4. A view of the Temple of Artemis at Lindos on Rhodes.

5. Pretoria from the Klapperkop Fort: one of the defensive ring of batteries designed to protect the city from attack but ultimately ineffective in the Second Boer War.

repaired by the now desperate defenders. Alexander considered giving up the siege and proceeding to Egypt, a sentiment apparently shared by most of his commanders (Diod. 17.45.7; Curtius, 4.1.1–2), but after some deliberation he returned to the attack on account of pride and an unwillingness to allow Tyre the privilege of defeating his endeavours. A final assault was therefore launched and appears to have been concentrated on some parts of the walls only accessible from the sea, a point confirmed in the later sources such as Arrian (2.23–34). Alexander in his inimitable fashion was first across a bridge from his warship onto the walls followed closely by his devoted troops. At about the same time, says Diodorus, another breach was made in the city's walls where the mole allowed battering rams to be operated and the attackers also entered at this point sealing the fate of Tyre. The citizens put up local resistance blocking narrow streets in much the same way as is described in the sieges at Selinous and Motya and so the death toll mounted to some 7000, while another 2000 were executed later and 13,000 were taken alive to be sold as slaves.[71] Using his second source again Diodorus says that some of the Tyrians found refuge in Carthage (17.46.4), but many of those captured must have been released almost immediately since the city was soon repopulated.[72]

The account of the siege of Tyre features in all the sources for Alexander's military campaigns and is the most complex of the descriptions of the attacks he made on the cities during the years of his reign.[73] It must have been recorded very soon after the event by a writer such as Callisthenes who accompanied Alexander and who is known to have composed a historical account. Moreover, within living memory of the siege at Tyre others such as Aristobulus, Onesicritus and Ptolemy Lagus all composed their own histories. The magnitude of the assault and its length – it was seven months (January–August 332) before Tyre fell – and the pathos of its climax cannot have failed to impress later writers such as Diodorus and the sources he employed.[74] As noted before, Diodorus' account of Motya must be drawn from the histories of Philistus, Ephorus, and Timaeus. Philistus' account would certainly have been the earliest and perhaps composed very soon after the event and will also have contained a highly favourable view of Dionysius. Philistus' account also must have survived long enough – if it was not used directly by Diodorus – for it to be employed by the next generation of historians. His source or sources for the siege of Tyre are much more difficult to identify, although Timaeus would be the obvious candidate. For the siege of Motya, Diodorus provides the sole ancient literary evidence and for that of Tyre, Diodorus is the earliest extant ancient historian. Thus for both episodes his history is of vital importance.

The similarity in the descriptions of these quite discrete events can of course be accounted for by the lack of eyewitness evidence or familiarity with the battlefields and hence the development of topical elements that were woven into the more specific information about each individual episode. The geographical details of Akragas and Tyre certainly stand out as exceptional while the absence of any information that had a direct bearing on the events at Selinous is also notable. Himera and Motya lie somewhere between these two extremes; some geographical detail is given but mostly hazy information when it comes to details. That Motya can be said to have a particular link with Tyre makes absolute sense since they were both Punic settlements, although the latter was by far the greater city. Furthermore, the siege of Tyre was conducted by arguably the greatest general of all time, the siege of Motya by the greatest of the Sicilian tyrants; and thereby hangs an interlinking thread that requires some exploration.

On an initial reading it might appear to be a straightforward continuation of Sicilian Greek history following and building upon what must have appeared to contemporaries as an utterly amazing victory over the Athenians by Syracuse. The account is therefore a composite creation drawn from a number of independent sources, yet there is, I would suggest, a greater complexity here than simply a construction from various building blocks.[75] Freeman, for example, long ago spotted that something was not quite straightforward about Diodorus' account for he comments:

> The siege began, a siege which it would be hopeless to try and understand by a glance at the existing map only. (Freeman, 1894, 69)

If this was the simple siege of a modest sized town then consultation of a map and some degree of empirical research in and around the archaeological site should be sufficient but it clearly is not. Motya's situation today is very much as it was in antiquity. Unlike at Syracuse or at Tyre and also Alexandria where in each case the mole has expanded to join the mainland and island more closely, at Motya the reverse has occurred, which calls into immediate question the historicity of such as massive construction attributed to Dionysius in 397.

The similarities between the fortifications of Motya and Selinous, founded at roughly the same time (610 BC) are quite startling. Most commentators remark on the supposed sophistication of the walls in late Classical and Hellenistic Selinous (from about 408 to 250 BC), but they omit mention of the stepped nature of these 'fortifications' and the number of gateways in the walls of the settlement dating to this time. The larger and earlier settlement, which had been destroyed in 409/8, was a city of much greater extent but cannot have been that secure since it would have required a suitably large population to defend it and Selinous is not considered to have possessed many more than 10,000 inhabitants at its maximum.[76] Thus its inconclusive border feuding with nearby Segesta, 65 kilometres or just 40 miles to the north, in the years down to 415 BC show that these two cities were of similar size and military capability.[77] The later settlement at Selinous, which followed the sack of 409, and the Carthaginian reestablishment of a presence here was considerably smaller and confined to within the former acropolis. The outer suburbs, which far exceeded the acropolis in size, were all abandoned. Indeed the later occupation suggests that it was rather a fortress but this was a fortress with a difference. One the one hand it appears to possess quite sophisticated fortifications as noted above and this is certainly the case at the northern end of the site where the main gate is clearly in much the same mould as the Epipolai Gate in Syracuse (see above) and has all the hallmarks of third century defence techniques: a complex system of bridges, pits and ditches, the channelling of traffic into a narrow entrance, subterranean passages to allow defenders to make attacks on the rear of besiegers and to remove debris from pits and ditches if attempts were made to fill them for siege engines to engage against the walls. The landward side of Selinous was always its vulnerable quarter and it was through the northern walls and entrance that the Carthaginians stormed in 409, though this was probably in the outer fortifications about one and half kilometres (a mile or so) to the north of the acropolis. Moreover, while this is an echo of Agathoclean fortifications – found not just in Syracuse, but also in Gela and Heracleia Minoa as well – there is a deceptive weakness to the later site if it was simply meant to be a fortress. Fourth century Selinous came to possess no fewer than thirty-eight gates, either full entrance/exits or postern gates for foot traffic alone. Besides this the stepped wall overlooking the harbour may appear to be a sort of sophisticated battlement but is really just a set of rather steep but not unmanageable steps. It seems that the rather obvious has been ignored here and that except for the landward side northern gateway the defensive works here are rather weak and that it was instead meant to be a place that actually drew visitors in. The northern end could still be presented as something not to be tangled with but for the rest it was really a case of open house. It is not credible, for example, that the existing step arrangement of the walls at that particular point in the southernmost fortifications was covered to make a smoother surface like the Great Pyramids at Giza. The obvious should be accepted here that steps and gates were meant to be used and that either merchants laden with goods or buyers arrived and brought them up to the top of the steps or inside one of the numerous gates in order to trade. Selinous in its latest existence was therefore the same as

Motya had been down to 397, not much of a fortress and rather more a mart or emporium. Of course, there was a civilian population in both settlements, but not of a substantial nature, plus the garrison. Neither site was of the size or strength of the more major urban centres further around the southern and eastern coast of Sicily.[78]

It is interesting to note that while modern commentators have been struck by the similarity in the description of the sieges at Tyre and Motya they have not also noted that, from topographical detail that the latter was simply not on the same scale as that most powerful city of the Levant. Motya did not possess the formidable fortifications or the resources that are reported for Tyre. Moreover, it is clear that the literary sources for Motya not only relied heavily on the accounts of Alexander's siege of Tyre, perhaps also Miletus and Halicarnassus shortly before, but that they also had no acquaintance with their subject. Diodorus was writing probably in Rome and although a Sicilian Greek had never visited Motya, while Timaeus wrote in Athens and clearly had never ventured to western Sicily. Motya by then was already a desolated site and mostly abandoned.

The siege train that the sources attribute to Hannibal is most unlikely because this technical aspect of warfare really belongs to the Hellenistic period or certainly from the time of Philip II of Macedon and not to the last years of the fifth century. The Athenians in the siege of Syracuse (Chapter 2) clearly possessed none and innovation in this field cannot have taken place within a decade or so. Thus there is at Motya a confusion of detail belonging to different periods and the events at Motya contain material applicable to Tyre and projected backwards to make the narrative more dramatic and elaborate. The siege at Selinous meanwhile probably drew some details from the Macedonian sieges at Methone, Perinthus and Byzantium in the 350s and 340s. The population figures given for the cities by among other Diodorus have also been inflated, the exaggeration explicable again as a dramatic element in the text. Therefore, like the myth of Sybaris (see Chapter 1) a myth of Motya has also grown up in the modern literature promoted for the most part by the absence of any concrete evidence. Most ancient writers were not drawn to write about Motya because there was simply nothing to write about. It was in the end the destruction of a fairly minor trading post by a ruler of Syracuse who was determined to make as much of his victories as he could. And so Motya entered the historical accounts as a great triumph for Dionysius I. Finally if we return to Cluverius with whom we began, he was, after all, correct in his comment about Motya. It did not exist as it was recorded by Diodorus for this island did not contain a powerful and populous city like Tyre or even one of a more modest *polis* such as Selinous or Heracleia

Minoa. In fact, Motya was a small trading outpost of the Carthaginians. It was not well fortified, nor was it particularly wealthy but it did possess both strategic and symbolic value because of its position situated just off the western coast of Sicily. The wonder is that it survived a siege of about nine days and that it did not surrender or was destroyed more quickly. That it should have been the object of a siege is not to be wondered at, however, because if Dionysius had been able to hold on to this acquisition it would have brought the Sicilian Greeks a harbour on the west coast and would have allowed virtually unhampered sailing around the entire island. He failed in his endeavour because the Carthaginian presence was transferred to the more defendable site at Lilybaeum and there it remained a thorn in the side of the Greeks until the Romans wrested control in 241 BC.[79] Arguably, Diodorus following in a line of distinguished Sicilian Greek historians – Antiochus, Philistus and Timaeus – wished to preserve for posterity an episode that was to be presented of similar magnitude to the siege of Tyre. The result was that Motya, which was in fact a fairly minor affair, offered an ideal opportunity for what, it must be said, was a high degree of creative writing.

Chronology

410	Border disputes between Segesta and Selinous (Diod. 13.43.1)
	Segesta requests aid from Carthage (Diod. 13.44.4)
409	Hannibal attacks and destroys Selinous (Diod. 13.57.6)
	Himera destroyed by the Carthaginians (Diod. 13.62.4)
409/8	Hermocrates reoccupies Selinous (Diod. 13.63.3)
408	Hermocrates killed in Syracuse (Diod. 13.75.8)
407	Carthage founds a settlement at Therma, near the former Himera (Diod. 13.79.8)
406	Hannibal and Himilcon elected joint commanders by Carthaginians for an invasion of Sicily (Diod. 13.80.2)
406	The Carthaginians attack Akragas (Diod. 13.85.1)
	Hannibal dies at Akragas during a plague (Diod. 13.86.3).
	Akragas taken by Himilcon after an eight-month siege on 21 or 22 December
	Dionysius elected general by the Syracusans
405	Dionysius at Gela (Diod. 13.93.1)
397	Dionysius completes preparations for a new campaign against the Carthaginians
	Segesta besieged by the Greeks

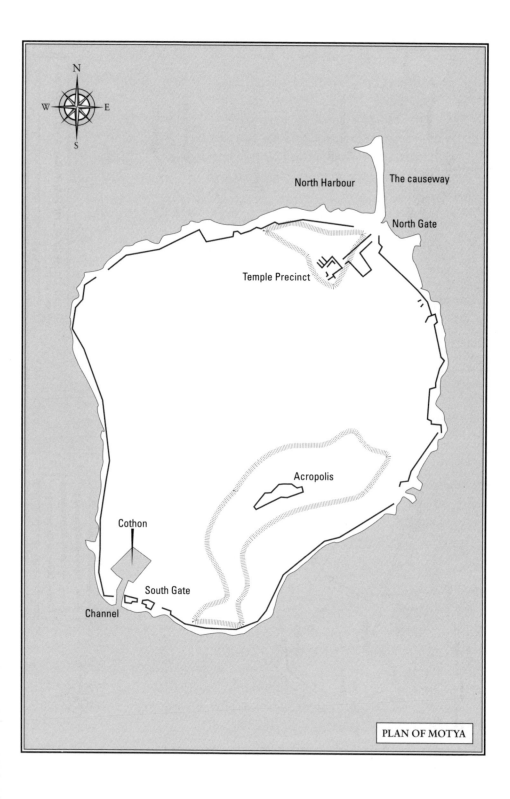

PLAN OF MOTYA

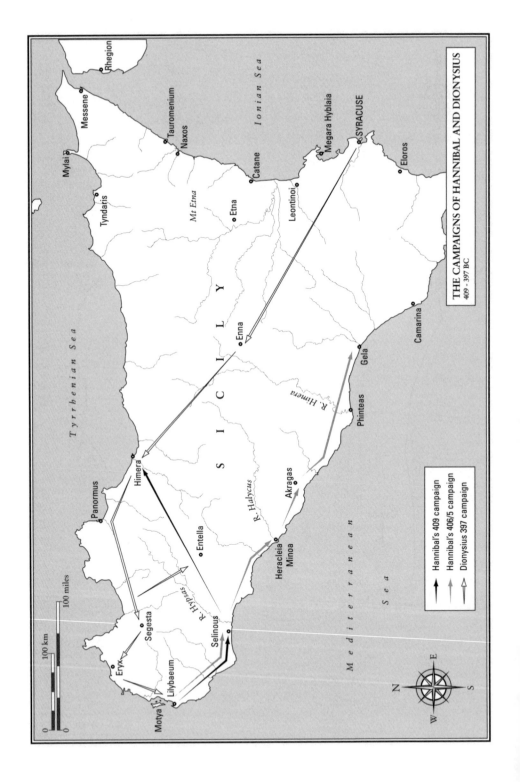

THE CAMPAIGNS OF HANNIBAL AND DIONYSIUS
409 - 397 BC

Hannibal's 409 campaign
Hannibal's 406/5 campaign
Dionysius 397 campaign

Ionian Sea

Tyrrhenian Sea

Mediterranean Sea

S I C I L Y

Rhegion
Messene
Mylai
Tyndaris
Tauromenium
Naxos
Catane
Mt Etna
Etna
Leontinoi
Megara Hyblaia
SYRACUSE
Eloros
Enna
Camarina
Gela
R. Himera
Phinteas
Akragas
R. Halycus
Entella
Heracleia
Minoa
Himera
Panormus
Segesta
R. Hypsas
Eryx
Lilybaeum
Motya
Selinous

100 km
100 miles

N E S W

Chapter Four

Aquae Sextiae and Vercellae (102–101 BC): Marius' Victories over the Germans

His victories over the Germanic tribes, the Cimbri and Teutones,[1] in two successive campaigning seasons between the summers of 102 and 101, rightly secured for Gaius Marius a place in the pantheon of the very greatest and most successful Roman generals.[2] This chapter will recount these military campaigns, but will also seek to answer the question of whether, as Marius and literary sources for his life would lay claim, he obtained his victories through personal martial excellence or whether he actually gained these notable successes through a combination of astute management of the military capability at his disposal and acute handling of the logistical problems encountered in pursuing any military adventure, not to mention poor tactical planning by his enemy? Thus to put it more succinctly: was Marius a warrior in the mould of Alexander the Great or even Mithridates of Pergamum (see Chapter 5) or was he the first of the accomplished managers of battles and battlefields winning his wars even before they were fought? I will illustrate that the second claim is much more likely to be historical and the first an example of ancient propaganda. It is nearly twenty years since I first argued that Marius was a greater politician than he was a general and in the intervening time I have not seen fit to alter that opinion in any way except that it has increasingly occurred to me that the intellect necessary for a highly successful civil career was also the basis on which his notable military successes were accomplished.[3] Marius was not a great warrior but he was or rather became a superb manager of tactics and strategy, learned almost certainly in the campaigns against Jugurtha the king of Numidia between 109 and 105. His role in this war graduated from legate to his commander when he was more active in the field to the sort of management that can be identified in his later role as vanquisher of the Germanic tribes for which he rightly earned the title 'Third Founder of Rome' from a grateful and very relieved citizen body.[4]

It is also the aim here to place these battles in both a more realistic temporal and regional context since Marius' great victories over the Germanic tribes came as the climax of a long and bitter war that extended for over a decade and affected the entire western sector of Rome's empire. This aspect is often overlooked when the focus is on Marius alone. He was the last in a series of commanders who fought against these tribes. Moreover, in the wider geographical context, the Cimbri especially are attested as roaming from Illyria in 114/3 into the Alpine lands by 109, throughout Gaul by 105 and into northern Spain between 104 and 103 before returning to northern Gaul and ultimately reaching the Po Valley by the winter of 102 via one of the Alpine passes. This tribe must be one of the most travelled of any ancient group before the Huns of the fifth century AD. And their marauding, which had a profoundly negative impact on the communities of the time whether they were Roman, Greek, Gallic, or Iberian, was brought to an end by Marius whose career, somewhat retarded at its outset, reached its apex as a result of his successes at Aquae Sextiae and Vercellae. Both issues will be highlighted in the following discussion. Finally, in most discussions of the conflict with the Germanic tribes the emphasis tends to focus on a broader picture of Roman warfare or imperialism or politics in this period of the republic and therefore much of the detail about these campaigns and especially the battles has been sacrificed. The intention here is to try and rectify an otherwise incomplete picture.

In Sallust's *Bellum Iugurthinum* (85) Marius is given a major speech by the historian where the speaker supposedly placed great stress on his personal expertise in battle, and that he was able to display the honourable scars – his *honestae cicatrices* – that he had on his body as a result of his warrior prowess.[5] However, when Marius became consul at the age of fifty in 107 it was many years since he had physically seen action in the field. As a much younger man he had served under Scipio Aemilianus in the war against the Numantines in Spain between approximately 134 and 133 in which he no doubt was able to prove his heroism, although that particular campaign had consisted mostly of a siege.[6] Thereafter, Marius is not attested as serving in a war until possibly a posting as proconsul to *Hispania Ulterior* following his praetorship in 116, by which time he would not have been fighting in the front line of any conflict. His background as a 'new man' or *novus homo* in political life, the first of his family to reach the consulship, obliged him perhaps to draw attention to his worthy deeds, which were different to those of established senatorial family members. In reality there was little or no difference between Marius and an aristocrat such as Metellus whom he was about to succeed in North Africa other than the prominence their families had achieved in recent years. Marius was from a wealthy and privileged stratum of Roman society and his ambitions lay in military success and political eminence in Rome. Towards that objective both the war against Jugurtha the Numidian king (107–105) and the war against the Germanic tribes (104–101) the second of which is the focus here, were springboards.

Marius served as the senior legate or staff officer to the commander of operations against Jugurtha, Quintus Caecilius Metellus (consul 109), for almost two campaigning seasons during which time he appears to have been popular with the troops under his care and with whom he adopted an easygoing relationship (Sall. *Iug*. 64.5). Certainly, by the beginning of the second campaigning season he was seriously considering a canvass for the consulship and not only did he exploit his popularity among the citizen legionaries (Plut. *Mar*. 7.4), he also made overtures to Roman merchants and business figures in Africa asking for their support.[7] Sensing that there was a good chance of success in the elections for the consulship for 107 he asked his general for permission to return to Rome in order to present himself as a candidate both to the presiding official and to the electorate.[8] Metellus, who later acquired the name 'Numidicus' for his successful conduct of the war after celebrating a triumph in Rome in 107, on the whole is well regarded by ancient commentators, especially by Cicero who clearly admired this political figure. However his *hubris* or excessive pride is decried in some later moralizing tracts, including that of Sallust for his haughty attitude towards his subordinate when he said that Marius would be ready for election as consul when his own son was of the required age.[9] Marius was probably the first senator from his family while Metellus could trace his pedigree back to the First Punic War, 150 years before, not it should be stated, therefore, a family of great antiquity among the Roman elite but sufficiently respectable for him to look askance at any potential newcomer to the highest political office in the *res publica*. After a series of incompetent appointees Metellus was a better calibre general and had considerable success against Jugurtha, defeating the King on a number of occasions and forcing his enemy to rely more heavily on guerrilla tactics. It could well be argued that when Metellus was replaced by Marius after his two years as commander in the field there was actually little left to accomplish other than mopping up operations for which the latter required another three years. Metellus' successes were acknowledged by the Romans through the grant of an honour of celebrating a triumph on his return to the city.[10] He later clashed with the tribune Saturninus and the praetor Servilius Glaucia who were intent on ensuring the passage of radical legislation by forcing all senators to swear an oath to support the new laws.[11] Metellus alone of the entire senatorial body refused and was exiled in 100.[12] His action, which cost him dearly, was later regarded with admiration by writers such as Cicero who compared his own tribulations and exile with this earlier politician. Metellus' son campaigned vigorously for his recall, which he achieved in 98. Marius, who had supported the laws and the activities of Saturninus and Glaucia until they went too far in their ambitions in 100 and then suppressed them and their supporters, left Rome for Asia rather than see his former commander return to the city. Metellus, however, played no further role in politics in Rome and indeed in the summer of 108 he was not in a position to prevent Marius from becoming a candidate for the consulship, although he might have offered his support to another candidate though this does not appear to have happened.[13]

The advent of the Cimbri at the frontiers of the Roman Empire dates back to a number of years before Marius' election to the consulship. This tribe is first mentioned by a Roman historian under the date 114 and as being present in Illyria. The epitome of Livy (Book 63) says the following:

Cimbri, gens vaga, populabundi in Illyricum venerunt: ab his Papirius Carbo consul cum exercitu fusus est.

The Cimbri, a nation of nomads, came to Illyria for the purpose of plunder and by these the consul Papirius Carbo with his army was put to flight.

The number of times this is noted by Roman writers clearly points to an occasion of some significance in their history. The Cimbri, at once an identifiable menace, became one of the more threatening enemies the *res publica* was to face before the barbarian onslaughts of the Later Empire. Much was evidently made of their possible origin, which was not of the Mediterranean or its hinterland. Plutarch who gives considerable coverage to the Cimbri says that some ascribed their origin to Central Asia and hence were related to the Scythians (*Mar.* 11.4), others that they had descended into the Roman world from the northern seas because they were blue-eyed (*Mar.* 11.3), and still others thought that they were descendants of Cimmerians (*Mar.* 11.6–7).[14] All such ideas according to Plutarch were conjecture for no evidence existed to confirm one theory above the others. As far as the size of the tribe was concerned Plutarch gives a figure of 300,000 men of fighting age alone and at least an equal number of non-combatants (*Mar.* 11.2) and that measured in terms of bravery and audacity they proved to be irresistible in battle as events had proved. Plutarch brushes aside those events because his focus lies with Marius. By the time Marius was appointed commander of the Roman defence of Gaul the Cimbri had clearly become more than just a thorn in the side of a giant empire. Initially these nomads had attacked some Roman allies in Illyria, whether along the coast or inland is not recorded and the details are obscure, yet there was sufficient concern in Rome to despatch the consul Cn. Papirus Carbo with an army to deal with these marauders.[15] Still, this did not take place immediately and probably indicates that complaints about the Cimbri arrived at Rome late in 114 and so Carbo, one of the consuls for 113, will have departed on his mission only in the late spring of the year of his consulship. It is apparent that Carbo had some difficulty locating this enemy, for the Cimbri were no longer in Illyria. Finding an enemy army in modern warfare is difficult enough but in the ancient world covering huge tracts of forested land in search of one's opponents even with the use of trained scouts would have posed great difficulties for the consul. Furthermore, the Cimbri in question who had attacked Illyria were a large raiding party, perhaps as many as 30,000 warriors, rather than the whole tribe in migration, proved elusive. And indeed Carbo only caught up with the Cimbri in the late summer as the invaders were moving north away from Illyria into Noricum (modern Austria).

What happened next caught the attention of ancient writers and has engendered mostly negative modern comment.[16] Appian has the fullest account, although this is hardly more than a fragment from his history of the *Gallic Wars* (13). He seems to have missed any connection with Illyria and suggests instead that the Cimbri had attacked allies of Rome in Noricum and that a Roman military response would therefore have been fully justified.[17] When the Cimbri became aware of a Roman army nearby they reportedly then sent envoys apologizing for their error and said that they had not known of the treaties between the people of Noricum and Rome and they promised to refrain from attacking these in future. Since the tribe was then nomadic this was quite an easy promise to make and Appian does not indicate that the Cimbri were prepared to make reparations or return their plunder. On the other hand, Carbo is said to have accepted this excuse and sent the envoys away with Roman scouts who were instructed to lead the Cimbri on a long route back to their compatriots.[18] This left time for Carbo to launch an attack on the main body of the marauders, a move that completely backfired on the Romans. The Cimbri not only offered a highly competent defence, but forced the Romans onto the back foot and indeed a rout was only avoided by a timely thunderstorm, under the cover of which Carbo's army was able to retreat but in some disorder. Appian claims that the Cimbri disappeared into Gaul, although this is more likely a device to link this episode with the next time this tribe came into conflict with the Romans. Carbo's lack of honour receives scathing treatment and he certainly paid a high price for his actions. But what other course was he to take? Allowing the Cimbri to go away without any redress whatsoever for their incursion might well be taken as a sign of weakness and invite further attacks. A robust response was actually necessary and was clearly expected by the Cimbri who were obviously not taken by surprise at the Roman behaviour and this would most certainly have been the course of action they would have taken. The idea of the noble savage beset upon by the perfidious Greco-Roman sophisticate betrays nineteenth century idealism rather than a sure appreciation of how warfare is fought then and now. Unfortunately for Carbo he lost his battle and that was why he was prosecuted on his return to Rome; had he gained a great victory any disreputable behaviour would have failed to surface. As it was, he avoided a conviction, although for precisely what is neither stated nor can one be easily sought, by committing suicide.[19]

For some years there is no report of the whereabouts of the Cimbri and they presumably found some land extensive enough for at least a temporary home. They had approached the Alps from the north by 109 and again may have come into conflict with Rome somewhere in Gaul. The details are again not forthcoming except that there was a request, which was rejected, for land within the empire on which to settle. This came either before (Liv. *Per.* 65) or after a battle (Flor. 1.38/3.3) in which the consul M. Iunius Silanus was defeated either during the summer of 109 or 108. The problem with this episode is that it may only have indirectly been with the Cimbri for the literary sources also mention the Teutones and a tribe called the Tigurini. Livy states that Silanus was defeated by the Cimbri; Asconius' commentary on Cicero's speech *pro Cornelio* agrees,[20] but Florus seems to have believed that there was an alliance of Cimbri, Teutones and Tigurini. Florus undoubtedly used Livy as his source and Livy remains only as an epitome so it is possible that the Romans were faced with a grand coalition of Germanic tribes as early as 109. However, the defeat, although serious, was plainly not regarded as a particularly threatening event and certainly not of the hysterical pitch that occurred in late 105. On balance therefore this episode refers to the earliest movement of the Tigurini from the Alps, perhaps under pressure from the Cimbri, into the upper Rhone valley and close to the Roman province. At Lake Geneva only a small stretch of water later separated the ancestral lands of the Helevetii, who claimed descent from the Tigurini, from the *imperium* of Rome (Caes. *B.G.* 1.7) and it may have been at this potential flashpoint that the engagement took place.

In 107 a much more serious event occurred when the Tigurini defeated a Roman army commanded by the consular colleague of Marius, L. Cassius Longinus, who was killed along with many of his senior officers. The Roman survivors were allowed to go under a truce says the epitome of Livy after they gave hostages to ensure good behaviour and half of their belongings.[21]

This defeat occurred near Agen, which lies on the River Garonne in modern Aquitaine. At the time this was inside the territory of the Nitiobroges (Liv. *Per.* 65), which lay adjacent to the lands occupied by the Volcae Tectosages and quite close to the sea (Orosius, 5.15).[22] This shows that the Tigurini had moved far to the west of the Rhone and had probably been pursued by the Roman army commanded by Cassius Longinus. The Tigurini, having dispensed with the opposition posed by Silanus, had felt free to wander but the Romans who had become accustomed to controlling by proxy the state of play beyond their frontiers through client kingships and ties of friendship must have viewed this movement as too hazardous to be allowed to continue. Again the details are not alluded to in the surviving texts partly because of the focus on Marius and his campaign against Jugurtha. Jugurtha was never a threat to Rome but possibly Roman interests in North Africa; the movement of the Tigurini could easily, and did as events proved, destabilize the entire north western frontier. It may well be that Livy devoted considerable detail to events in Gaul but it is also possible that these were rather suppressed in the desire to portray Marius' earlier career as worthy of what came later. However, the magnitude of the Roman disgrace can hardly be denied. The Romans must have been shocked for they immediately ordered a new army levied and despatched under Q. Servilius Caepio who had a good record from a provincial command in Spain.[23]

The location of the battles lost by Silanus and Longinus illustrates the great instability that had by 106 affected this whole region for at least three years, and by then called for some even more concerted action by the Romans. Indeed at first they accomplished some limited successes, but not it seems against the Tigurini who appear to have dropped out of sight. The consul Servilius Caepio was given a province that extended beyond the Rhone frontier and he attacked not the Tigurini but the Volcae Tectosages who had been giving aid to this tribe, whether willingly or under compulsion is not said, but perhaps because on account of ancient common ties. There is a suggestion that the Volcae were in a state of internal unrest at this time, perhaps associated with the movement of the Tigurini, and Caepio took advantage of this weakness. The Volcae must also have had some treaty with Rome by this time but such a connection would have been regarded as void because of the local infighting and the broader chaotic picture. Caepio marched his army west of the Rhone and stormed the capital of the Volcae at Tolosa (modern Toulouse), which he captured and destroyed. Far from pacifying the area, however, this simply inflamed the situation even more, for the Tigurini, if they had been tackled at all, seem simply to have returned to their former territory high above the Rhone valley.

The River Rhone is a crucial geographical element when it comes to trying to retrace the area of the battles first at Arausio and then at Aquae Sextiae and it is worth dwelling a while on the river's importance as a trade and communications route in this period. The Rhone rises in the western Alps above Lake Geneva into which it feeds and from which it exits running first in a westerly direction before flowing south at its confluence with the Saône. From there it flows into the Mediterranean, which it reaches through an extensive delta. The Rhone had become *de facto* the north-western frontier of the Roman Empire after the conquest of that region, Provence today ('The Provincia'), by the end of the 120s, which in time became the province of *Gallia Transalpina*. Roman involvement here became inevitable for there was a long history of hostility with a tribe called the Ligurians who lived along the coast from north-western Italy into southern Gaul. The suppression of those Ligures living east of the Alps in the first half of the second century did not bring about permanent peace because their cousins on the western side of the Alps maintained their independence. Thus the Romans were drawn across the Alps especially when summoned by their longstanding ally Massilia, which was threatened not only by the western Ligures but also the Gallic Saluvii and Vocontii. One of the consuls of 125, M. Fulvius Flaccus, operated in southern Gaul, which marked this new intervention by the Romans.[24] He was followed immediately by C. Sextius Calvinus (cos. 124) who penetrated as far as Rhone as the name of the Roman colony at Aquae Sextiae (modern Aix-en-Provence) clearly illustrates, the foundation of which was intended to keep the Saluvii and Vocontii pacified (Liv. *Per.* 61).[25] But more importantly, a policy can be identified in the intention of ensuring the security of the Massilia by keeping a tight hold on the interior. The Massilians were clearly not in a position to defend their own territory, which is perhaps surprising since the city had been one of the most influential of the Greek settlements in the western Mediterranean from the sixth century BC at least.

Still it was the conflict with the Allobroges that caused the Roman Empire to be extended formally to the Rhone and beyond. The Allobroges were a powerful tribe with homelands south of the Rhone as it flows out of Lake Geneva towards the Saône and had alliances with other Gallic groups west of the river.[26] In 123 following the Roman defeat of the Saluvii their southern neighbours, the Allobroges, gave safe haven to that tribe's king and refused to surrender him to the Romans when requested to do so. This refusal became the pretext for another military campaign which the senate entrusted to the consul of 123, Cn. Domitius Ahenobarbus, who apparently defeated a huge gathering of local tribes (Strabo, 4.2.3) at Vindalium (near modern Avignon). And either as a result of this victory or a prelude to the successful conclusion of the campaign the construction of one of the great trunk roads of the Roman Empire the *Via Domitia* was begun.[27] Ahenobarbus must have remained as proconsul in the area until he was replaced by Q. Fabius Maximus (cos. 121) who undertook the final defeat of the Allobroges.[28] During a hard-fought campaign Fabius Maximus finally had a similarly spectacular success in battle against a combination of Allobroges and their allies the Arverni. The former were brought into the empire, while the latter were given client status just across the Rhone frontier. The details are scant and the magnitude of the warfare is somewhat understated in the literature, which tends to comment mostly on the number of enemy casualties. The celebration of the Roman victories is indicated by the triumphs awarded to Ahenobarbus in 121 but to Fabius Maximus possibly as late as 117.[29] The most significant outcome of these hostilities was not only the emergence of the province of *Gallia Transalpina*, but a permanent Roman presence across the Rhone delta. The newest Roman colony called Narbo Martius (modern Narbonne) was established from 118, eventually becoming the capital of the province, which was renamed *Gallia Narbonensis*.[30] Therefore, the war with the Allobroges had lasted six years and when the Cimbri arrived in southern Gaul they found a region barely recovered from that upheaval.[31]

Matters may have been bad enough on the north-western frontiers of the empire, but everything became immeasurably worse with the disaster at Arausio (modern Orange). Q. Servilius Caepio (cos. 106) had been granted the province of *Gallia Transalpina* but evidently with sufficient ambiguity about its terminus to allow him to cross the Rhone and intervene in the affairs of the Volcae Tectosages. This is clear from his activities at and around Tolosa, and this command was prorogued for 105. In addition and rather unusually for the Romans, probably since the Cimbri's movements must have been monitored after their defeat of Cassius Longinus in 107, the province of Transalpine Gaul was assigned to the new consul Cn. Mallius Maximus.

The consul's military credentials are unclear and not attested. He was a *novus homo* who must have benefited from the success of Marius and it ought also to be assumed that he had sufficient experience of commanding armies since he was appointed rather than his colleague P. Rutilius Rufus who had very recently served as a legate to Metellus Numidicus in the war against Jugurtha and who remained in Rome.[32] However, the two generals became quickly embroiled in a personal quarrel since it was a little unclear who should be in command of the operation. Caepio as proconsul had an army of about 40,000, while Mallius Maximus who reached Gaul in early summer came with an army of about the same number. The two were expected to cooperate and act against any incursion from the Cimbri, which must by then have been expected. The two armies initially remained independent of each other, again a highly unusual and risky strategy. The Romans were used to sending out a general with a new levy, if needed, who would then take overall command of all forces on the ground. It is possible that there was some concern about the ability of Mallius Maximus, although nothing is noted in the sources except that Cicero, writing much later and with hindsight (*Oratio pro Plancio*, 12), is highly critical of this politician's background and character.[33] Caepio was a tried and tested commander but he seems also to have possessed a prickly character and, it is claimed considerable pride, although one should be aware of the *hubris* and *nemesis* element in any Greco-Latin narrative text, but he seems to have found his match in Mallius Maximus. A new man to politics perhaps but he was certainly sure of the etiquette and prerogatives of a consul for he considered himself the commander-in-chief of this campaign and Caepio as his subordinate. Caepio had taken up a position on the right bank of the Rhone. Mallius Maximus at Arausio then ordered the proconsul to join him so that they might present a united face to the Cimbri. At first Caepio refused mainly because he would place himself in a subordinate position by vacating what had become a roving command beyond the frontier.

Arausio is dated to 6 October 105, which was late in the year for a tribe to be migrating in search for a suitable permanent or even a temporary home. Gaul was already well populated and there were few large open areas that could easily accommodate a tribe the size of the Cimbri. It therefore seems more likely that the Cimbric army was, as had been the case at Noreia over a decade before, a marauding party, and so the number mentioned in some accounts, is probably inflated.[34] Plutarch (*Mar.* 11.2) claims his figure for the total number of Cimbri (11.8) was a conservative one in comparison to that given by other writers, although he fails to name these sources. And this assertion comes from a writer who is intent on enhancing the magnitude of Marius' victories and as such his use of figures in this context must be suspect. Overall, it is notable that Greek and Roman writers give huge estimates for Gallic armies and casualty figures, probably because these are offset against the difficulty the Romans encountered in subduing the region.

The capture and murder of Mallius' senior legate the former consul, M. Aurelius Scaurus, is both an intriguing detail about Arausio but also another instance of tactics that appear baffling because of the lack of information provided by the sources. The epitome of Livy (*Per.* 67) places this event immediately before a report of the main engagement. Quite what Scaurus was doing is simply conjecture.[35] He was evidently in charge of a column of troops, perhaps not that large a detachment, and he may have been either looking for the location of the Cimbri or shadowing them as they moved within range of his commander's army at Arausio. The defeat of Scaurus' troops and his capture and subsequent murder by the Cimbri must have taken place just of days before Arausio because the sources seem to agree that this episode caused the consul to summon Caepio from the west bank of the Rhone.

Caepio had been moving north after his sack of Tolosa, whether in pursuit of the Tigurini, elements of the Volcae or in anticipation of a conflict with the Cimbri is not stated. He evidently made camp across river and contact was established with Mallius' group, but the commanders were not on friendly terms from the start. As a result of the loss of Scaurus and his troops Mallius summoned Caepio to cross the Rhone and join him at his camp.[36] Caepio was unhappy about doing so because he wished to retain his independent command but finally crossed the river and made camp close to that of Mallius but refused to obey the latter's orders. At this point the Cimbri, having already displayed their power with the victory over Scaurus, but still reluctant it seems to fight so large a combined Roman force, sent envoys to Mallius requesting land as they had done in 109 when they encountered Silanus. The request was rejected by the consul. There is some uncertainty in the sources about just who received this embassy. The text of Granius (17) looks rather confused and seems to suggest that it was Caepio who was approached and who abusively threw out ('*contumeliose submovit*') the Cimbri who as a result were justifiably inflamed by this display of *hubris* and this made them inclined to fight with greater vigour. Caepio's infamy as a result of Arausio and accusations made against him later for embezzlement and then his exile have plainly influenced Granius' account and therefore the more sober interpretation of Dio (27.91.3) ought to be preferred.[37] He states that the mutual jealousy and dislike between the two commanders had been kept secret but was exposed when the Cimbri sent their ambassadors to Mallius, and Caepio objected that he had not been consulted. As a result he would not participate in Mallius' plan of action against the invaders. The battle as it unfolded soon after was a quite straightforward and rather rapid affair without much novelty or display of tactics by the Cimbri. Partly because the two Roman forces remained divided and did not offer battle but chose to remain on the defensive in their camps, they were simply swamped. Caepio, who first may have brought his troops outside his camp and formed up with his back to the river, was attacked and routed and lost his camp. Then the Cimbri moved a little to the south to take the camp of Mallius, who offered no battle at all, although since this camp had a means of retreat to the south there were almost certainly far more survivors from this second round of fighting.[38] Oddly enough the Romans fell into adopting a siege-like mentality and their rout is more reminiscent of later Roman successes over Gallic tribes taking refuge in their hill top forts. Had the Romans played rather to their strength and made a combined effort and drawn up a correct line of battle they would have had a greater chance of avoiding disaster, but this was not to be seen against the Cimbri until Vercellae four years later.

Quintus Sertorius, later famous as the Roman renegade who set himself up as an independent ruler in Spain in the 70s, was a young soldier serving in the cavalry in the army commanded by Servilius Caepio. He lost his horse and was wounded in the first debacle. To save himself he swam away from the Roman province to safety, according to Plutarch (*Sert.* 3.1) and towards the west bank of the Rhone.[39] He is said to have been among the few to escape alive as the total for those killed by the Cimbri range from 60,000 to 80,000. Bearing in mind that this would account for the two Romans armies almost in their entirety some exaggeration is clearly indicated. Both Mallius and Caepio survived the joint defeat and probably with sufficient numbers to maintain some defence of Roman interests in southern Gaul. Luckily for the Romans the Cimbri did not follow up this great victory in the way expected. And so Mallius Maximus and Servilius Caepio remained with the remnants of their respective commands for the time being.[40] Mallius' consular colleague P. Rutilius Rufus must have been given the task of overseeing the protection of Italy during his year in office was in Rome. His duty was also to preside over the elections for 104, most of which he must continually have postponed in order that Marius, who was widely regarded as the only possible candidate with sufficient military experience to avert an invasion of Italy, could complete the campaign in North Africa and return to Rome to present himself at the hustings. The elections usually scheduled for mid-summer would have required more than just panic to defer them and the most obvious course would have been to appeal to unfavourable auspices. Tribunes and aediles of the plebs would have been elected by the *comitia plebis tributa* at the usual time during July or August, but the *Comitia Centuriata*, which elected the curule aediles, praetors and consuls, did not convene before the autumn of 105. This is implicit in the literature, which points to Marius' election to a second consulship being coterminous with the battle at Arausio and the capture of Jugurtha. Therefore, the elections were not held at the usual time of the year and the electorate, with the votes being heavily weighted with the wealthiest members of the community, were prepared to wait and see rather than vote for more untried candidates.

Marius' election to a second consulship was therefore not a revolution but rather a calculated move by a highly perceptive citizen body about where its strengths and weaknesses lay and in whom its survival and future prosperity could best be entrusted. The votes of wealthy citizens carried far more weight than any others since they exercised their rights first, only a majority of centuries in the assembly was needed for success and so poorer citizens potentially more open to demagogic persuasion were rarely required in the process. Marius' second consulship was promoted by those in the community with the most resources and the greatest power and he cultivated that support. His evident success in North Africa compared with the failures of other senators in the field highlighted his ability.[41] Sallust concludes his account of the war with Jugurtha (*Iug.* 114.4) with the telling comment that the 'the hope and strength of the state resided in that man alone'.

Jugurtha was surrendered by the Mauretanian king Bocchus to Marius' legate Sulla at the very end of the campaigning season in 105. Indeed Sallust (*Iug.* 114.1) says that this event occurred at the same time ('*idem tempus*') as the defeat at Arausio and so only shortly before the onset of the winter. The Roman settlement of the region, which would have taken several months more, needed Marius' presence for some time before he could feel it was appropriate to leave for Rome.[42] Unlike in 108 there was, of course, no need for haste since his election to the consulship was allowed *in absentia*; not an unprecedented event, but one not recently enacted.[43] He arrived in Italy only very late in December and remained outside the city as was the custom in order to celebrate his triumph over Jugurtha on 1 January 104 on the first day of his second consulship (Sall. *Iug.* 114.3).[44]

With two Roman armies cooperating together, in theory at least, in the Rhone Valley there should have been only great optimism that the Cimbri's wandering along the frontiers of the empire would at last be terminated. There was absolutely no reason therefore that Marius could in the summer of 105 look forward to a second consulship and the idea that there was some sort of obvious progression from the Numidian command to that in southern Gaul can be quickly discounted. Moreover the war against Jugurtha was only won with the capture of the King. The defeat of Servilius Caepio and Mallius Maximus – note that the tradition of Cannae has also crept in here with the generals of patrician and *novus homo* backgrounds at odds with one another – came as a complete surprise.[45] Hence the account of panic, again with Cannae very much in the mind of the writer, which notes that Rutilius Rufus issued an order, perhaps a decree of the senate, forbidding overseas travel to any young men who, by implication, might have sought to escape fighting against the Cimbri in the event that this tribe arrived on Italian soil (Gran. 21).[46] This decree dates to sometime in October 105 and the similarity of the material looks either like a deliberate anachronism by Granius or an uncritical use of his source, which may well be Livy.[47] A moralizing passage from another writer of the Second Sophistic looks all too likely.

However, Diodorus (34/35.37) whose history is the earliest extant source for the period, albeit in fragments, appears to have compared the disaster of Arausio with the defeats of Papirius Carbo in 113 at Noreia and Iunius Silanus in 109, not with Cannae, so that analogy may have been found in Livy's source, Valerius Antias. Diodorus goes on to write (36.1) that when the second slave rebellion in Sicily was announced at Rome in early 104 there were no military forces available for a rapid response to this latest problem in the provinces. However, this was not a novel situation since the Romans were still used to holding an annual levy and Diodorus tells us little about real conditions in Italy and especially in southern Gaul.[48]

It is assumed that Rutilius Rufus took other action as well in response to this military disaster. Valerius Maximus writing in the first century AD (2.3.2) appears to give some indication that Rutilius Rufus initiated some military reforms in light of the Cimbric victory over the Roman legionaries. The text is interesting for it says that Rutilius employed instructors from the gladiator school of a certain C. Aurelius Scaurus to train his troops. Valerius Maximus was neither a historian nor, as far as is known, a writer versed in military arts. Nor indeed is he specific about the time of this episode, yet his information is taken to show a development in Roman military training. It possibly is just that but a note of caution might be sounded since the name of the owner of the gladiator school is problematic. The name Aurelius Scaurus is not a common one; a M. Aurelius Scaurus was the consul in 108 and killed either just before or during the battle at Arausio, and a C. Aurelius Scaurus was a praetor in 186,[49] and is almost certainly a close relative. It is possible that, if Rutilius was galvanized into action after Arausio, then his contact was with a brother or cousin of the former consul, but no date is given and the episode could just as easily refer to preparations during the levy for the Numidian war in 109 or even earlier.[50]

Even if Valerius Maximus indicates some positive and determined reaction by the consul, Rutilius Rufus' activities were short-lived since his term of office expired barely ten weeks after Arausio. His levy of troops in late 105 can barely have begun and if, as one must assume, he had taken charge of such matters these duties were quickly transferred to Marius in January 104.[51] Frontinus (*Str.* 4.2.2) gives a somewhat different but equally tantalizing picture since he claims that when Marius had the opportunity to choose between two armies, one of which had served under Rutilius Rufus the other under Metellus and then ('*postea*') under himself, he considered the former although less in number ('*quamquam minorem*') more certain in discipline ('*certioris disciplinae*'). The date seems to point very definitely to the end of 105 or the start of 104 and if taken in conjunction with Valerius Maximus' evidence might convincingly illustrate the attraction of the new training regime supposedly instituted by Rutilius Rufus. However, there is, in fact, quite another way of looking at this evidence supposing Valerius Maximus to be at the very least vague if not unhistorical. Some of the soldiers in Marius' army had been *capite censi*;[52] not many, but a significant percentage. Of those levied by Rutilius Rufus at the end of 105 more will have possessed the usual census qualifications and hence were more respectable citizens. This must be the meaning of Frontinus' statement since any new recruits in 105 could not possibly be better trained than those veterans of the war against Jugurtha, while the argument that these new troops might have been subjected to a longer period of training in Italy during the consulship of Rutilius Rufus is simply not convincing since those levied in the spring of 105 will have accompanied Mallius Maximus to the Rhone frontier. There was no need for a large number of troops to be held on garrison duty in or near Rome in 105 because the outlook for the war was not then pessimistic. The smaller number of troops mentioned by Frontinus also points to a late emergency levy in 105 rather than an army on permanent station in Italy during that year.

There is no record of Marius' activities between the first day of January 104 and his arrival in southern Gaul, an event that cannot have taken place until late in the spring or early summer of that year (Plut. *Mar.* 13.1). By that time the Cimbri are said to have dispersed (Plut. *Mar.* 14.1). Before his departure from Rome, as in 107, Marius must first have conducted his own levy of troops for the war against the Cimbri but using perhaps also those already enrolled for that purpose by Rutilius Rufus. No post-election speech of Marius is preserved, although one was no doubt delivered to the populace, and it will surely have brimmed with confident assurances that his victory over Jugurtha was about to be repeated against an enemy who lacked the guile of the Numidian king. Given the outpouring of despair and grief that appears to have enveloped Italy and Rome after Arausio, Marius must have worked hard to repair the damage done by this latest in the series of defeats (Sall. *Iug.* 114.2).[53] When he eventually left for Gaul his colleague C. Flavius Fimbria was left to oversee domestic affairs.[54] Marius either accompanied his army overland, a route that would have taken about two weeks even along the *Via Domitia*, or went ahead of his force by ship to Massilia. Massilia, outside the Roman province, was not his base for operations, however, and instead he went inland to Arelate ninety-four kilometres (about 60 miles) north-west.

Arelate (modern Arles) was strategically sited at the lowest bridging point on the Rhone at the head of the delta, which begins a few kilometres downstream, and is at the point where the river divides into its two main channels. Today Arles is an important cultural and commercial centre but in 104, although it had been a trading centre for some centuries, after the Cimbric invasion it was probably little more than a fortified encampment with a market alongside the river.[55] From Arelate to Arausio is just sixty-six kilometres (roughly forty miles), but plainly there was no attempt to re-establish a Roman presence in this neighbourhood because the Cimbri were long gone. Mallius Maximus and Servilius Caepio had probably buried their dead and retrieved what they could from their ruined camps but there was no point in Marius moving his new army here for any further conflict with the invaders who were now far to the south. It is reported that the Cimbri had trekked towards the Pyrenees and perhaps by way of the La Perthus Pass had crossed into Iberia (Plut. *Mar.* 15.1). Certainly when Marius arrived in his province there was no war, although there must have been a great swathe of devastation caused by the influx and passage of the victorious Cimbri as they moved south during the winter or early spring of 104 (Livy, *Per.* 67).[56]

Why then did Marius not pursue the enemy and why was he so confident that they would return? The answer to the first question was that his brief was presumably confined to the defence of the province and his command was not a roving one as had been assigned to Servilius Caepio in 106/5. The answer to the second question must lie in the availability and efficacy of Roman intelligence network existing in the region as alluded to by Plutarch in his biography of Sertorius (*Sert.* 3.2) where he relates that his subject became a spy and acquired a proficiency in the languages of the local Gallic tribes to gather information probably regarding the whereabouts of the Cimbri. Plutarch does not say that Sertorius had direct contact with the Cimbri but that he fulfilled a vital role and that afterwards was an outstanding soldier in the war.[57] Sulla, too, who served as legate and later a military tribune during the campaign up to Aquae Sextiae, also appears to have spent time in undercover work for Marius and used his diplomatic skills to win some Gallic tribes over to the Roman side.[58] Moreover, there were also the contacts Marius maintained across the Golfe du Lion from Marseilles to Rhodes (Roses) and Emporion (Ampuries near modern L'Escala) and other towns in northern Iberia, not least since his brother M. Marius was proconsul of the province of Near Spain (*Hispania Citerior*) for the duration of the wars against the Germanic tribes (104–101).[59]

Although today because of modern political frontiers regions tend to be regarded as in one country or another, in the ancient world such artificial divisions did not necessarily apply. Southern Gaul and northern Spain were little different in the composition of their populations: Greek towns and cities along the coast and a variety of tribes of Gallic or Celtic origin inland and a largely laissez-faire attitude between the two. It was into this established and quite static world that the Cimbri blundered and came close to destroying at the end of the second century BC. There are no details, although the epitome of Livy appears to be quite specific about the overall effect and that nothing withstood the tidal wave of warriors who poured down the Rhone valley after Arausio and across the flat plain towards the Pyrenees. In the path of the Cimbri lay Arelate and Narbo as well as other smaller settlements, and all were levelled. Narbo Martius, founded about 118, was probably without fortifications or a sizable population. There was perhaps just time to evacuate the town before the Cimbri arrived, perhaps not. Casualty figures among civilian populations are rarely of interest to the historian in the ancient world.[60]

The surprising fact that we learn about the peregrinations of the Cimbri in northern Spain is that they suffered serious defeats at the hands of the Celtiberians. This is quite astounding information given that they had defeated four Roman armies in the previous decade or so. Where did the Cimbri go and why did they return to Gaul? Since it is likely that the Cimbric army that defeated Mallius and Caepio at Arausio in October 105 consisted of a formidable raiding party and did not include non-combatants, they were able to move more quickly to reach their objectives. These Cimbri probably spent the winter to the west of the Rhone delta where they had destroyed Narbo and Nemausus and other small towns before proceeding over the Pyrenees in early 104. The obvious and inviting targets were the coastal settlements of north-eastern Spain, which may have succumbed to Cimbric attacks, but there were other possibilities and a prolonged conflict with the Celtiberians suggests that the invaders moved south-west rather than in an easterly direction. The overall state of the Iberian Peninsula was far from settled in this period. There had been frequent warfare mainly towards the south-west against the Lusitani where one proconsul, L. Calpurnius Piso Frugi (pr. 112), had been killed and where Servilius Caepio (cos. 106) had earned his triumph in 107.[61] However, the area was far from pacified and the arrival of the Cimbri seems to have exacerbated a tense situation and the Romans, apparently overstretched because of threats to their security elsewhere, were unable to rectify the position. Appian in his history of Spanish Wars states that by 102 the Romans, with invaders approaching northern Italy and a major slave rebellion in Sicily, had no troops to send to Spain and had to rely on poorly supported legates who must have been under instruction to organize military support from the local communities. The Cimbri once they had suffered a defeat by the Celtiberians returned to southern Gaul, probably in 103, for this group was reunited with the main tribe in the territory of the

Vollocases or Parisi in the valley of the Seine and set out again from there in early summer 102. The Cimbri were therefore in northern Spain for less than two campaigning seasons (104–103). They left behind a destabilized region, which was to suffer incessant warfare and devastation for nearly a century.[62]

Thus when Marius arrived in southern Gaul in the early summer of 104 the Cimbri had departed but they had not disappeared, and the Romans knew where they were and that they would return but not when. With M. Marius just across the Pyrenees based at Tarragona, his elder brother Gaius would be able to use any intelligence about the movement of the Cimbri to his advantage. Marius also knew he had time to ensure that he had an effective fighting unit to deal with the marauders on their arrival back in southern Gaul. This is what Plutarch is alluding to in his life of Marius when he gives what might appear to be trivial material about Marius' activities in Gaul. In fact, Plutarch is giving information about what he considers a good general ought to do if he has the opportunity, but he also provides interesting evidence for the composition of the army and its evolution.

For example, the nickname 'Marius' mules' Plutarch claims (*Mar.* 13.1–2) came about because his troops were ordered to carry their own supplies on their backs instead of having these brought up in the supply train and that these men did whatever they were told in a most contented manner. This is dwelt upon as a new departure in Roman military training.[63] Such innovations intended to improve the mobility of troops in response to a rapidly moving enemy such as the Cimbri, and while making perfect sense, had been introduced into the Macedonian army by Philip II by the 340s and maintained by Alexander the Great, so the concept was not at all novel by Marius' time. And, indeed, Plutarch does voice a little scepticism about the name if not the training, which he claims was introduced while Marius was en route to Gaul. This suggests that Marius was in a hurry to reach his province, although Arausio had taken place at least six months beforehand. Once there all may have been disrupted but there was no enemy to tackle. Therefore says Plutarch (*Mar.* 14.1–2) Marius trained his men both physically and mentally to face the challenges ahead and especially so that in getting to know their general they knew what to expect from him and he from them. The rather lax attitude he had adopted in Africa with the men under Metellus' command had therefore been replaced by a stricter and harsher approach, although Plutarch has omitted all mention of Marius' command against Jugurtha except for the King's capture. It still suggests that the troops under his command in 104 were recently levied and had not served with him in the Numidian War who would have known Marius well enough after serving for at least three campaigning seasons (107–105).

The construction of a twenty-five-kilometre long canal (16 miles) between Arelate and Massilia was quite a different exercise and is said to have been intended to allow traffic between the two centres because the main channel of the Rhone was silting rapidly at this time. The canal continued in use throughout the Greco-Roman period as Strabo (4.1.8) notes and it brought great prosperity to both communities. The canal was given to Massilia by Marius and this city is said to have become wealthy on its revenues, although its maintenance must also have been expensive since the channels of the Rhone were subject to quite rapid fluctuation. In fact, this canal also silted up so that in modern times yet another channel has been constructed in this very changeable environment (see plate). The canal that became known as the *Fossae Marianae* had at least a triple purpose besides commerce.[64] Since there was no warfare at that moment and idle hands might have been a source of trouble for Marius in his wait for the enemy, this construction was an ideal occupation and focus for his soldiers. Plutarch seems to place the canal's date to after Marius' election to his fourth consulship (*Mar.* 15.1), which would have taken place in the summer of 103 over a year after Marius had first arrived in the region.[65] This is certainly possible, although that would also mean that Marius' initial camp may have been further east at that stage, perhaps at Aquae Sextiae and not Arelate. The canal was also, of course, a means by which large quantities of supplies could be transported by a quicker and more direct route than overland from Massilia. And, finally, it also acted as a further identifiable line of defence which might force the Cimbri to cross the Rhone north of the delta at the point where Marius concentrated his forces.

As it was the canal became almost a negligible factor in the subsequent fighting for the Cimbri must have taken a route through the territory of the Volcae Tectosages without coming close to the Rhone valley and this must have occurred in the summer of 103 at about the same time that Plutarch says that the Arelate to Massilia canal was being excavated. Quite why they should have ignored the Roman presence is again a matter of conjecture but some possibilities might be raised. The Cimbri had suffered some serious defeats at the hands of the Iberian tribes and this would have left them less enthusiastic and confident about another encounter with any new army in readiness and commanded by Marius whose reputation will have gone before him. The Cimbri may also have suffered significant losses in their numbers and so were in need of reinforcement from those whom they had left behind in northern Gaul. It is interesting too that they were not to be seen again in this part of the ancient world. Perhaps their leaders no longer considered that their future lay there and that they should set their ambitions on another goal with Italy a leading contender as a new objective.

The return of the Cimbri must have caused the following to happen, nonetheless. Sometime during the summer months of 103 Marius transferred his main camp from Arelate to Valentia (Valence) on the confluence of the Rhone with the River Isère (Orosius, 5.16). This move was surely governed by the movement of the Cimbri north from Spain and by their unexpected route. From Valentia (Valence) to Lugdunum (Lyons) and the confluence of the Rhone and Saône is one hundred kilometres (about 62 miles). And the headwaters of the Saône lead more or less directly into the valley of the Seine where the Cimbri found a temporary home among the Parisi. And then suddenly, the Germanic tribes were approaching, but these did not, in fact, include the Cimbri. The Cimbri had met up with at least two other Germanic tribes in northern Gaul (Liv. *Per.* 67: 'in the land of the Vellocasses'),[66] and it is possible that the Tigurini, or some of them, were also in this area having moved north after their victory over Cassius Longinus in 107. The sources suggest that a grand council was held in which these tribes agreed to cooperate with each other in order to defeat the Romans and invade and seize Italy (Plut. *Mar.* 15.4).

The arrival of the Teutones and the Ambrones, who had never set foot in the Rhone valley, obviously made them more vulnerable than the Cimbri would have been if they had come south again. The choice of routes allocated to the tribes raises interesting points. The Cimbri either struck out across the north European plain or more likely perhaps accompanied the Teutones and Ambrones to near Lugdunum and then headed up the Rhone to Lake Geneva and the Alps. It is interesting to note that the Cimbri preferred the northerly route, yet having already defeated the Romans had a distinct psychological advantage that the others did not possess. They seem not prepared to risk another battle against this enemy in that area. So was it a case of the Cimbri seeking a softer option and leaving the latest round of fighting to others after their reverses in Spain? They no doubt provided the Teutones and Ambrones with a great deal of information about the Romans and their military capability and liable modes of attack and defence. However, there is no better preparation for a war than some previous experience of the enemy and in this respect those Germanic tribes moving towards the army of Marius were bound to have some weaknesses that the Romans would be able to exploit. Meanwhile, Plutarch says (*Mar.* 15.4) that it was decided that the Cimbri would move east towards Noricum and from there force their way into Italy by defeating Marius' colleague Q. Lutatius Catulus (cos. 102) who was guarding the Alpine Passes and in particular the Brenner. Plutarch is therefore, unusually, being highly specific in his dating given that Catulus cannot have taken up his position in Cisalpine Gaul until the late spring/early summer of 102. What he says is naturally governed by hindsight in that Catulus was later worsted against the Cimbri in the early winter of that same year, but the text is meant to suggest concerted action by the Germanic tribes and some ongoing offensive strategy against the Romans cast in a purely defensive mode. The sources are also quite clear that there was an elaborate plan for an invasion of Italy carried out by a pincer movement of two gigantic armies moving from the west and north to overwhelm the defending Roman forces, which they greatly outnumbered. This elaborate plan may, of course, be the creation of later writers keen to draw the contrast between the anguish of the defeat at Arausio and the euphoria of the later triumphs over the Germans. Such an approach is certainly not out of keeping with the sort of sentiments to be expected from writers of military history in the Greco-Roman world.

This defensive mode of the Romans is further illustrated and accentuated by the decision of Marius, even with two years of planning behind him, not to risk a single all-out engagement as the invaders approached from the north. Plutarch (*Mar.* 15.5) claims their numbers were vast and that their appearance and language were quite unfamiliar to the Romans. They encamped near the Romans and offered battle over what appears to have been several days. The Roman legionaries were, however, ordered to remain inside their fortified camp where they are supposed to have endured the taunts and insults of the Teutones and Ambrones. It transpires that Marius' tactic was to make these tribesmen less intimidating by allowing his men to acquire a familiarity with them. His troops initially thought that this apparent display of cowardice was unworthy of Romans but Marius restored calm by stating that he was waiting for the appropriate portents for victory (Plut. *Mar.* 17.1–3). The Teutones and their allies attacked the Roman camp,[67] but unlike the Cimbri at Arausio they were unable to make any headway. They also lacked perseverance and soon lost interest and instead decided to move on to Italy, which they now regarded as undefended and expected no more trouble from this Roman outpost. Plutarch relates that his sources say that the Germanic tribes with all their non-combatants and wagons marched in a continuous column past Marius' camp for six days.

As soon as the invaders had moved on Marius left Valence and shadowed them as they moved south-east, probably overrunning Arelate, a march lasting two to three days for such a large body of people, on their way. The rate of advance by the Teutones and Ambrones, unlike the Cimbri's rapid movement in 105, was very leisurely and it seems that they took quite some more time to reach Aquae Sextiae, another sixty kilometres to the east, where apparently unaware of, or unconcerned about, the Romans they made camp and as events showed failed to post scouts. Plutarch (*Mar.* 18.3) has Marius decide that he must now do battle since Italy was within easy reach of the invaders. Marius ordered a camp be constructed that was well fortified on higher ground, but without access to water except that which was close to the camp of the Teutones and Ambrones. When the soldiers complained about this lack of water Marius is supposed to have responded with the advice that they should look for water at the camp of the enemy but that the price would be their blood. The troops were busy fortifying their camp but their slaves and other camp followers went in search of water, taking arms with them and prepared to fight to obtain it. Some of the Ambrones were enjoying the hot spring water, while others having finished with their bathing were eating in their camp. Fights inevitably started up and the Roman soldiers concerned about their servants began to run down to give help. Among the first to arrive at the stream were some allied troops from Liguria who were almost natives to this place. The Ambrones, on the other hand, seeing that there was now likely to be a hostile engagement were forming up in large numbers. Plutarch claims that there were more than 30,000 fighting men (*Mar.* 19.2) and that these had gained a ferocious reputation for their fighting ability.[68] These were rested and had just eaten and formed up in an orderly way to meet their opponents with whom they exchanged insults and it is said that they chanted a similar war cry. Yet the Ambrones seem to have lost cohesion as a body because in their movement towards the Ligures they had to cross a stream. Those who crossed first became isolated and fell early victims to the Ligures in fierce fighting. The Ligures were clearly hard pressed nonetheless for the regular Roman legionaries soon came to their aid from the camp. This arrival accelerated the rout of the Ambrones who were, surprisingly perhaps, annihilated where they were crowded together in the stream while the remnants fled back to their wagons followed closely by the victorious Romans.[69] There the camp was overrun with a massacre of the non-combatants, although Plutarch suggests that Roman casualties were not slight, and a good number of the tribesmen made it to safety with the Teutones who were camped further away, and dusk precluded further hostilities.[70]

The Romans returned to their camp and kept a careful watch for a response from their enemy. However, the Ambrones spent that night in mourning during which time they exhibited their grief by what Plutarch describes as a 'bellow almost like that of a wild beast' (*Mar.* 20.2). The Romans, including Marius, spent an anxious night but when it became clear that there was to be no rapid counterattack they took the next day to prepare for battle as did their opponents. On the second day after the rout of the Ambrones, Marius drew up his army in battle formation outside his camp above the river valley where the Teutones and the survivors of the Ambrones had their camp. They were in a rush to engage with their enemy and exact revenge for their recent losses but made it difficult for themselves by attacking uphill in a terrain made more exacting by its rough and broken nature, typical of limestone country, with scattered woodland wherever there was sufficient soil for the growth of trees (see plate). Marius instructed his men not to break ranks or fire any missiles until the enemy came close. When arrows, javelins and smaller missiles hurled from slings had done their job the Roman began to fight at close quarters and push the Teutones and Ambrones down the hill. During the preceding evening Marius had ordered one of his legates, M. Claudius Marcellus, to station himself with three thousand legionaries ('hoplites') in a copse (Plut. *Mar.* 20.4).[71] Frontinus (*Str.* 2.4.6) adds the pertinent detail here that Marcellus was posted in the wood during the night and that his 'small' force consisted of both infantry and cavalry, but that this number was bolstered by the addition of servants who were also armed, and pack animals disguised as cavalry. The fact that Marius was able to send out such numbers without being observed is highly revealing about the lack of scouts or intelligence on the part of the Germanic tribes who elsewhere could apparently make grandiose plans for an invasion of Italy but then commit the most basic errors or judgement and preparation. The sudden emergence of this relatively small but noisy group of Roman soldiers at the rear of the main Germanic massed ranks caused some panic to infect their lines, as Frontinus says (*Str.* 2.4.8), and although it seems unlikely that Marcellus intended to surround 30,000 with his 3000 troops caused sufficient havoc at some point out on one of the wings to produce the required result, the breakup of the Germanic ranks, which then led inevitably to a disorderly withdrawal. The Roman charge tore into the camp of the enemy, the contents of which were given to Marius by vote of his soldiers. Plutarch comments that such a generous gift was considered by some to be unsuitable given the serious threat to the *res publica* at this time (*Mar.* 21.2). He does not name his source but a less than enthusiastic writer about Marius such as Catulus, his consular colleague of 102, or Sulla, both of whom wrote memoirs, might well be responsible for such a comment.[72]

The battles at Aquae Sextiae (there were really two quite separate engagements) took place over at least three days in the middle of the summer of 102.[73] The casualty figure for the Germanic dead is enormous and surely hugely inflated partly to offset the already high figure given for Arausio but also because this victory had to be seen to be infinitely more impressive than the previous Roman defeat. As usual the figures given by ancient writers vary. Livy (*Per.* 68) records 200,000 dead and 90,000 taken prisoner. Velleius (2.12) claims more than 150,000 dead, and Plutarch that 100,000 were killed or sold as slaves. The common message is, however, that the Teutones and Ambrones were extinguished as an ethnic group (Florus, 1.38.11: '*sublatis*'). Plutarch further adds that the citizens of Massilia used the bones of the dead, which will have lain unburied, as fertilizer for their vines, and that they reaped bumper harvests for many years afterwards.[74] Marius celebrated a great sacrifice with a huge pyre consisting of captured arms and equipment and while this was taking place messengers arrived from Rome to announce his election again *in absentia* to a fifth consulship. The honour was immense but the job only half done!

Q. Lutatius Catulus had been assigned a holding position in Cisalpine Gaul since Roman intelligence had obviously indicated that some of the Germanic tribes were intent on attempting a pincer movement to outflank the western Roman defences. The Cimbri were to link up with the Teutones and Ambrones somewhere in the PO Valley before heading south into the Apennines, and once across them Rome, the ultimate prize, was their destination.[75] Most sources place Catulus in the Adige (Atiso/Athesis) Valley, which leads up to the Brenner Pass, a long established route from the plains of northern Europe to the Mediterranean. However, Plutarch's evidence is not categorical (*Mar.* 23.2–6) and states only that the River Adige was the site of much fighting between this Germanic tribe and the Romans who were forced to withdraw to some unspecified point further south. Plutarch dramatically describes the arrival of the Cimbric warriors in early winter snowstorms, sliding naked down the steep snowy slopes of the Alps on their shields (cf. Florus, 1.38.11–12). Catulus had already withdrawn from the Alpine valleys to collect his troops at one spot. He built forts on either side of the river and connected these with a bridge. The Cimbri attempted to isolate one of the forts by damming the flow with felled tree trunks or piling great rocks into the bed of the river. The bridge connecting the forts was damaged by the great logs and this so unnerved the Roman soldiers in the forts, presumably on the same side as the attackers, that they began to make their way in complete disorder across the river to where they believed safety lay. Catulus who was with these troops is credited with keeping a semblance of order instead of allowing chaos to rule. Plutarch (*Mar.* 23.5) claims that this behaviour showed what a good commander he was in bringing most of this army to safety rather than looking after his own skin or dying in the attempt to win hopeless glory against overwhelming odds. The statement seems rather trite and probably originated in Catulus' memoirs of his own conduct in the wars against the Cimbri.[76] The Romans did manage a withdrawal without too many casualties, but it is evident that they abandoned the entire northern half of the Po Valley, leaving it in the hands of the invaders who are said to have caused widespread devastation (Plut. *Mar.* 23.6).[77] Thereafter, the Cimbri spent the winter of 102/1 camped in the Veneto (Florus, 1.38.13) and enjoyed the benefits of its climate and produce. Indeed, Florus says that spending the winter here had a debilitating effect on the prowess of the Cimbri who were physically compromised by the delights of good food and wine in much the same way that the Teutones and Ambrones had languished in the hot spring waters of Aquae Sextiae and had so let their guard down that they were the easy victims of an ambush. It is a little odd that a Roman writer appears to be diminishing the value of the victory of Marius but Florus may have picked up negative reports of this sort from his main source, Livy, who probably devoted a great deal of space to the arrival of Cimbri south of the Alps.[78]

Marius returned to Rome towards the end of 102 to announce his victory to the citizen body in person. They had already voted him a second triumph but Marius declared that he would forgo this honour until the problem of the Cimbri was overcome and he had completed his brief in full (Livy, *Per.* 68). So he then moved immediately north of the Apennines to join his forces with those of Catulus, although Marius remained, as the current consul, the senior commander for the coming campaign.[79] In comparison to his arrival in southern Gaul, where conditions were initially quiet, in the Po Valley an encounter with the Cimbri could not long be avoided. However, there seems to have been some reluctance on the part of this tribe to engage the Romans. If the intention had been to pull off this spectacular form of a pincer-movement extending over many hundreds of miles and over many months it had plainly not gone to plan. The Cimbri had apparently been delayed in their trek and left much later in 102 than the Teutones and Ambrones, and yet it they were to go via the Tridentine Alps (Dolomites) they had by far the greater distance to cover and they were also the largest tribe and so probably moving at the slowest pace.[80] Arriving by the Adige Valley or one of the eastern Alpine passes actually makes little logistical sense and it is curious that the Cimbri did not travel with their allies south as far as the confluence of the Saône and Rhone and then gone by the far shorter route via Lake Geneva and the Great Saint Bernard Pass into the Duria Valley then into upper course of the Po. This route would have brought the idea to fruition more speedily if all other matters also went according to plan. It is noticeable that the details given by the ancient sources will not fit the geography.[81] The Teutones and Ambrones were defeated in the summer of 102, by August at the latest, and the Cimbri, 'having begun late' (Plut. *Mar.* 15.5) are said to have arrived in the Adige Valley by the late autumn of the same year. The Cimbri had travelled from Gaul to Rhaetia or Noricum in about three months when they had wandered for years in the opposite direction and then wintered far from any conceivable rendezvous with their allies. By the following early summer, however, they were nowhere near the Veneto but in the north-west sector of the Po Valley and heading, it seems, away from Italy. The Cimbri were probably looking for their allies and not prepared to face the combined legions of Marius and Catulus, although they had not flinched to attack two consular armies four years before. It may have been the reputation of Marius, although at this stage they are said to have been ignorant of the fate of the Teutones and Ambrones. The Cimbri once again sent envoys to the Romans demanding land not just for themselves, but also for their allies and even for towns to live in (Plut. *Mar.* 24.3). When Marius asked who their allies were these representatives of the Cimbri said they meant the Teutones, a statement that was greeted with much mirth. On being informed that they need not wait for their allies since these already had land – or rather earth for they now lay underneath it – the Cimbri were outraged and refused to believe the Roman claims of victory until some of the chiefs of the Teutones were paraded in shackles.[82]

There was no excuse for delaying a confrontation any longer and it was the Cimbri who were the first to attack, but as with the Teutones and Ambrones, they made little headway against the fortified camp of the Romans (Plut. *Mar.* 25.1). Plutarch introduces a digression at this juncture about an innovation in the javelin, which was by then standard equipment of the Roman legionaries. He says that a new design for which Marius was responsible was first employed by his troops in this campaign. Plutarch claims that the javelin in general use, which had its head fastened to the staff by two nails, was replaced by another that had one iron nail and one wooden plug. On impact the javelin head therefore snapped away from the shaft and made it unusable for the enemy.[83] Whether or not Marius was indeed the inventor of this new design is perhaps less important here than the fact that his biographer devotes as much attention to the logistics of battle and war as to the actual fighting, which illustrates again the managerial side of the general more than his warrior prowess. This is further exemplified by the next episode in which it is reported that Boiorix, one of the chiefs of the Cimbri, rode up to the Roman camp with his entourage and challenged Marius to decide on a day on which they might settle their claim for Italy (Plut. *Mar.* 25.2–3).[84] This action is clearly based on the challenge to single combat between opposing leaders or their champions, an invitation that Marius was obviously not going to be drawn into. The day for battle was, nevertheless, chosen and the place named as 'Plain of Raudium' (*Campus Raudius*),[85] a site identified by some today as being situated not far from Verona.[86] However, the battle itself later became known as that at Vercellae, and modern Vercelli lies much further east and higher up the Po Valley, not at all close to Verona. The actual battle therefore cannot be identified conclusively and can only be assigned to some point in northern Cisalpine Gaul, but probably at some distance from either the Po or the Adige rivers since neither seems to have played a part in the tactics of either side nor are they mentioned in any ancient account of the battle.

The dawn is said to have broken with misty conditions (Florus, 1.38.15), as might well be experienced in the Po Valley even in August; and Marius, unusually for recent Roman generals, decided to take the offensive. He had placed Catulus with the legions under his command in the centre with instructions to gradually fall back as the need arose (Plut. *Mar.* 25.5). Although this tactic was commonly employed Plutarch claims that Marius gave this order so that Catulus and his legions would not become engaged with the enemy and that the glory would then fall to the former alone. Plutarch is specific in his totals for Roman forces deployed, assigning 20,000 and 300 to Catulus in the centre and 32,000 to Marius, which were divided between the two wings (Plut. *Mar.* 25.4). These figures, Plutarch says, he obtained from Sulla's memoirs who was present in this battle since he was perhaps Catulus' senior legate.[87] Marius commanded the right wing again, a common enough practice among generals in the Greco-Roman world. We are not informed about the identity of the person who commanded the left wing. Some speculation is possible here and M. Claudius Marcellus, for example, would have been a good candidate for this responsibility since he had been a successful commander at Aquae Sextiae the year before and obviously had sufficient seniority. It can certainly be argued that whoever was in command of the left wing must have been someone who had Marius' complete confidence and, as events show, needed to have close communications with the senior commander.

The Cimbri advanced from their camp in a single block of infantry, which was 'thirty stadia' along each side of the square, an astonishing six kilometres or 3¾ miles (Plut. *Mar.* 25.6). There were also 15,000 cavalry in armour and, although Plutarch does not state specifically where they positioned, they appear to have been in front of the infantry since they went into action first and so do not appear to have formed the wings to the larger body of foot soldiers. Moreover, these Cimbri did not advance in a straight line but, possibly having acquired some experience from their various encounters, moved forward obliquely to the right. The intention was to draw the opposing left wing away from the centre and to open up a gap into which the Cimbri could pour and then attack the Roman centre from the rear.[88] Plutarch states that the Roman commanders, by whom he presumably means Marius and Catulus, who were both offering sacrifices for victory at that moment, saw the strategy but were unable to prevent their own troops who thought the enemy was in retreat and began to pursue them in what must have become a disorderly charge. A dust storm thrown up by these 15,000 cavalry brought a premature end to that episode, but it also resulted in the two armies losing contact with one another.[89] Plutarch comments that Sulla declared that this was an ominous portent for it threw the whole affair into confusion (*Mar.* 26.3). Quite clearly the Roman intention was to employ their wings to envelope the Cimbri but Marius, leading the right wing, missed the enemy in the dust storm, and apparently spent some time wandering around. In the meantime, the Cimbri engaged the Roman centre where most of the fighting occurred. Catullus is supposed to have written (Plut. *Mar.* 26.5) that the dust worked to the Roman advantage since the Germanic tribesmen were unaccustomed to the heat, which drained their energy, and, since there was only limited vision, the legionaries could not see the disparity in numbers between themselves and the enemy, which gave them greater confidence to carry the battle against their opponents. The Cimbri were forced back with huge losses since their warriors were chained together in lines to prevent gaps opening up in their lines but this would also have contributed to an even greater loss of life once a rout began. And the centre of the Roman army pursued the Cimbri back into their encampment where a grisly massacre ensued of any fighting men, their wives and children if they had not first committed suicide. Yet Plutarch says that 60,000 prisoners were taken and double that number were killed (*Mar.* 27.1–3).[90]

It is a curious feature of the ancient accounts that, while modern commentators assign this victory directly to Marius, there is actually no reference to him after his departure into the dust storm. In Plutarch's account he only reappears when an acrimonious debate took place, although he evidently took no personal part, about who was responsible for the victory and whether it was Catulus' troops or those of the senior commander. He was, nonetheless, active after the battle in bestowing honours on certain troops for conspicuous bravery and is recorded as granting Roman citizenship to two troops of allied infantry from Camerinum in Umbria.[91] These soldiers were almost certainly on the right wing serving directly under Marius, but precisely what their act of heroism may have been is not stated. That Marius was able to award such an outstanding honour as full citizenship to such a large group of individuals on the battlefield suggests that his plan of encircling the Cimbri actually paid off and that his troops were actually just as much involved in the fighting as those of Catulus, and that Plutarch's reliance on hostile evidence has coloured the account of this episode.[92] And it should always be remembered that it was Marius who received the sole credit for the defeat of the Cimbri and the signal honour of another triumph, although he celebrated this event jointly with Catulus towards the end of 101 before he took office as consul for a sixth time (Livy, *Per.* 68). Marius' activities during the engagement have therefore been suppressed in the ancient literature.

According to Appian (*Gall.* 14) Marius 'ordered the bodies of the Cimbri be untouched until it was light supposing them to be covered in gold ornaments'.[93] Sadly, this fragment of Appian does not reveal whether or not the dead warriors of the Cimbri were heavily adorned with symbols of their former success and wealth. Gaius Marius undoubtedly gained much personal wealth from leading the campaigns against the Germanic tribes and his double victory over them. His career reached its height in his sixth consulship in 100, which a grateful Roman electorate bestowed on him in gratitude for saving Rome and Italy. Like many other political figures, Marius' career did not prosper once that threat was removed and his glory days were soon forgotten, although in later times his name remained forever associated with the fearsome Cimbri and Teutones.[94] The vanquishing of the tribes after the stupendous success of certainly the Cimbri was a relatively simple affair and it has to be asked in conclusion how could these invaders of the Roman empire having inflicted such damage be exterminated in the end, apparently so easily and in just two battles? Conflict in the ancient world was often concluded in a single hostile engagement, which resulted in the vanquished either suffering territorial loss or surrendering its identity. However, by the time of the Macedonian invasion of the Persia Empire and the Roman wars with Carthage, long campaigns with numerous battles had become commonplace. The intermittent warfare with the Cimbri over more than decade follows this second phenomenon and with it one can see that this Germanic tribe became too sure of itself with regard to the Romans and this enthusiasm infected the Teutones and Ambrones, although the leadership of the Cimbri ought to have taken into consideration its defeat by the Celtiberians. They do not appear to have done so and instead of being able to absorb another defeat they suffered obliteration. Marius exploited that pride or *hubris* and became the *nemesis* of the Germanic tribes. He did not defeat the Germanic tribes by a great display of bravery or active leadership on the field of battle, but rather by thorough and rigorous planning, military intelligence and firm and perceptive command. In many respects Marius was a new breed, the manager of campaigns not a Homeric warrior, and that was an innovation in its own right.

Chronology

114   First mention of the Cimbri
113   Late summer – the Roman defeat at Noreia
109/8 Defeat of Silanus by the Cimbri/Tigurini
109/7 Marius senior legate to Metellus in Numidia

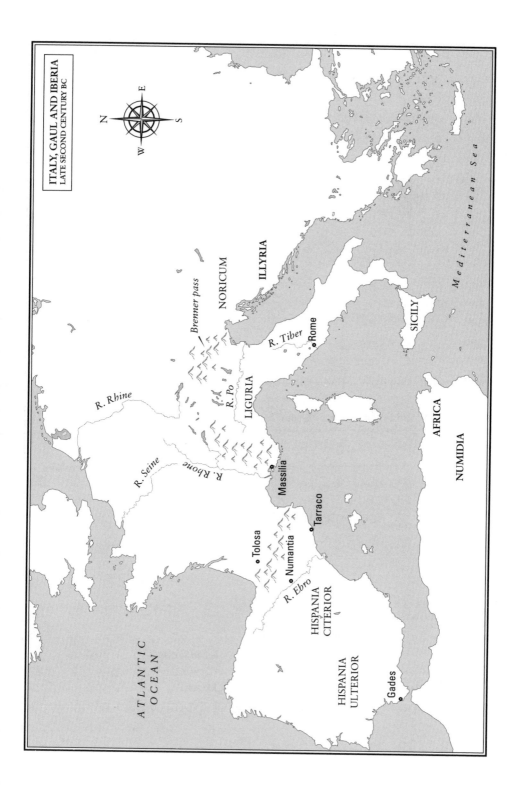

ITALY, GAUL AND IBERIA
LATE SECOND CENTURY BC

N
E
S
W

ATLANTIC
OCEAN

R. Rhine

R. Seine

R. Rhone

Brenner pass

NORICUM

R. Po

ILLYRIA

R. Tiber

Rome

LIGURIA

Massilia

Tarraco

Tolosa

Numantia

R. Ebro

HISPANIA
CITERIOR

HISPANIA
ULTERIOR

Gades

SICILY

AFRICA

NUMIDIA

Mediterranean Sea

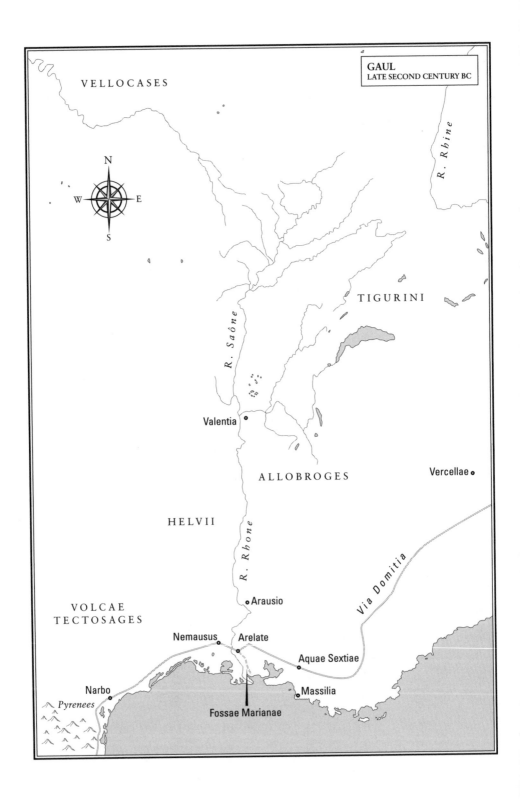

VELLOCASES

TIGURINI

R. Rhine

R. Saône

N
W   E
S

Valentia

ALLOBROGES

Vercellae

HELVII

R. Rhone

Via Domitia

VOLCAE
TECTOSAGES

Arausio

Nemausus   Arelate

Aquae Sextiae

Narbo

Pyrenees

Massilia

Fossae Marianae

GAUL
LATE SECOND CENTURY BC

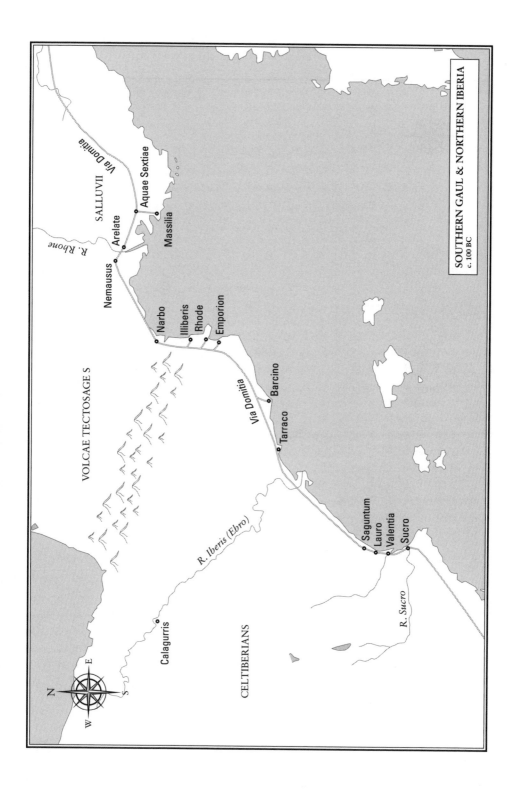

SOUTHERN GAUL & NORTHERN IBERIA
c. 100 BC

R. Rhone

SALLUVII

Via Domitia

Aquae Sextiae

Arelate

Nemausus

Massilia

Narbo

Illiberis

Rhode

Emporion

VOLCAE TECTOSAGE S

Barcino

Via Domitia

Tarraco

R. Iberis (Ebro)

Saguntum

Lauro

Valentia

Sucro

R. Sucro

Calagurris

CELTIBERIANS

N
E
S
W

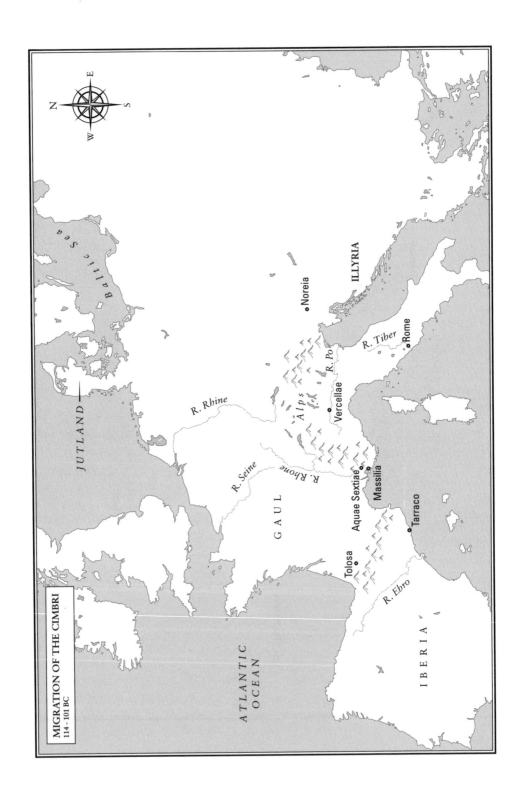

MIGRATION OF THE CIMBRI
114 - 101 BC

Baltic Sea

JUTLAND

R. Rhine

R. Seine

GAUL

R. Rhone

Alps

Noreia

ILLYRIA

R. Po

R. Tiber

Rome

Vercellae

Aquae Sextiae

Massilia

Tolosa

Tarraco

R. Ebro

IBERIA

ATLANTIC
OCEAN

N
E
S
W

Chapter Five

Julius Caesar, Mithridates of Pergamum and the Relief of Alexandria (47 BC)

I n tracing this battlefield, the focus of discussion switches to the problem of chronology and order of events, next to the relief column as a climactic event to a siege and finally to comparable distances covered by relief columns, specifically here but also elsewhere in bringing sieges to a conclusion. Some attention will also be devoted to the possible military forces employed by the adversaries in this affair. Relatively little note has been taken of this episode in Julius Caesar's career except for his well publicized relationship with Cleopatra, the Egyptian queen.[1] Their notorious love affair is reckoned to have started at this time, and they remain two of the most famous and familiar figures of world history. However, the backdrop to this love affair is a siege and arguably that was more important an issue than the amorous intrigues of certain protagonists. The warfare has been relegated to the background and regarded as somewhat minor when measured against Caesar's many and varied triumphs. Yet this siege of Alexandria and its conclusion took place over a period of six months, during which time the outside world heard little or nothing from the man who was its sole ruler.

Cicero who had joined Pompey in Greece after Caesar began the civil war and had escaped unscathed hoped to return to Rome, but was forced to wait at Brundisium until his request was confirmed or denied by Caesar. In a letter to his closest friend, Pomponius Atticus, dated 14 May 47, Cicero states that Caesar seemed to be detained in Alexandria and ashamed of writing about the situation there.[2] A month later, on 14 June, Cicero again in much more detail catalogues Caesar's apparent disappearance in Alexandria, more because it affected his own position in Italy than for any great concern about the other's state of health. Interestingly enough, the information provided by Cicero goes some way to illustrate that communications between Egypt and Italy were hardly straightforward and that the whereabouts of even the most prominent persons in the ancient world could be the subject of intense speculation and uncertainty. Cicero says:

Illum ab Alexandria discessisse nemo nuntiat constatque ne profectum quidem illim quemquam post Id. Mart. nec post Id. Dec. ab illo datas ullas litteras …

Nobody has announced that he has departed from Alexandria, or indeed that anyone has set out from there after the Ides of March, or that any letters have been sent from him after the Ides of December.[3] (Cic. *Att.* 11.17a)

This means that Caesar, who was ordinarily a prolific writer of letters besides being a busy author, had by then been completely silent for half a year while the inhabitants, or at least the ruling elite, of the whole Roman Empire waited with baited breath about their future. What had been happening in Egypt and why had events there so absorbed the new ruler of the empire; was it simply love or were there other more deadly challenges to be faced?

First of all there is a desideratum to place the siege of Alexandria in a firm chronological context. Because the divergence between the Roman civic calendar and the solar calendar had become so great by this time using the former alone to understand the date of events and what appears achievable by especially armed forces in military campaigns becomes almost a nonsensical exercise. The Romans, like the Greeks, were fully aware of the real extent of the year and to take into account the discrepancy between the division of time in days and months they added an intercalary month after January every now and again. In the increasingly unstable political climate of the first century BC this practice had somehow been forgotten by the Roman senate, which decreed such measures. Therefore, by the late 50s real time and official Roman time had become seriously out of kilter. Indeed when Caesar crossed the Rubicon on 10 January 49 it was actually sometime in November 50; and the decision to invade Italy from Cisalpine Gaul at that precise moment was forced on Caesar for two closely inter-connected reasons. He could not allow his opponents led by Pompey to have the time to levy and train an army to face his own, and unless he moved very rapidly he knew that this would be allowed them because the weather would enforce a delay to the campaigning for the passes through the Apennines and hence the route to Rome would be closed for up to three months. Caesar's reforms to the calendar, which brought it back into sync with the solar year, did not occur until 45 and so the entire period of the civil war and coverage of the events during it are affected by this rupture between nature and the civic year. When Caesar arrived in Rome, officially it was March 49 but really still only January and hence he had not only beaten the winter weather, but also caused such panic among his enemies by the speed of his attack that with their abrupt and chaotic departure they had left Rome and its institutions, such as the public treasury, entirely unguarded and the city in utter chaos.

It may seem a relatively unimportant point to labour but the chronology of events especially as they are affected by the seasons is arguably fundamental for understanding how, when and why things happen. Thucydides, probably the greatest of all writers of historical prose, was well aware of the various difficulties that a given time of the year imposes and makes the point of noting the military campaigns of the Peloponnesian War that he covered (431–411 BC) by the changes of the seasons. And it is certainly worth noting in connection with the siege of Alexandria, as we shall see.

By starting his campaign before the winter closed in Caesar forced his rival onto the back foot almost immediately. Pompey left Rome the moment he heard that Caesar had crossed the Rubicon,[4] and before the next summer was obliged to withdraw from Italy entirely since his army was not in readiness for the crucial battle with Caesar. He accomplished this relatively easily from Brundisium and although he had some measure of success in the initial confrontation on the other side of the Ionian Sea following this tactical withdrawal, it was always going to be an uphill struggle for him against the flair of Caesar's generalship and the experience of his legions. It should come as no surprise therefore that Caesar defeated Pompey at Pharsalus in Thessaly in the summer of 48 BC, roughly nineteen months after he had crossed the Rubicon. The surprise if there is any is that this victory took so long to accomplish. The battle occurred not, however, in late summer but in early to mid-June. Pompey fled from Greece with hardly any land forces intact, but still in control of a strong fleet and headed east to Mytilene on Lesbos from where he sailed due south to Egypt where he hoped, with much of the summer still before him, to regroup and raise a new army and train this new force during the winter months ahead. Nevertheless, on his arrival at Pelusium he was murdered on the beach,[5] the date the middle of July. Caesar knew that he had to chase down Pompey precisely in order to prevent this reforming of his enemy's forces and if possible to capture his former son-in-law alive.[6] After a brief visit to Asia where he spent some days at Ephesus (*BC* 3. 105), he set off on Pompey's trail using a fleet to transport a relatively small detachment of his army, but more than his opponents had with them.[7] He arrived outside Alexandria about ten days to two weeks after he had heard of Pompey's death, therefore towards the end of July. There he was presented with Pompey's head, which he ordered to be buried with all due honours (Plut. *Pomp.* 80. 5–6).[8]

Then almost immediately Caesar became embroiled in the latest Egyptian civil war, this time between Cleopatra VII and Ptolemy XIII; and Alexandria in its first ever seizure by a foreign power became divided into military camps where the Romans in one quarter were effectively barricaded by Ptolemaic troops and a hostile population. The origin of the current internecine strife lay in the terms of the will of Ptolemy XII Auletes who had four children, two boys and two girls, who survived him, and he had stipulated that the elder son and the elder daughter should succeed jointly to the rule. This was, in fact, a recipe for disaster given the recent history of Ptolemaic Egypt, which had been plagued with nearly a century of civil war among members of the ruling dynasty. As long ago as 131 BC tensions among the ruling family had caused severe instability in the state, on that occasion when Ptolemy VIII Euergetes and fallen out with his sister Cleopatra II.[9] Although these were reconciled in 124, periodic episodes of family bloodletting occurred, each one undermining further the authority of the Ptolemies and the regard in which they were held by the people. Ptolemy XII had been expelled by the Alexandrians in 58 and he had fled to Rome where with massive bribery he was able to obtain military intervention on his behalf and a short-lived restoration in 55 until his death in 51. Cleopatra was the eldest sibling by far and clearly ambitious to rule alone, while Ptolemy, titular king, was under the influence of a number of advisers such as the eunuch Pothinus and the Greek tutor Theodotus.[10] When Caesar arrived Cleopatra was twenty-one, her brother was just thirteen. Pompey had put in at Pelusium since Ptolemy was there and not in Alexandria and he was there facing Cleopatra who had recently been expelled from Egypt because of her quarrels with her brother and was now apparently intent on an invasion of Egypt (Caes. *BC* 3.103; Plut. *Pomp.* 77.1). Quite where she went in search of support is not stated, but one might surmise that she visited Jerusalem and sought the aid of its de facto ruler, Antipater, who was to play an important role in later events, and who may well at this time have made an informal alliance with her in preference to Ptolemy or rather his advisers. Still, she cannot have had substantial forces at her disposal as becomes clear, and the military capability of the King was also almost certainly not as strong as it is subsequently made out to be.

Caesar had wisely avoided Pelusium, perhaps alerted to the fracas that would await him if he had decided to put in at the harbour there, and he sailed instead directly to Alexandria. Here, even though Caesar states that there were at least seventy-two Ptolemaic warships in the vicinity (*BC* 3.111), which presumably could keep a watchful eye on the sea-lanes, he seems to have taken the city's government completely by surprise since he was admitted and took up residence in the palace quarter next to the harbour (*BC* 3.106–112).[11] The lack of preparedness of the Alexandrians is further emphasized by Caesar (*BC* 3. 112) when he says that the narrow entrance to the harbour could easily be controlled by a garrison on the Island of Pharos (see map). The forces accompanying Caesar were also not that impressive for the conqueror of Pompey but although he encountered some opposition from the garrison at Alexandria his troops were clearly more than sufficient since the Egyptians were under strength, the greater part of the King's army being at Pelusium.[12] Caesar had with him about 800 cavalry, and 3200 heavy infantry drawn from two legions, which had been quartered, and probably still were, in Thessaly and Achaea. These were presumably two of the legions from his Gallic campaigns rather than two of those of the defeated troops at Pharsalus, which had since sworn allegiance to Caesar. The fact that he was able to take up residence and billet his troops throughout the city at first (*BC* 3.106) indicates that his occupation of Alexandria was mostly peaceful and that the forces available to the Alexandrians were at least inferior even to his, and if not in actual numbers certainly in their training. The casualties suffered by the Romans at this time seem to have been the victims of mob attack rather than from any official opposition in the city.

Still Caesar must have perceived a future threat, for he states that he immediately sent out requests for reinforcements, which were to be provided from those remnants of the legions that had fought against him at Pharsalus (*BC* 3.107; cf. *BA* 1). This came on top of the arrangements he had already made for additional troops to advance overland from Asia (more below); and later on by occupying the Pharos Island (*BC* 3.112) he safeguarded future supplies brought in by traders and any troops transported by ship. Furthermore, Caesar was not able to leave Alexandria initially, although ultimately he almost certainly had no desire to leave until the entire affair in every permutation was concluded to his satisfaction. The reason that Caesar gives for remaining in the city (*BC* 3.107) was that he was by then virtually a prisoner because of the Etesian (or annual/yearly) winds (*etesiae*). These northerly winds invariably blow from about the middle of May through to mid-September in the eastern Mediterranean and can achieve severe storm force and hence could greatly hinder or even completely prevent ancient shipping. This again points to the need for accuracy in the dating since had he arrived in Egypt only in the autumn these winds would simply not be an issue for the movement by sea.[13]

Cleopatra must have arrived very soon after Caesar also by sea since the overland route was blocked to her while her brother was either in the city when the Romans landed or again very quickly afterwards. Neither could afford to be away from Alexandria when Caesar was there. The romantic story told by Plutarch about Cleopatra's arrival may be true or an embellishment put around later.[14]

So Cleopatra, taking with her of all her friends only Apollodorus the Sicilian, sailed in [a] small boat and landed at the palace after dusk and in order to escape notice she lay down flat inside a sleeping bag which Apollodorus tied up at the top and carried her indoors to Caesar. And they say that it was by this trick that she first charmed Caesar ... (Plut. *Caes.* 49.1–2)

By whatever means she took it was essential for her to be in the palace in person so that she could at least attempt to win concessions for her cause against that of her brother. In this of course she succeeded very well. It is also suggested by Plutarch (*Caes.* 48.5), that Caesar had actually invited her to return to Alexandria, which means therefore that the celebrated scene of their first meeting was engineered by them both.[15] At first Caesar appeared to be even-handed in calling for a copy of the will of the previous king to be produced and stressing the legal status of both parties to joint rule and that he, as a friend of their King, should be available for arbitration but this, in fact, was simply a reiteration of the intentions of their father. Cleopatra may well have been pleased with this settlement; the King who was under Caesar's protective influence may also have been amenable had not the ambitious Pothinus intrigued against the Romans. He clearly believed, however unrealistically, that he could engineer a triumph against the Romans because of their few numbers; his own position it must be remembered was now very insecure with Cleopatra accepted once again in Alexandria, and so not only did he voice hostile remarks about the occupiers, but he also sent messages to the army at Pelusium. Here the officer in command was the Egyptian Achillas, one of Pompey's killers, and he acted quickly.

At the same time the King is said to have vented his anger at what he regarded as Caesar's partiality by tossing away his diadem and appearing before a mob claiming that his kingship had been taken away from him. Stripping the King of his rule by the representative of a foreign power did not go down well with the city mob and, although probably stage-managed by Pothinus, appears to have led to serious rioting in the streets. The affair features neither in Caesar's account nor in that of his continuator, but in the much later Dio (42.35.2; cf. Flor. 2.13.58–59), and it is conceivable that it may have coincided with the arrival of Achillas who, at the summons of Pothinus, led the Egyptian army back to Alexandria where he was admitted.[16] With the presence of a real threat to Caesar the initial move was to ask the King to send envoys to the army commander stressing that Ptolemy was agreeable to sharing power with Cleopatra, as his father had wished. The envoys were Dioscorides and Serapion, influential members of the royal household, but they were seized on Achillas' orders; one managed to escape while the other was killed (Caes.

BC 3.109).[17] Caesar presents an analysis of the forces he was facing and gives a total figure of 20,000 for this Egyptian/Ptolemaic army, and also provides a breakdown of its composition, which shows it was a typical Hellenistic army comprising quite discrete units, unlike the more uniform heavy infantry of the Roman legion.[18] Among Achillas' army were some Roman legionaries who had been posted in Alexandria by the proconsul of Syria Aulus Gabinius (cos. 58) in 55 when he had restored Ptolemy XII Auletes to his throne and who had then been retained by the King to ensure his rule.[19] Caesar is quite scathing about these men whom he describes as having ceased to consider themselves Roman and who had forgotten the standards of their former training and command and who had, in effect, gone native (*BC* 3.110).[20] Still these men were probably the core and ablest section of Achillas' force and undoubtedly well paid to fight fellow Romans. Besides this element – perhaps a thousand all told – the rest are described as a motley group drawn from Syrian thieves, former Cilician pirates, exiles and runaway slaves. There were also two thousand cavalry, perhaps drawn from the Alexandrian elite or from Arab allies, although these cannot have been that effective in the sort of close combat that took place in the city's streets. Caesar, on the other hand, appears to have employed his cavalry quite sparingly in the fighting.

Yet Caesar considered that this force, because it contained veterans of recent wars, constituted a far greater threat than a hostile civilian population, but it should also be remembered that the author would wish his audience to regard the opposition as formidable even when it was perhaps not that strong. The fighting now accelerated and the Romans had to endure a major assault on their position around the palace as Achillas' troops occupied the greater part of the city. Caesar's legionaries built palisades and covered walkways that blocked off streets leading to the palace quarter and reduced the area they had to defend in line with the small number of the besieged. However, the Romans also wanted to have access to the countryside in order to ensure some supplies could enter this sector of the city, although no details are provided on how this was achieved if indeed it was (*BA* 1). On the other hand, Achillas also had clear objectives, to overrun the Roman positions and in a concomitant move, which seems to have involved members of the local community, to retrieve the Alexandrian warships from their berths in the harbours. Ancient shipping was usually hauled up onto the beach rather than allowed to ride in the water as in a modern port, and there were also boat sheds that often accommodated more than one ship where the vessel could be dried out and repaired. The port at Alexandria will almost certainly have appeared very much the same as the harbour at Syracuse as it is described by Diodorus. He says (Diod. 14.42.5) that Dionysius, the ruler of Syracuse between 405 and 367 BC, constructed around the larger of the city's two harbours no fewer than 160 sheds and that most of these, described as expensive constructions, were designed to take two boats at any one time, suggesting that more than 300 triremes or even larger shipping could be housed there for repair and safe-keeping.[21]

Caesar claims that the warships in Alexandria's harbours were mostly quadriremes or quinqueremes, but these were clearly not manned since Achillas' men were intent on seizing them while the Romans were equally keen to see them go up in flames. These warships were almost certainly in boatsheds or in dry dock, and some may not even have been immediately serviceable. But where were these ships? The two harbours – the Great Harbour and the Harbour of Eunostus – stood adjacent to one another separated artificially by the causeway joining Pharos to the mainland.[22] However, had the Alexandrians managed to launch the majority of these they would have far outnumbered the Roman fleet, which comprised as few as twenty-five warships and transports mostly from Rhodes or Ionia (*BC* 3.106). It is certainly possible that Achillas intended that an attack against the palace would leave the harbour relatively lightly guarded and that it would therefore be vulnerable and an easily accomplished objective. Caesar, no mean tactician himself, had plainly seen the potential problem here and drew men away from his landside barricades to deal with attackers in the port. He knew that if he lost control of the sea he would be in a highly perilous position and although he was not able to leave because of the adverse winds once the seasons changed he could vacate the city. If Achillas gained the Alexandrian warships this choice became closed. Thus although Caesar provides little detail he does indicate that around the harbour there was a stiff fight,[23] but that the Romans accomplished their aim of burning the entire Egyptian fleet, both ships in the harbour and those on land, and that since he could not gain control of the whole harbour area he ordered troops to land, presumably from ships that had been launched, onto the Pharos Island.

Caesar at this point in his account gives interesting details about the famous lighthouse on Pharos, one of the wonders of the ancient world, but which actually stood almost until the modern era.[24] The lighthouse was over four hundred metres in height and its light, which was from a wood-burning furnace reflected by huge burnished bronze shields, could be seen several kilometres out at sea. His comments on this construction give some insight into the fact that although a commentary about warfare Caesar still considered digressions of this sort important to his narrative, but perhaps more importantly he gives topographical details, which add to the picture of the unfolding events in the battle in the harbour. He states (*BC* 3.112) that the Pharos Island lies a little less than one and half kilometres (slightly more than a mile) off the mainland to which it had been joined at about its midway point by means of a narrow causeway. In doing so the earlier Ptolemies had created an inner harbour almost circular in shape, which was easily defendable and secure because of its narrow entrance. This was situated – still is – beside the lighthouse, which was also fortified as was the other side of the entrance the *Diabathra* (see map).[25] Over the years the island became another suburb of the city but was no less strategically important for that.[26] This is why Caesar's troops landed at the lighthouse in order to control the entrance and exit of any shipping. He does not state that any fighting took place here only that the local community was used to pillaging any wreckage that came ashore. The Romans are said to have established a garrison while in other parts of the city on the mainland the fighting came to an inconclusive halt.[27] Caesar ordered that the positions the Romans held be strengthened in the expectation of further attacks (*BC* 3.112).

Up to this point the entire royal family was sharing the palace with Caesar, but now Arsinoe, the other daughter of Ptolemy XII, chose this particular moment to abscond from the palace with her mentor or adviser, the eunuch Ganymedes.[28] She joined Achillas and his army, although they were soon at loggerheads, each trying to gain absolute control of their troops through lavish bribes. Ptolemy, however, remained in the palace under close surveillance in case he too tried to join his army, but also because Caesar could use him as a bargaining tool if necessary.[29] Pothinus, who still exercised personal power over the King, was also actively engaged in encouraging Achillas to press home his attacks on the Romans. Couriers from Pothinus to the Ptolemaic forces were intercepted by the Romans and so Caesar ordered his execution. And at this point Caesar's own account (*BC* 3.112) breaks off with the words: 'These were the beginnings of the Alexandrian War.'[30]

The *Bellum Alexandrinum* then takes up the account with a slight overlap, by stating that Caesar had already sent for fresh troops and supplies and took great care to fortify his sector of the city. He had sent instructions for additional ships from Rhodes, Cilicia and Syria, archers from Crete and cavalry from the Nabataean Arabs (*BA* 1). On the other hand, the Alexandrians had summoned reinforcements from the surrounding districts and had also made every effort to ensure their own protection from any Roman incursion. There was a general perception among the city's population that if they did not win this fight their independence would be at an end.[31] Moreover, their spirits were buoyed up since they knew that Caesar was isolated from any outside aid. Still, they had to act quickly. In achieving these aims, in Achillas the belligerents had a reasonably competent commander but he soon fell victim to the intrigues of Ganymedes and Arsinoe who had him murdered and then took command of the army (*BA* 4).[32] And it was Ganymedes who devised the next strategy to try and break the Roman resistance. The water supply at Alexandria was drawn from the Nile by means of aqueducts and then stored in underground cisterns. In these tanks the muddy water settled and could then be used for household purposes. And the whole city possessed this subterranean network; this underground network of water channels was its lifeblood, allowing an urban culture to flourish and supporting such a large population.[33] The palace quarter was naturally connected with this network of conduits and cisterns, but Ganymedes ordered that these channels be blocked up and water pumped from the sea be introduced into the cisterns in the Roman held part of the city. The water on the perimeter of the Roman-held section of the city began to turn salty, which puzzled the besieged since the water further into this area remained clean, however, within a very short time the water in the entire zone became undrinkable. The prospect of no drinking water took its toll on the mental state of the defenders (*BA* 7) who were suddenly plunged into the depths of despair, fully understandable given the hot climate and the time of the year when temperatures in Egypt can soar above forty degrees Celsius (100°F). Caesar immediately restored command by his usual unflappable approach to crises when he ordered wells to be excavated at once, and even if they found nothing supplies, including water, could be transported in by ship without fear of attack since the Egyptians were now lacking a fleet.[34] Withdrawal from Alexandria was not possible since there would be insufficient time for the Romans to embark until their positions were overrun by the enemy who could easily catch them in the harbour. In any event, fresh water was soon found and the whole scheme of Ganymedes came to nothing (*BA* 9).

Just two days later, the author of the 'Alexandrine War' is quite specific; it was reported that some of the extra troops summoned by Caesar had arrived in the vicinity, but because of the gales were unable to enter the Great Harbour and had instead beached further along the coast.[35] This force consisted of the Thirty-Seventh Legion (*BA* 9), which had been despatched by Caesar's proconsul in Asia, Cn. Domitius Calvinus (cos. 53), and which also carried supplies of food and badly needed armaments. The legion had been one of those raised by Pompey prior to the Pharsalus campaign and hence had fought against Caesar but which, instead of being cashiered and returned to Italy, was ordered to join him to fight other veterans of Pompey among the Egyptian besiegers. These had arrived safely enough but were in a serious predicament themselves since they did not have access to water. Still, they managed to alert Caesar, sending messengers in a small boat, possibly by cover of darkness. How these reached the harbour when it was impassable for larger vessels is not related, but a small boat might be more manageable in the adverse conditions than the huge transports, which needed to employ their sails, and could perhaps not tack because of the shallows and unpredictable currents across the Nile Delta. When Caesar received the information about the reinforcements he was now forced to act. He evidently decided to take personal command of the Roman fleet and to go out and to see for himself the state of these stranded troops (*BA* 10). Taking just the crews and no marines or heavy infantry aboard he sailed out of the harbour, taking the besiegers unawares perhaps since no confrontation is mentioned, although Dio (42.38) maintains that the Alexandrians were actively employing warships for frequent attacks on the harbour.[36] He then put in at a place called the Chersonese or Peninsula, probably around midday, as was usual ancient nautical practice, and sent foragers ashore but these encountered enemy cavalry, and some were captured. Since these told the Egyptians that Caesar was personally in command of the Roman fleet but had no heavy infantry they believed that this was an excellent opportunity to intercept him, and they manned their available ships and sailed at once. Understandably Caesar was not at all keen to risk battle when he was at a disadvantage not only because of his lack of a military complement but also because it was by then rather late in the day and his pilots did not know the area well enough to fight in poor light. He therefore ordered that the fleet beach at an easily defensible spot. Some of his ships remained at anchor, one of which from Rhodes on the Roman right wing had become detached from the rest of the line. This prompted rapid action from the Egyptian squadron, which immediately attacked while Caesar felt obliged to go and rescue his wayward ship. The Rhodians are said to have fought bravely and seem hardly to have needed help. With night approaching the enemy withdrew in some disorder with the loss of four of their quadriremes, one of which had been sunk. The author of the *Bellum Alexandrinum* (11) states that the Romans would have destroyed the Egyptian fleet had night not intervened and as it was the enemy was demoralized by this reverse. Caesar, on the other hand, was able to retrieve the beached convoy and the legion it was transporting, and tow the merchant ships into the harbour at Alexandria a day or two later.

Caesar arrived back sailing 'against a gentle breeze' but from which direction? If he was stranded in Egypt by strong northerly or easterly winds then it ought to follow that the mostly transport ships sailing south from Asia had been blown off-course to the west of Alexandria and were unable to make it back unaided. If Caesar sailed westwards in the direction of Cyrene and towards Paretonium, which is mentioned (*BA* 8) as a possible source of supplies, then he too would have encountered the unfavourable winds on his return. And where along the west coast might the extra Roman forces have landed? Chersonese is a name commonly used to describe many coastal headlands and is also the name given as Caesar's stopping point en route to his beached troops. Yet where might this feature along the west coast? Maps reveal no obvious peninsulas in the area to the west of the Nile Delta, but there are several possibilities situated to the east, one of which near Canopus is perhaps a suitable lunch break for Caesar's fleet. His foragers were attacked by Egyptian cavalry and these are much more likely to have been active in the east between Alexandria and Pelusium rather than west of the city. Unless they were shadowing Caesar's movements even when it is asserted that his departure had apparently been unnoticed, cavalry are perhaps less likely to have been on the move in this direction. Caesar was not absent for long, no more than two to three days, which probably indicates that the supply convoy had beached close to Alexandria, and perhaps between the city and Pelusium. In addition, the winds seem to have abated, suggesting a time later in the summer or in early autumn, by which time Caesar could perhaps have withdrawn from the city but evidently had no intention of doing so.

The Alexandrians were initially despondent about their losses but Ganymedes seems to have galvanized them or their leaders into action again by constructing a new fleet, even though they had already lost 110 warships (*BA* 12). Clearly there was no desire for a peaceful conclusion to the hostilities at this stage. In fact, the Alexandrians decided to refurbish some guard ships, which were used to collect harbour dues, and repair old ships that were in dry dock and within days they had re-launched and made battle-ready twenty-two quadriremes and five quinqueremes (*BA* 13). The Romans had more ships – thirty-four in total – but only ten were quadriremes, the remainder were smaller. However, in a battle in the confines of a harbour with its lack of space for manoeuvres the smaller vessels actually had the advantage. Both sides surprisingly were confident of success. Caesar seems to have ordered his fleet out of the Great Harbour and around and then to the west of the Pharos (*BA* 14) and drew up for battle: the Rhodian contingent of nine warships (the quadriremes probably) were on the right wing, the eight warships from Pontus on the left. Between the two wings he deliberately placed his remaining ships some distance to the rear, so presenting to his enemy what may have appeared to have been a defensive posture rather like an open box in the shape of a rectangle, but which could also be a trap to snap shut on any unsuspecting opponent who entered the box. The Alexandrians adopted a much more positive or offensive battle order. All twenty-two quadriremes were drawn up in a line with the five quinqueremes as a reserve, but they also brought out a large number of small boats, the crews of which were armed with firebrands and given orders to cause terror and chaos by directing these towards the Roman warships. The role of small boats, in effect dinghies, in ancient battles is rather overlooked but most battles fought on the water in antiquity took place close to the shore and to harbours and their cities. The citizens of these settlements needed little encouragement to take part in view of the potential gain to be made from plunder, and the participation of small craft was no doubt an important element, but rather defies the neat strategies favoured in modern commentaries.[37] The lack of real organization in ancient sea battles is generally quite apparent and only the most basic tactics could be relied upon. Caesar's strategy here was probably influenced by his lack of numbers while the Alexandrians had little in the way of tactics at all. Just a short distance separated the two sides but this area was straddled by a shoal so whoever initiated the hostilities had to advance through this treacherous obstacle and risked becoming isolated from the other ships and easy prey for the other side. The Rhodians commanded by Euphranor, described as a brilliant captain and an exceptionally brave soldier, offered to lead the right wing into the attack. When four of the Rhodian ships had crossed through the shallows the Alexandrians advanced their ships but were held in check by Euphranor and his crews while the rest of the Roman fleet – all tactics now abandoned – poured through to join their fellows. The space for fighting was very tight and so all thought of employing any forms of nautical skills fell away and a melee developed. Once again, the author of the *Bellum Alexandrinum* probably had Thucydides' account (7.71) of the hopes and fears of the protagonists in the battle between the Athenians and the Syracusans in the Great Harbour at Syracuse in 413 BC in mind when he wrote:

> The prize in this contest was not at all equal for if our men were thrown back and defeated no way of escape lay by land or sea. If they won a victory the outcome of the general affair was still uncertain, but if the Alexandrians won the sea battle they would win complete control of the sea and if they lost they would still be able to try other ways to win the war. (*BA* 16)

The Romans and their allied troops and crews, mostly Asiatic Greek, are said to have fought with determination against the Alexandrians whose navy had a long reputation for excellence in battle and eventually got the upper hand capturing one of the Egyptian quinqueremes and a bireme with soldiers and crews and sunk three others and lost none of their own.[38] The Alexandrians withdrew to their part of the city and were able to escape only through the intervention of the citizens who crowded the walls and bombarded the pursuing Romans who therefore could not get close and the Egyptian crews suffered no further losses by retreating almost certainly into the Habour of Eunostus to the west of the Pharos.

To prevent further incursions into the Great Harbour from the Eunostus side, Caesar now decided to secure the Pharos and the causeway leading from the island to the city. Caesar had already placed a garrison on the island, or so he claimed (*BC* 3.112), and by doing so had controlled the entrance to the Great Harbour from the sea since he already must have controlled the *Diabathra* or the manmade mole that formed the eastern side of the port. However, it is also possible that he had been forced to withdraw his soldiers prior to the battle with the Alexandrian fleet. It is quite plain from the account in the *Bellum Alexandrinum* that he no longer held, had never held Pharos, or had been forced at some stage to give it up.[39] This would also indicate that he did not control even the whole of the Great Harbour and certainly not its adjacent facility (see map), yet the explanation given is rather obtuse: the reason was to prevent what had previously occurred from happening again, specifically the sea battle and the events that led to it. The Alexandrians had evidently been able to utilize old ships from one or other of the harbours, which certainly lends support to the argument that Caesar actually occupied much less of the city that he himself stated, and that he had been unable to accomplish a more decisive victory against the Alexandrian fleet because it had been able to withdraw under the protection of the city walls by which are meant those walls joining the Pharos to the mainland along the *Heptastadion* or causeway.[40] Since at either end of the causeway there were pontoon bridges that allowed access between the two harbours the Alexandrians by holding this sector were also in a position to launch attacks into the Roman held area, a weak point in the Roman defences and worrying for Caesar. Whatever the precise motivation for the Romans' latest move, Caesar believed that his landward defensives were secure from any attack launched within the city and sufficiently well guarded, probably as a result of the recent reinforcements to take personal command of this latest venture. He ordered ten cohorts of heavy infantry,[41] together with lightly armed troops and some Gallic cavalry to board small boats and cross the harbour to the Pharos. He also instructed a number of his warships – the larger quadriremes – to sail around the island and so make the attack a two pronged one.[42]

To begin with the Alexandrians countered the initial Roman assault on the rocky shore of the island by throwing missiles down from high buildings where the attackers entered streets. But, once the Romans gained a foothold, the inhabitants of the island fled while other Alexandrians evidently on board ships defending the seaward side of the island from the Roman fleet immediately beached and returned to defend their homes. This proved unsuccessful and the island fell rapidly with six thousand of the people living there taken as prisoners, probably mostly women, the elderly and young, since those fighting, if not killed, appear to have swum for safety across the harbour. Caesar ordered many of the civilian buildings demolished and a fort constructed at the pontoon bridge on the island side of the causeway. The Alexandrians had garrisoned the other end of the *Heptastadion*, so capture of the island was only a job half done since they still possessed the means to enter and cause damage to shipping in the Great Harbour. But at this stage it is interesting to note there is no mention of a central command structure on the Alexandrian side, although presumably Ganymedes and Arsinoe were in titular command. The defence of Pharos and the causeway seems to have been more a spontaneous reaction of the citizens living in this section of Alexandria, rather than any overall defensive plan. Indeed there was by this stage some reaction against the leadership of Arsinoe and Ganymedes. Had Caesar now been content with his gains the Alexandrians might have turned on one another, but as it was he decided on a major offensive for the next day because he could see the advantage of controlling the entire causeway and the gateway that led into the city. This was set in motion, not with an infantry or cavalry advance along the causeway against the gateway into the city, but by launching ships from the Roman held area of the Great Harbour and moving them towards the lower gate. The troops garrisoned there were soon driven back through the sheer number of missiles directed against them from Caesar's ships. Then three cohorts of legionaries were landed, which was as many as could easily be accommodated in the narrow area around the gate and the rest remained on board. A barrier was then erected (*BA* 19) to defend the Roman troops while the connecting waterway between the harbours was blocked up with stones. This did not go unnoticed and there was a rapid counterattack by the Alexandrians who drew up their troops on an open stretch close the causeway and the bridge, and also called up old hulks that were used as fireboats and directed these towards the Roman ships containing the troops. If the Romans possessed only the Great Harbour side of the causeway this would indicate that the Alexandrians still had a foothold here, although it seems more likely that Caesar, now in possession of the whole of Pharos Island, had sent ships into the Harbour of Eunostus as well and these were obviously much more vulnerable to attack. However, as events showed it does appear as if most of the action was in the Great Harbour since the Alexandrian attack threw the over-confident Romans into some disarray because some of those not initially involved including rowers left their ships to join in the fight or to watch the action. The Romans had the upper hand but when some of the Alexandrians also left their ships and could not be dislodged from either near the gateway or the causeway others joined them and began to push the Romans back. A stampede began as Caesar's troops and the other allied combatants recognized the threat developing around them as more and more Alexandrian soldiers came ashore from their ships and quite unexpectedly a rout began. The regular Roman troops fortifying the gateway they had just taken now saw their own comrades in the rear now starting to flee, and while facing a barrage of missiles to their front now feared they would also be left isolated and attacked from behind. So these too abandoned their positions and rushed back in a panic to the Roman ships where there was now a life and death struggle to board and get away to safety. Some were killed in the flight to reach the ships while others died when they clambered aboard any sort of craft, many of which were overloaded and sank or were capsized in the melee.

> Some were fortunate to get to the warships which lay at anchor and which were in readiness for action and managed to find safety, and a few raised their shields above their heads and swam out to the ships which lay further out in the harbour. (*BA* 20)

Caesar had a very lucky escape since he was caught up in this surging wave of terrified men each trying to find a way from the enemy. He made it to his own ship, which must have been lying at anchor at the causeway and managed to get aboard among a crowd of soldiers whose discipline had completely collapsed and who if they had any thoughts at all were simply for self preservation. A ship at anchor may appear to be salvation but in reality it could also be a death trap because if the boarding was chaotic or too many clambered onto the deck there was every chance of the ship capsizing. Caesar knew this and could see for himself the panic that had overwhelmed his troops and who were now filling the ship beyond its limit.[43] So he jumped overboard and swam out to one of the ships a little further out in the harbour and which had probably left the dangers of the causeway as the rout began. From there we are told he ordered small boats to put out and rescue any of his men struggling in the water, but his ship went down with the loss of all on board. Altogether four hundred legionaries were killed in this defeat and as many again of the sailors and rowers who had foolishly joined in or had wanted a ringside view of the fight. The Alexandrians regained their gateway and reopened the channel into the Great Harbour so the Roman enterprise was futile, although it is not said that Caesar lost control of the *Heptastadion* and Pharos, and presumably holding this extra sector of the city partly made up for the casualties suffered on this occasion.

The author of the *BA* says that this reverse did not have a negative impact on Roman morale and that in subsequent fighting Caesar's troops were more often victors than vanquished, although no concrete advance appears to have taken place from their previous lines of defence. Still, as a result of this impasse the Alexandrians arrived at a new strategy. They decided to send a deputation to Caesar – whether Arsinoe or Ganymedes approved this measure or were even consulted is not related – to ask that their King be reunited with his people. They also affirmed that, since Arsinoe and Ganymedes no longer had their confidence, they would obey whatever the King wished even if that included a peace with the Romans. Up until now Caesar had clearly believed that the King's presence inside the Roman sector of the city was of crucial importance to him since he could represent his own participation as one of friendly ally rather than that of oppressor or would-be conqueror. He was therefore in a dilemma as to what the best course of action should be. Here the *BA* has some scathing criticisms of the Alexandrians and, for the author, their notorious duplicity.[44] Caesar finally considered that if Ptolemy was allowed to leave the palace he would take one of two courses: he would either bring the Alexandrians to the negotiating table or he would take up the leadership against the Romans. Ptolemy is said to have been reluctant to leave but once he had done so he took over the command of the Egyptian army with great enthusiasm, perhaps from a hatred of his sister Cleopatra. Caesar is reported to have believed that Ptolemy's move was at least likely but that to have a king as an opponent was more creditable than a young girl and a eunuch.[45] However, the Romans were not put out with the loss of the King among their ranks, while the Alexandrians did no better in the fighting. The besiegers must also have been made aware that pro-Roman forces were gathering in the north and advancing down the coast towards Sinai. To forestall this succour the Alexandrians now attempted to starve the Romans into surrender, by employing a naval blockade of food supplies, which were still arriving into the Great Harbour.

Caesar felt he had to respond to this latest tactic by ordering his fleet to break this latest deadlock, although on this occasion he did not take personal command but entrusted this task to Ti. Claudius Nero (*BA* 25).[46] The fleet sailed in an easterly direction hence the time of the year must by then have been autumn if not early winter of 48/7 since the winds no longer posed a problem and it reached Canopus.[47] Here it found the Alexandrian fleet and battle lines were drawn with the Rhodian contingent on the right wing, which immediately attacked. The Rhodian commander Euphranor, true to his character, played a leading role in the engagement and rammed and sank one of the Egyptian quadriremes and then pursued another but became detached from his compatriots and was surrounded. He fought bravely but was outnumbered and without aid he was killed and his ship was lost. The narrative ends abruptly and it can probably be assumed that the Roman fleet came off worse in this fight and withdrew to Alexandria leaving the enemy blockade in place. Although a setback, as later events showed, the strategy of the besiegers was unsuccessful. The siege then became a standoff between the two parties.

The arrival of the Thirty-Seventh Legion may have to some extent represented an initial relief column but these troops had merely joined the other Roman forces already in Alexandria, while the main force necessary to turn the scales of the conflict was still far away. The siege by then had lasted into the autumn of 48 since the second half of July. It was only in November 48 that relief appeared close to Pelusium in the person of Mithridates of Pergamum who had arrived at the frontier of Egypt after a march that had apparently encompassed the Roman provinces of Asia, Cilicia and Syria, and much besides.

The questions that now need to be addressed here are these. How was this private individual able to raise troops along this route, what were his resources and what was his official capacity? What sort of troops could have been under his command and how was he able to obtain a victory over Ptolemy's garrison at Pelusium whereas Caesar with all his resources and talents was unable to throw back his opponents in Alexandria itself? What was Mithridates' contribution to the subsequent battle in which Ptolemy's forces were routed and the King killed? How serious was the opposition to Caesar in Alexandria, and how much propaganda has been generated by the presentation of the material in the *BA* and which found its way into the later literature? Finally, what was the role and influence of Antipater of Judaea?

According to the *BA* (26.1) a local notable named Mithridates had been deputed to levy troops in Cilicia and Syria as reinforcements for Caesar even before the latter had set out for Alexandria in July 48. But just who was this man Mithridates with his Persian-sounding name who was clearly not a Roman official or a serving Roman army officer? He was a prominent citizen of Pergamum and apparently had the reputation for being a warrior. Therefore, he may have fought at Pharsalus but not on the side of Caesar for while Pompey drew his infantry troops mostly from Italy, his lightly armed soldiers and his cavalry were almost certainly drawn from a wide variety of sources, which would have included Asia Minor. If Mithridates fought in this battle he served among the cavalry, perhaps as one of its senior commanders, and had then been pardoned for his participation following Pompey's defeat. On the other hand, he may well have stood aloof from any involvement in this latest bout of Roman civil war, although it may well have proved difficult or indeed impossible for any provincial magnate in areas controlled by Pompey, his allies or governed by his subordinate commanders. Ephesus was the seat of the proconsul of the Roman province of Asia but Pergamum the city of the former Attalid kings who had ruled this region between 282 and 133 BC retained its place as a major urban and cultural centre. Its civic leaders were well connected not just within the province but throughout the East and in Rome itself. In his usual brief coverage of the cities and regions of the world as he knew it, Strabo noting Pergamum's place in Mysia and its illustrious history also relates that Mithridates was one of the leading citizens of Pergamum of his day. Not only that, for he was connected to the kings of Pontus and the tetrarchs of Galatia. His mother was a daughter of Adobogion, a member of the ruling family of the Galatian tribe the Trocmi, who is said to have been a concubine of Mithridates VI Eupator the king of Pontus (120–64 BC). His father was the Pergamene aristocrat, Menodotus, but Mithridates was named after the King, which clearly gave rise to the rumour that he was actually of royal blood.[48] Indeed as a child he had spent time at the court of his namesake who was one of Rome's most persistent and cunning adversaries. This is likely to have been when the king of Pontus was resident in the city after his ordered invasion of the Roman province of Asia in 89 BC until he was expelled from there by Roman forces about three years later.[49] This would also suggest that by 48 Mithridates was not a young man and indeed appears to have been a close contemporary of Caesar with whom he is said to have been on very friendly terms. Indeed, Caesar made him tetrarch of Galatia after the battle of Pharsalus but their friendship may go back many years to when the former was a junior officer serving in Asia in the 70s.[50] Caesar is known to have been in Bithynia and in Rhodes and could easily have become acquainted with Mithridates at that time. A longstanding *amicitia* between the two seems certain given that Mithridates was entrusted with so crucial a task in 48. Furthermore, that he was given such an essential task at all clearly illustrates not only the lack of Roman officials who had either Caesar's trust or the talent to carry it out but also the instability in Asia Minor where the imperial provincial administration had been entirely disrupted by the ongoing civil strife.[51]

Moreover, Mithridates was not simply a famous provincial but for Caesar to leave him to organize an army must indicate that he had considerable expertise in this area as well. The *BA* is also clear on this point, saying that he was held to be in the mould of the Hellenistic king and warrior, largely the creation of Alexander the Great, and exemplified by Mithridates VI himself.[52] Thus Mithridates was fully aware of the duty expected of him and knew how to go about organizing a military expedition and had the connections, and presumably the personal finance and patronage, across Asia Minor to successfully complete this assignment. He could clearly call on his Galatian subjects to provide the bulk of any military force and their contribution was most likely to have been in the form of cavalry for which this region was famous.[53] Indeed this was not a levy of citizens for a Macedonian type phalanx or a Roman legion; instead, this will have been almost exclusively a cavalry force raised either by the Galatians or from the urban elite of the cities along the route. Its composition becomes clear enough when it is described in action at Pelusium and afterwards. The service is likely to have been voluntary if drawn from among elite households and payment, if any was promised, was likely to have no more than the prospect of plunder and if moveable wealth was supplied to Mithridates in the shape of coined money then this too will have come from independent and local contributions and not from the Roman state. Caesar probably did not have access to large funds so the movement of an army relied to a great extent on goodwill, compulsion or the promise of largesse. This relief column was therefore almost a private affair, and quite unlike a modern equivalent of that launched by a centralized state as the Rome Empire was to become.

The *BA* states that the force was a large one and that Mithridates had been effective in his assignment. Understandably perhaps the author of the *BA* shows no interest in the logistical problems involved in the mounting of a successful relief column because his focus is firmly on Caesar's activities. Thus Mithridates appears as if out of thin air on the Egyptian frontier and yet this advent came plainly at the end of an arduous and difficult expedition from Ephesus.

The distance travelled by the Roman relief column needs some attention since it was substantial. From Ephesus to Alexandria by sea is approximately eight hundred kilometres (approximately 500 miles) and could take as little as five days with a favourable wind. Overland, however, it is nearly double this distance and an army, even one mostly composed of cavalry, will have covered hardly as much as forty kilometres (25 miles) a day because of its baggage train; and that distance would be compounded by halts to collect further troops and to allow the horses and pack animals to feed. It is obvious that an expedition of any magnitude would have taken several weeks if not months. The process of raising additional troops necessarily would have slowed the progress. Alexander's campaign from crossing the Hellespont in the early summer of 334 took nearly two and a half years (May 334 to November 332) to reach Egypt, admittedly fighting on the way but a good indication of the distance and the difficulty of advancing overland for any army especially when facing opposition.[54] Of course cavalry could easily be transported by ship, which had been shown as early as the Persian invasion of Attica at Marathon in 490 BC and the vessels available over four hundred years later were considerably larger, yet there seems to have been no provision for this. Mithridates' route would have kept him quite close to the sea while the cities he visited would for the most part have possessed harbours. Moreover, Caesar had ordered a legion to be brought to Alexandria by sea so why no fleet for this venture? There are several possibilities: the size of this force was too great for a fleet to carry – it is possible that about 20,000 men and horses were involved, that there were insufficient ships available and they could not be constructed in time from cities with huge debts on account of the civil war, that the sea route was unsafe since Caesar's opponents still possessed a serviceable fleet that might pose a threat – although these had regrouped in Africa, and that Mithridates only acquired a sufficiently threatening forces late in his recruitment. The last reason needs some examination for it is Josephus who provides a clue.

Therefore, the relief column probably arrived outside Pelusium in Roman civic time in January 47, actually November 48, which means that Caesar had been virtually cut off from the outside world from the end of July for more than four months. Pelusium (near the modern city of Port Said) was roughly 250 kilometres (160 miles) from Alexandria, and still possessed the garrison that had been installed there by Achillas to counteract Cleopatra's attempt at returning from exile. The fight for this fortress was brief but hotly contested. The occupation of Pelusium by an invading force always posed a serious threat to the security of Alexandria and Egypt as a whole. Ptolemy and his advisers knew that this problem had to be met quickly and effectively or Mithridates would be outside Alexandria and that they would become the besieged not the besiegers. The author of the *BA* (26) compliments Mithridates on his tactics of surrounding the fort and in making a determined and continual assault, which he managed by sending in fresh troops at regular intervals to allow the defenders no respite. Pelusium was taken within the day and Mithridates placed his own garrison there before continuing his advance towards Alexandria. Josephus tells a rather different story for he states that in the attack it was Antipater who displayed the greatest bravery and was, again very much in the Alexander mould, the first into the breached walls and in the frontline of the fighting (*BJ* 1.3.189).[55] Once Mithridates had expelled the defenders and installed a garrison to ensure no possible attacks on his rear, he advanced southwards perhaps on the east bank of the Nile and crossing the river at or near Memphis. Antipater is again said (*BJ* 1.4.190) to have been instrumental in easing the way forward, which was defended by Egyptian Jews. Josephus does not give details and the episode is perhaps unhistorical but there may have been some encounter with Egyptian forces at the river near Memphis – the *BA* has another version of this engagement. On account of Antipater's presence and his influence with these Jews any opposition was overcome peacefully and they seem to have thrown in their lot with the invaders who then appear to have entered and taken Memphis without any further fighting. The relief column, according to Josephus, then moved downstream towards the Delta along the west back, which allowed easy access to Alexandria. The contemporary account does not, however, mention this at all and although in agreement with Josephus about the ease of conquest up to the Nile places the invaders on the east bank and still to cross the Nile before being confronted by the Egyptian army. It is interesting that there is such a gulf between the two sources and if the earlier is likely to have been more accurate then the later was perhaps motivated again to show the usefulness of the Jews to the eventual Roman victory. If we follow Josephus' account we have the King leading his army, or the greater part of it, out of Alexandria either intent on taking aid to Pelusium, the fall of which may not yet have reached Ptolemy, or to retake the town and throw back the invading army. Since Mithridates is said to have turned (περιελθὼν) the Delta (*BJ* 1.4.191) the opposing armies met again with Ptolemy now on the east bank and Mithridates on the west. Thus here was a recurrence of the battle at Issus in 334 when Alexander outflanked Darius, and the positions of defender and invader were reversed. The manoeuvre was perhaps purposely modelled on Alexander's tactics, which he had also employed against Porus at the Hydaspes River in 327, but it also places Mithridates in this Hellenistic heroic ruler mould, which was his heritage. Ptolemy, on the other hand, was obliged to cross the Nile to engage his opponents or run the risk of losing Alexandria without a fight.[56] Yet the invading army came under heavy pressure on its right wing where Mithridates was in command while Antipater on the left wing was victorious and came to the aid of the Pergamene who was in retreat. Antipater attacked the Egyptians from behind, routed them and captured their camp; and he lost a mere eighty men while Mithridates' casualties numbered eight hundred (*BJ*. 1.4.192). Mithridates is said to have delivered unconditional praise of Antipater in his later report to Caesar, who apparently not present, repaid this glorious achievement, granting numerous honours to the hero.[57]

The defence at Pelusium was a brief episode, and the final battle that occurred over two days, as it is described in the *BA*, is also a far more one-sided encounter than that dwelt upon by Josephus to the benefit of the Jewish contingent not mentioned at all in other accounts. The writer of the *BA* could be relating the history of another war for he has Mithridates pacifying the Egyptian countryside as he passes through to the Nile and the King in response sending out a substantial armed force of his own to the Delta in order to intercept Mithridates as he attempted to cross the river. Some of the Egyptian troops crossed the Nile and attacked the relief column, which suggests something of a breakdown in discipline and command or that these were lightly armed troops on reconnaissance. These were thrown back into the river and into their boats by Mithridates who appears to have made a crossing since he engaged these defenders again and sent messengers to Caesar to inform him of the latest developments. Ptolemy appears to have received similar reports, which drew him out of Alexandria with his main army, but Caesar left Alexandria at the same time in order to meet up with Mithridates. However, they evidently took quite different routes mainly so Caesar would not have to engage the Egyptian forces before he was in possession of superior numbers. Ptolemy, meanwhile, moved his army by the most direct route from Alexandria to the Nile just below Memphis and made camp. Yet the author of the *BA* (28) asserts that Ptolemy transported his army by ship, which seems at least a little improbable when cavalry, chariots, and even infantry would have moved more easily overland. Ptolemy is also said to have had a large fleet at his disposal which, considering his supposed severe losses, also appears exaggerated. Caesar's route, also by sea, seems that much more roundabout and complicated, either sailing first west and then doubling back to confuse any Egyptian spies and perhaps eventually making land to the east of the Delta. Yet he is said to have joined Mithridates before Ptolemy made any attack. If, as Josephus maintains, Mithridates was already on the west bank of the Nile then it is seem probable that Caesar made landfall to the west of the Delta and marched overland from what is described as 'Africa' (*BA* 28).

Ptolemy's camp was on a hill overlooking the river and when he heard that Caesar was in the vicinity he sent out cavalry units and lightly armed troops to intercept him. Quite how the Egyptians thought that these would be effective against Roman legionaries is puzzling but perhaps reflects the sort of troops at the King's disposal. It is said that Ptolemy hoped to prevent Caesar from crossing a tributary of the Nile some seven miles away. This stream had steep banking and it was intended that the Egyptian troops, probably a mix of archers and javelin throwers, would attack from a distance only.

Caesar's cavalry, which may by now have been reinforced with those of Mithridates, found fordable places while the infantry cut down trees to bridge the stream, which was clearly not that wide.[58] The Alexandrians seem to have been caught by surprise at the speed and ingenuity of the Roman forces and, making no attempt to repel their enemy at the banks, immediately fled with very heavy losses. Caesar decided to attack the King's camp immediately to take advantage of any confusion that would be caused by those fleeing from their recent defeat. However, seeing that this camp was well fortified and guarded, he changed his mind in order that his troops could take some badly needed rest after their battle, so instead instructed that they encamp close to their enemy. The King had made a fort in a village near his camp, which was connected to it by some walls and these became the objective of the Roman assault on the next day. Attacking Ptolemy's head quarters made sense and a massive loss to the Egyptians should the Romans be victorious here. Caesar therefore threw all available manpower at the fort and the connecting walls and was quickly successful expelling and chasing the defenders into the main camp but instead of attacking the main fort from inside connecting the fortifications a more general assault from all sides seems to have occurred. On one side the camp faced inland and, although easily accessible, was well defended, the other side faced out over the Nile and only a small strip of land separated it from the river. The Roman attack on this side was hampered not by the number of defenders but by the fact that the attackers were vulnerable not only from missiles hurled by those inside the camp but also from other Egyptian units stationed on numerous warships anchored on the river. Following the initial success the Romans were finding suddenly that they had a real fight on their hands when Caesar noticed that a section of the camp at its highest point had been left undefended by its guards who had either gone further down the walls to join in the fighting there or simply to watch more exciting proceedings. Caesar ordered one of his officers named Carfulenus to lead a number of cohorts against the highest point of Ptolemy's camp and these quickly engaged the few guards in that sector.[59] This new assault caused such consternation among the defenders that confusion quickly set in followed rapidly by panic and this spurred the Romans on to such an extent that the fortifications were overthrown on three sides almost simultaneously, although it is said that Carfulenus' detachment led the rout and killed many of those attempting to flee. Many others were killed as they leapt from the fortifications towards the river when a section of the walls collapsed; others escaped jumping over the dead bodies of former comrades. Some escaped in the ships. Ptolemy is said to have found refuge on one of the anchored ships but this capsized when it was engulfed with other fugitives. Florus, probably using Livy as a source, says that the body of the King was discovered in the mud where he had fallen (Flor. 2.13.60),[60] but other writers claim that the body of Ptolemy XIII was never found (Plut. *Caes.* 49.5).

The date of the final battle is given as 14 January 47, which actually means it took place in late November 48 BC.[61] But the affair was not even then completed for now Caesar immediately set off to Alexandria with his cavalry, certainly now very much enhanced by the presence of Mithridates' forces. This must have been accomplished perhaps by the next day or so and evidently took the Alexandrians entirely by surprise. They knew nothing of the outcome of the fight on the Nile. Unsurprisingly, the citizens of the city capitulated at once faced with an enemy much superior in numbers and with no other forces to call upon. The besiegers had become the besieged and they sent envoys suitably dressed as suppliants to Caesar fearful of a sack and looting of the city. He reassured them that nothing of the sort would be allowed and he progressed through the city streets and entered the Roman lines where he was greeted with great enthusiasm by his own men; the besieged at Alexandria had been relieved. The siege had lasted rather more than four months. Cleopatra and her younger brother, Ptolemy XIV, were confirmed as joint rulers of the kingdom.

The relief of Alexandria and the complete destruction of the besieging forces in 47 BC is a most unusual if not a unique episode certainly in antiquity if not in all military history. It was the case that Q. Tullius Cicero had been besieged in his winter quarters by Nervii in the winter of 55/54 BC for several days (*BG* 5.39–49) until saved by Caesar himself leading a relief column. Although the predicament was solved in a similar fashion, the Nervii lifted their blockade in order to face the Roman reinforcements and were subsequently defeated and dispersed; this siege had been against a military establishment not a city. On the other hand, for untimely relief columns, there is no need to look further afield than Thucydides' failure in 422 BC to relieve Amphipolis, which fell to the Spartan forces under Brasidas, which had been besieging the city. Thucydides does make the point, in his own account, that he actually saved the nearby harbour at Eion from similarly being taken by the enemy. Still, the apparently inept command cost him dearly and he was exiled. Troy, it will be remembered, endured an enormously long siege, possibly the longest in history, and the fact that no relief column came to the aid of the Trojans, considering their apparent alliances in and around Asia Minor, is notable to say the least.[62] Similarly the three-year sieges of Carthage between 149 and 146 and Numantia 136–133 ended in disaster for their inhabitants without any aid appearing for the besieged. While, when the Athenians besiegers of Syracuse in 413 had themselves become the besieged, a relief column did indeed arrive but to no avail it and, it along with the rest of the Athenian-led forces, perished in one of the greatest turnaround situations in the history of siege warfare (see Chapter 2).

It is remarkable how very few sieges in antiquity reached a happy conclusion for those besieged through the timely arrival of a relief column or a tactical withdrawal by the invader. In fact, it is quite the opposite, which is attested, and almost exclusively the list is one of besieged cities either forced into surrender or taken violently and subsequently destroyed. Some were occupied following short attacks such as Eretria on Euboea, which was betrayed after seven days of defence against the Persians in 490 (Herodt. 6.101). Others, such as Potidaea in the winter of 430/29, endured well over two years of close investment by the Athenians before it negotiated a truce and its civilian population was allowed to depart into exile (Thuc. 2.70). Similarly, the siege of Plataea, which had begun in the summer of 429, ended nearly two years later with a surrender of its garrison of about 225, composed mostly of Plataeans but with some Athenians, all of whom were executed (Thuc. 3.68).[63] Others, like Miletus, Halicarnassus and Tyre, all suffered violent damage when they were stormed by Alexander the Great during his invasion of Asia Minor and the Levant between 334 and 332. Miletus and Halicarnassus were relatively brief but the siege of Tyre went on for six months before it was stormed and a large part of its population was massacred. However, an outstanding exception to what appears the usual course of events was at Syracuse, which endured four lengthy sieges between 414 and 212 BC and was only taken by the Romans after both the Athenians in 413, and the Carthaginians in 396 and 309, had been repulsed with heavier losses to the besiegers than to the besieged.

On the other hand, compare the following famous events in more recent history when sieges have had happier endings for the besieged but not necessarily for the besiegers. During the Indian Mutiny in 1857 the residency at Lucknow with a garrison of about a thousand was besieged from July throughout the following summer months until a relief column broke in and the entire force evacuated in November of that year. Elsewhere in the British Empire, the wars in Southern Africa provide perhaps some of the most celebrated rescue of those besieged. In fact, the entire Second Boer War (1899–1900) consisted mainly of three notable sieges of British garrisons, all of which were raised through use of the relief column. Thus at Ladysmith in Natal, a siege by the Boer forces from 28 October 1899 lasted until the British garrison was reinforced on 27 February 1900. The relief of Kimberley in the Northern Cape, besieged from 14 October 1899 until relieved on 15 February 1900, was effected almost simultaneously by a substantial army led by General Earl Roberts. Meanwhile, Robert Baden-Powell, better known as the architect of the 'Scout Movement', commanded the besieged at Mafeking from 13 October 1899, to be relieved only after more than seven months of continuous investment by the part-time Afrikaner soldiers on 17 May the following year.[64] At almost precisely the same time, halfway around the world, in Peking, during the Boxer Rebellion, a peasant uprising manipulated by the Chinese imperial court and which became directed against foreign intervention in China, the legations of the mostly European powers represented in the city were besieged from the 20 June 1900 until relieved over two months later on 15 August. A relief column consisting of European, Australian and Japanese contingents marched from the coast and suppressed the entire insurrection. And finally, of course, how can one forget any good Hollywood cinematic drama that involves the American Wild West, cowboys and Native Americans? The attackers are usually driven off with heavy losses with the arrival of the almost predictable relief column of usually a cavalry detachment of the army, which is usually heralded by suitably martial and patriotic music.

Modern mechanical and technological advances have meant that the relief column need not come by boat, horseback or on foot. Thus mechanized road traffic was responsible for the relief – or rather the lifeline – of Leningrad (St Petersburg) between 8 September 1941 and 27 January 1944 (872 days), while a continuous airlift by the Western powers ensured that the blockade of Berlin from 25 June 1948 to 12 May 1949 was a failure.[65] Even in modern times, however, there have been occasions in which attempts to relieve the besieged have been frustrated. The notoriously unsuccessful attempt to relieve Khartoum arrived two days too late on 28 January 1885 and after its commander, General Gordon, and the garrison had been massacred after a siege that had lasted from 13 March 1884 to 26 January 1885. And more recent events such as the Russian siege of the German army in Stalingrad in the winter of 1942 or the French debacle at Dien Bien Phu in Vietnam in 1954 following a siege of fifty-four days (13 March to 7 May) show how the siege remains an integral element in the strategies of warfare.

Some analysis is now needed of the distances involved in those modern sieges and their relief columns mentioned above compared with the distance that Mithridates covered from Ephesus or Pergamum to Pelusium. In terms of distances travelled how does the route of Mithridates compare with that of more modern examples of the relief column? The motorization of warfare altered the whole scale of movement even in the early part of the twentieth century. However, up to 1914 there are more similarities than differences with the ancient world. Thus Ladysmith is situated only 247 kilometres (about 150 miles) from the port of Durban, which remained in British hands and from where a relief might easily be organized. Still, initial reinforcements were repulsed by the Afrikaners at Colenso on 15 December 1899 and it was only after protracted fighting around the town that the British eventually forced their way when their enemy retreated under cover of a thunderstorm nearly two months later. It is worth noting that once the railway link between Ladysmith was cut by the Afrikaners the situation was hardly different to that experienced by a besieged town in antiquity, although the distance from the coast to the town was not that great. Mafeking and Kimberley, on the other hand, could have been relieved from Johannesburg, which remained in British hands throughout the Boer Wars, but had, in fact, to be reinforced from the Cape since there was a shortage of British troops in the Transvaal. Both sieges were extremely protracted considering the manpower available to the British, which ought to have allowed for a much more rapid suppression of the enemy. They also controlled much of the rail link from Cape Town, but the distance involved is certainly comparable to that faced by Mithridates when he left Ephesus.[66] And like Mithridates, Generals Roberts and French had to employ almost exclusively cavalry in the last stages of their advance on Kimberley and while within reasonable reach Mafeking was not relieved for nearly a further three months, and therefore illustrative of the intense fighting and the stubbornness of the opposition to the British in this region.[67] What is notable is that the distances between Ephesus and Alexandria, Cape Town and Kimberley and Mafeking are not only similar but that the logistical difficulties encountered – fodder for animals, supplies and armaments for troops – and the rate of advance in a largely pre-mechanized society is certainly identical. Furthermore, Mithridates had neither trains nor employed transportation by sea and therefore his achievement becomes more remarkable in that context. The British were able to use the recently introduced steam power and railways in both Natal and the Cape provinces to move their troops and horses some distance but when these became unavailable, either because they were in enemy hands or had yet to be constructed, they were nearly in the same state as an army in the ancient world.[68]

The British simply needed to transport their troops from the coast inland. The delay to relieve all three besieged towns in Natal, Northern Cape and in the western Transvaal was caused by a combination of shortfalls in the size of the British army in South Africa, the transportation of reinforcements from Britain, and the intensity of the resistance organized by the Afrikaner forces. The might of the British Empire like that of its Roman predecessor might be expected to prevail. The Romans, however, were still in the throes of a civil war and there were clearly limits to the number of troops available to Caesar even if he was the Empire's ruler. Many of his staunchest opponents, such as Cato, Metellus Pius Scipio and Titus Labienus, were regrouping in North Africa and Iberia. Dealing with the Egyptian problem compounded a shortage of manpower meaning that Mithridates, once he had called upon his Galatian resources, had to recruit while he marched. He first had to cross Asia Minor heading towards Cilicia, a region only recently subdued by the Romans under Pompey in the mid-60s where a pirate culture had been forcibly suppressed and where many of its adherents had been transferred to more landlocked pursuits. Some no doubt had sworn loyalty to Rome and Pompey and given up their adventurous habits, and indeed some may not have been keen to enlist in a war against his supporters but others would have relished participation in another war. The *BA* (26) specifically notes Cilicia as on Mithridates' route, probably because it was fruitful recruiting ground. Less certain would have been the support in Syria perhaps, which had been an independent kingdom until 63 and where enthusiasm for Roman rule may have been lukewarm among its elite. Here, it is worth noting that when Crassus had invaded Parthia from Antioch in 53 and had been on the receiving end of one of the worst military disasters in Roman history, it was his quaestor, C. Cassius Longinus, who had led 10,000 of the defeated army back to the safety of Syria and had organized the successful defence of the province from Parthian attack until he returned to Rome in 51.[69] Cassius had been an ally of Pompey in the civil war and was particularly vigorous in his command of the latter's fleet causing havoc in Sicily and around southern Italy just at the same time as Pharsalus. Thereafter he surrendered to Caesar, was pardoned and may even have been with Caesar in Alexandria or perhaps had been required to remain in Ephesus or had even accompanied Mithridates.[70] The citizens of cities such as Antioch may well have been informed of Caesar's benevolent treatment of Cassius – one can now see the rationale behind Caesar's decision not to exact revenge on many of his former enemies – and this would have produced a much more positive attitude towards service in an army proceeding to the former's succour. Therefore while proceeding via Cilicia and Syria along the regular route from Asia Minor there was clearly some planning involved in the direction that the relief column took. From Syria Mithridates proceeded south through Coele-Syria (Bekaa Valley) and into Judaea. There he certainly met with Antipater, the chief minister and general of the Hasmonaean ruler of Judaea, Hyrcanus II. Antipater, formerly a client of Pompey to whom he owed his current position, had wisely switched his allegiance to Caesar but this also meant that he would have been expected to provide material for Mithridates. Since Mithridates and Caesar were friends and Cleopatra had already been aided by Antipater, the connections between all four can only have been further cemented by the Jewish general's next actions. In his *Jewish History* Josephus, naturally enough, gives considerable prominence to Antipater's role in the relief of Alexandria and in his opinion his contribution was instrumental in its success. It is interesting to note, however, that Antipater's intervention only occurred when Mithridates was already at Ascalon and almost within sight of Pelusium. It is certainly possible that the high priest Hyrcanus in Jerusalem had signified a desire not to be involved, but Antipater who ruled over an autonomous Idumaea,

188 Fields of Death

which corresponds roughly to the southern districts of modern Israel, had no such qualms. It should also be remembered that he must have already given his support to Cleopatra against Ptolemy XIII so his allegiance would have been in no doubt. However, if Mithridates was delayed it might also mean that there was far less enthusiasm for Caesar's cause than the *BA* (26) claims and that, at this point, he had too few troops to advance into Egypt. If that is so then the problem was solved, says Josephus (1.3.187), by Antipater enlisting the support of the Arabs of nearby Nabataea, and providing from his own resources three thousand infantry.[71] If Josephus is accurate in stating that infantry were a desideratum and supplied by Antipater this offer may have been crucial and the key to ensuring the success of the relief, since up to that point the bulk of Mithridates' force was almost certainly cavalry. Caesar's lacked cavalry certainly but probably also needed a larger number of infantry than he had at his disposal in Alexandria.

Mithridates received a suitably extravagant reward for his help when Caesar assigned to him the kingdom of the Bosporus after his victory over its king, Pharnaces, at Zela in Pontus in 47.[72] Mithridates, by then in his sixties, did not enjoy his elevation to kingship for long since in 45 he died, possibly fighting against Asander, another claimant to the Bosporan kingship who had after killing Pharnaces had assumed the title of king. This was a position he later retained when Augustus became the ruler of the Roman Empire.[73]

There are a number of important issues that deserve discussion in the conclusion. First, Cicero's letters to Atticus dated to May and June 47 must obviously refer to the spring of that year, March and April respectively, when Caesar had yet to leave Egypt for Syria and his appointment with Pharnaces at Zela later in that summer. His defeat of this self-proclaimed king of Pontus was very suitably '*veni, vidi, vici*' to celebrate the briefest of military campaigns, while his time in Alexandria was anything other than noted for its brevity. Although Caesar probably had a similarly appropriate and bombastic description of his victory in the Alexandrine War, it was only due to the unusual success of the relief column and it could so easily have become a case of '*victus est*' rather than victor. Second, it would be correct to argue that the battle at the Nile, which incidentally was a winter confrontation and illustrates once more the increasingly professional nature of warfare in antiquity in that it was no longer confined to summer months, was the last occasion of the Hellenistic Age in which there were present two opposing forces composed essentially of Asiatic Greeks plus native levies raised from Egypt, Syria, Judaea and Nabataea. The battle described in the *BA* essentially follows a familiar pattern of Caesar storming yet another hill top fort so perhaps the episode does not deserve to be described as a formal or pitched battle. The much later account of Josephus gives us a far more glamorous and heroic interpretation in which the role and participation of Antipater is emphasized and yet has all the hallmarks of the Homeric hero leading his troops in battle. After this battle the supremacy of Rome was so complete that in the next half a millennium wherever a confrontation occurred at least half the combatants on the field of conflict were Roman citizens or wished to be Roman citizens and all were drawn up according to Roman military regulations and tactics and armour. At the Nile the Roman element was relatively minor, although perhaps not necessarily unimportant but the outward face of the battle would have been as familiar to Alexander the Great and the Diadochi of the third century BC as it was to Caesar over 250 years later. Finally, it is interesting to note (*BA* 33) that Caesar left by the overland route and not by the sea, which may confirm that the Etesian winds had already returned and that the date was at least May 47 BC, and just before or more likely immediately after the birth of the Queen's child, probably his own.[74]

Chronology of events at Alexandria 48–47 BC

Mid–July 48	Pompey at Pelusium, Caesar at Ephesus, Mithridates assigned to raising an army
End of July	Caesar in Alexandria and admitted into the city
	Roman casualties due to rioting
	Caesar orders reinforcements
August 48	Arrival of Cleopatra
	Intrigue of Pothinus
	Arbitration of Caesar between Cleopatra and Ptolemy
	Ptolemy leaves the palace (Dio, 42.35.2) but returns against his will
	Sporadic attacks on the Roman positions and fights around the harbour
	Legation from Ptolemy to Achillas
	Arrival of Achillas with Ptolemaic army
	Ptolemaic army occupies greater part of the city
	Caesar focuses his defence on a section of the palace quarter, theatre and Great Harbour
	Fighting in the Great Harbour, Alexandrian fleet destroyed, Romans occupy Pharos
	Arsinoe and Ganymedes desert to Achillas
	Pothinus executed
	Caesar's own account breaks off (*BC* 3.112)

	Achillas murdered by Ganymedes and Arsinoe
	The water supplies to the Romans cut by Ganymedes
	Caesar involved in a sea fight following foraging probably near Canopus
September 48	Legio XXXVII arrives in Alexandria
	Fighting around the palace, harbour and Museion
	Caesar occupies the Pharos Island and fighting on the *Heptastadion*
	Alexandrians blockade Caesar's food supply
	Sea battle in which the Rhodian Euphranor is killed
	Ptolemy granted leave to rejoin his people
October 48	Stalemate in the city
November 48	Mithridates at Ascalon and troops received from Antipater
	Pelusium falls to the relief column and Memphis soon after
	Ptolemy goes to intercept the relief column
	Caesar sails west of the Nile Delta and marches back to the Nile at Memphis
	Caesar makes a successful assault on Ptolemy's camp
	Ptolemy and Ganymedes killed in battle on the Nile; Arsinoe captured
Winter 48/7	Caesar and Cleopatra sail up the Nile with four hundred ships (App. *BC* 2.90)
May 47	Birth of Caesarion
	Caesar departs Egypt after a nine-month stay (*BA* 33; App. *BC* 2.91) and probably after the Etesian winds had returned since he left overland to Syria
	Plutarch says that he left Egypt just before the birth of Caesarion (*Caes.* 49.5), but perhaps it is more likely that it was just afterwards.
45–41	Arsinoe imprisoned after Caesar's triumph in the temple of Artemis at Ephesus

Notable sieges in antiquity

538	Babylon captured by Cyrus the Great (Herodt. 1.191)
510	Sybaris (captured and destroyed)
510	Athenian Acropolis (defenders allowed to depart)
499	Sardis (lower city burned)
498	Amathus on Cyprus (relieved by Persian fleet)
498	Soli (walls undermined after four months of siege)

494–493	Miletus (surrendered and depopulated)
490	Eretria (surrendered and depopulated)
480	Athens (city and Acropolis destroyed)
465	Athenian siege of Thasos – Spartans were to invade Attica as diversionary tactic
465–455	Mt Ithome (negotiated truce and Messenians allowed to emigrate)
454	Athenian siege of the 'White Castle' at Memphis in Egypt – Persian relief column
442	Samos (captured and walls dismantled)
432–429	Potidaea (surrendered and depopulated)
427	Mytilene (capitulated and ringleaders executed)
429–427	Plataea (surrendered and destruction)
425	Spartans on Sphacteria surrender to the Athenians after a siege of seventy-two days (Thuc. 4.39)
422	Amphipolis (capitulated and population allowed to depart)
422	Eion (relieved by fleet commanded by Thucydides)
418–417	Melos (surrendered and all citizens executed)
414–413	Syracuse (April 414 to September 413) Athenian besieging force destroyed
409–8	Selinous and Himera captured and destroyed by Carthaginians
406–405	Akragas besieged and captured by the Carthaginians
404	Athens (April to September) capitulation and long walls dismantled
397	Motya (captured and destroyed)
396	Syracuse (Carthaginian besieging forces destroyed)
388-387	Rhegium captured by Dionysius of Syracuse after an eleven-month siege
386	Mantinea captured by Sparta and destroyed
381-379	Phlius captured by Spartans after twenty-month siege
356	Pydna and Potidaea captured by Philip II
353	Methone besieged and captured by Philip II
349-348	Siege of Olynthus, captured and destroyed by Philip II
340	Perinthus besieged by Philip II
340	Siege of Byzantium by Philip II
335	Thebes besieged captured and destroyed by Alexander
334	Miletus taken by Alexander
334	Halicarnassus besieged and captured by Alexander
332	Siege of Tyre (January–August) stormed by Macedonians led by Alexander

332	Siege and capture of Gaza (September–October) by Alexander
323–322	Siege and relief of Lamia
311–309	Syracuse (Carthaginian besieging forces destroyed)
305–304	The Rhodians withstand a fifteen-month siege by Demetrius son of Antigonus Monophthalmos.
214–212	Syracuse (captured and looted by Romans)
212–209	Tarentum besieged and captured by the Romans
211	Capua besieged and captured by the Romans
192	Pergamum (Syrian forces withdrew)
191	Phocaea (looted)
185	Pergamum (Bithynian forces withdrew)
146	Corinth (captured and destroyed)
149–146	Carthage (captured and destroyed)
134–133	Numantia captured and destroyed after an eight-month siege
87	Athens (captured and looted by Sulla)
	Pergamum (captured by Roman army under Fimbria)
75	Chaledon (besieging force withdrew)
	Cyzicus (besieging forces withdrawn by Mithridates VI of Pontus)
52	Alesia (Gallic revolt of Vercingetorix ended by Caesar)
49	Brundisium (Pompey besieged by Caesar and withdraws to Greece)
48	Dyracchium (Caesar blockaded by Pompey who withdraws)
47	Alexandria (relief column led by Mithridates of Pergamum)
AD 70	(mid-April to early September) Roman siege of Jerusalem, captured and sacked
73	Capture of Masada after a siege of six months
359	Amida (siege of seventy-three days) captured by Sassanid invaders

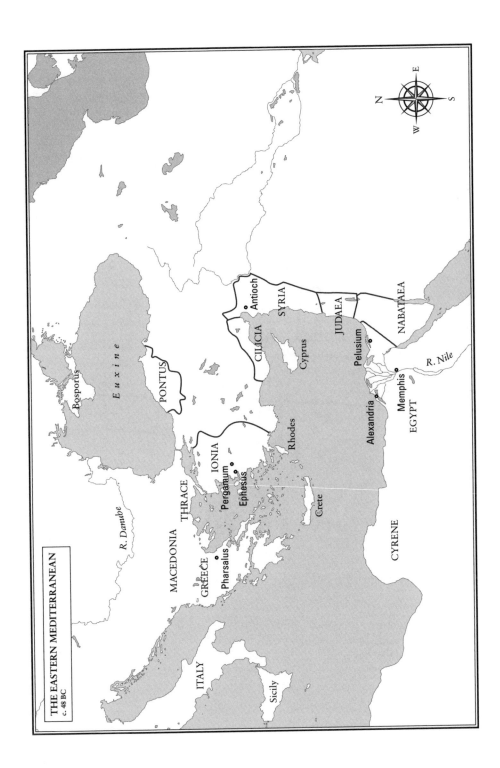

THE EASTERN MEDITERRANEAN
c. 48 BC

ITALY

Sicily

MACEDONIA

GREECE

THRACE

Pharsalus

IONIA

Pergamum

Ephesus

Bosporus

Euxine

R. Danube

PONTUS

CILICIA

Rhodes

Crete

Cyprus

Antioch

SYRIA

JUDAEA

Pelusium

NABATAEA

R. Nile

Alexandria

Memphis

EGYPT

CYRENE

N
E
S
W

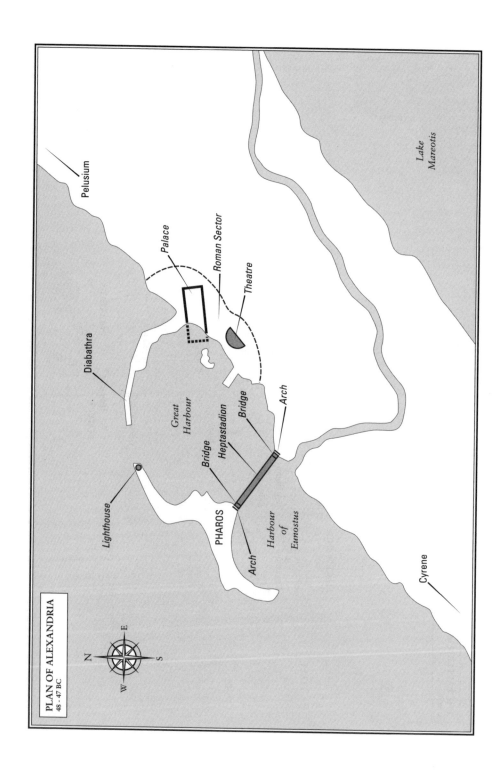

PLAN OF ALEXANDRIA
48 - 47 BC

Pelusium

Palace

Roman Sector

Theatre

Diabathra

Great
Harbour

Bridge

Heptastadion

Bridge

Arch

Lighthouse

PHAROS

Arch

Harbour
of
Eunostus

Lake
Mareotis

Cyrene

N
E
S
W

MITHRIDATES' ROUTE TO MEMPHIS
AND RELIEF OF ALEXANDRIA

N
W   E
S

Bosporus

Pontus

PONTUS

Pergamum
Ephesus   GALATIA

CILICIA   SYRIA

Rhodes

Cyprus

JUDAEA

Pelusium

Alexandria

CYRENE

Memphis

EGYPT   NABATAEA

R. Nile

*Red
Sea*

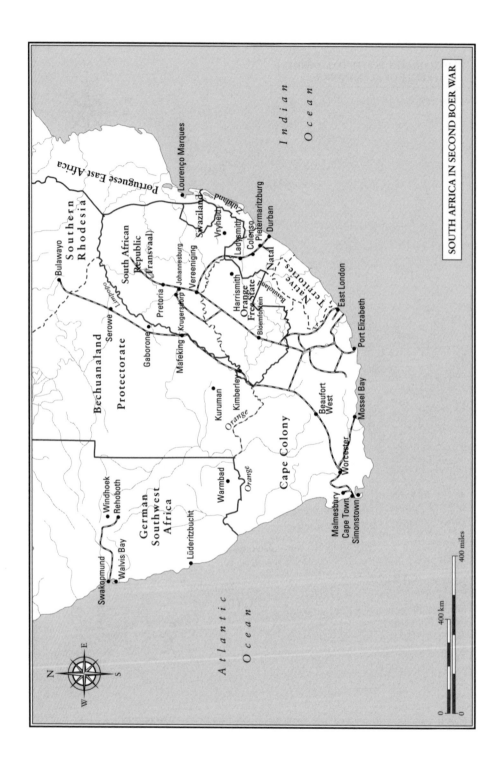

SOUTH AFRICA IN SECOND BOER WAR

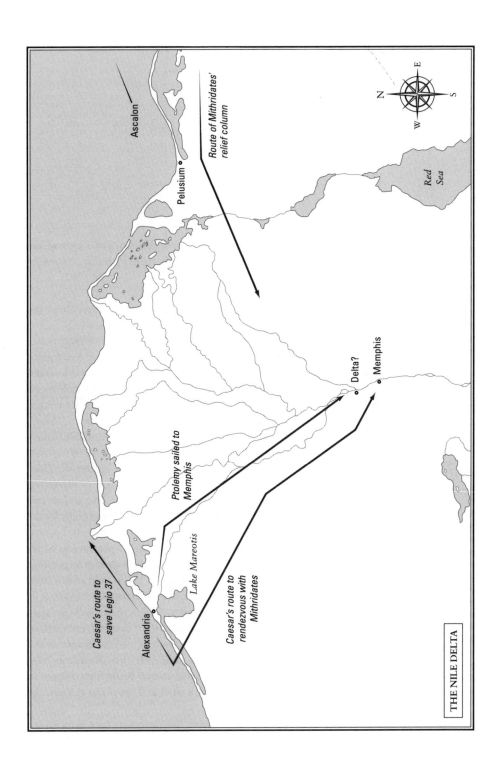

Ascalon

Route of Mithridates'
relief column

Red
Sea

N
E
W
S

Pelusium

Memphis

Delta?

Ptolemy sailed to
Memphis

Lake Mareotis

Caesar's route to
save Legio 37

Alexandria

Caesar's route to
rendezvous with
Mithridates

THE NILE DELTA

Notes

Chapter 1

1. H.V. Morton, *A Traveller in Southern Italy* (London 1969) 317–318. For a view of the area from the opposite direction, the Sila Massif to the south, see O.H. Bullitt, *Search for Sybaris* (London 1971) 2–3.
2. Morton, 1969, 394–395. Morton here refers to Athenaeus Book 12.
3. Elsewhere, 9.24, Aelian relates without any criticism the accepted tradition about the luxurious habits of the Sybarites.
4. From Heracleia (Siris) to Metapontum is just nineteen kilometres (12 miles) hence probably the reason for its relatively brief existence as an independent community because it was situated too close to a more powerful neighbour. Metapontum was founded within twenty or so years of Sybaris and these two sites have many striking resemblances: low-lying and inclined to flooding, wealth supposedly based on agriculture yet neither has yielded the physical remains of other Greek cities in Magna Graecia and Sicily. Metapontum, meaning the 'place beside the sea', had a much longer identifiable history but was a place of little importance by the first century BC.
5. The *Iliad* is an episode from the Trojan War involving the death of Hector the chief Trojan warrior. The *Odyssey* is about the homecoming of Odysseus, one of the Greek heroes, and the tribulations he endured before he reaches his home in Ithaca. Just two tales survive but it is clear that there many other such stories were circulated orally by the poets of this period.
6. We are much better informed about the dating of the earliest Greek presence in Sicily than in Italy because Thucydides, 6.1–6, in his coverage of the Athenian expedition (415–413 BC) against Syracuse in the Peloponnesian War begins his account with a brief excursus about the island's history, which he obtained from the history of Antiochus of Syracuse. Antiochus was probably an older contemporary of Thucydides and the latter must have employed this history as a source for Sicilian affairs, for example, information about the Lipari Islands, 3.88, eruptions of Etna, 3.116, and the earliest history of the Greeks in Sicily, 6.1–5. Strabo, 6.1.4, 6.1.6, refers to the same Antiochus when describing the cities of Magna Graecia and hence accessed the same source. Sadly Strabo is not as specific about the foundation dates of the Italian Greek cities as Thucydides is about the cities of the Sicilian Greeks.
7. Achaeans are noted as the founders in the eight century, but there were tales of an earlier settlement most likely of a legendary nature. The LCL edition (1934) 46 has the name 'Is of Helice' but also notes the problem with this assumption. Helice was destroyed by a tsunami in 373/2 BC.

8. Athenaeus, 12,519 b–c, states that the city possessed 5000 cavalry who paraded in saffron-coloured cloaks over their breast plates.

9. The towns would include its own harbours on both the Ionian and Tyrrhenian Seas such as Posidonia, Scidros and Laos while the states are likely to be those of local Italian tribes such as the Bruttii.

10. He states that Sybaris was inhabited for 210 years. Aristotle, *Politics*, 5.3, relates that the city had originally been settled by the Trojans after the end of the Trojan War and that the Achaeans were later arrivals.

11. Rhegium, dated to about 740, was slightly earlier while Pithecusae on an island opposite Cumae at the entrance to the Bay of Naples is considered the first dating to roughly 750 BC.

12. For more discussion of the cities in Sicily see further in Chapter 2.

13. We have no idea when Herodotus' evidence in Books 5 and 6 were composed but if in the 430s or 420s then conceivably when he was a resident in Thurii.

14. References to the ancient sources are to be found in the Bibliography. The translations are my own as are any errors.

15. On the links between these two *poleis* see H. Van Wees, *Greek Warfare: Myths and Realities*, London 2004, 6 and n.1. Herodotus perhaps considers the lack of reaction by those who had escaped from Sybaris bad form or a discourtesy to former allies, but there are evident sub-layers in the text.

16. Some Milesians fled west to Zancle and then the northern coast of Sicily says Herodotus, 6.22.

17. For example, Gelon of Syracuse and Theron of Akragas were allies and related by marriage in the second decade of the fifth century BC. Note also the connection between Periander of Corinth and Thrasybulus of Megara in the preceding century.

18. Cleomenes was the son of the second wife of the king, Dorieus the eldest son of his first wife. Anaxandrides had two wives, simultaneously an unusual pratice among the Spartans.

19. Later Greeks certainly found employment as mercenaries, some like Agesilaus (395–360) of Sparta in Egypt, others in southern Italy including his son Archidamus III (360–338) who died fighting for the Tarentines at Manduria.

20. Herodotus suggests that he raced himself, although tyrants such as Anaxilas of Rhegium, Gelon of Syracuse, winners of equestrian events in the 480s, employed professional drivers or riders, as indeed did Philip II of Macedon whose jockey won the equestrian event at Olympia in 356 at precisely the same time as the birth of his son Alexander.

21. Megacles, a cousin of Pericles, see family tree, p. 78.

22. Megacles archon in 631 put an end to the attempted coup of Cylon who aspired to become tyrant of Athens but he also ordered the murder of Cylon's supporters who were then suppliants in the temple of Athena Polias on the Acropolis, a crime which incurred exile.

23. Compare this statement with that of Athenaeus, 4.138d, which is probably also drawn from Timaeus, although he is not cited here.

24. The Sybarites were similarly attracted to the Etruscans for the same reasons says Diodorus, perhaps an explanation in ancient accounts for the activity of Sybaris in setting up satellite communities on the west coast of Italy around the Gulf of Policastro.

25. Pearson (1987) 34–35.

26. For Philistus see Pearson (1987) 19–36.

27. For Antiochus of Syracuse see the discussion of Pearson (1987) 11–18, and that Diodorus probably referenced this historian via Timaeus rather than firsthand, although note Diod. 12.71.2. Antiochus is noted by Dionysius of Halicarnassus (1.12.3) and Strabo (6.1.7).

28. For a detailed study see Pearson (1987) *passim*.
29. He was already born when Timoleon landed at Tauromenium, a guest of Timaeus' father Andromachus, in 345 on his way to Syracuse. Agathocles ruled at Syracuse from 316 to 289. Timaeus spent about fifty years in exile dying perhaps as late as 250 and his history covered Sicilian affairs down to 264, Polyb. 1.5.1; Pearson (1987) 37.
30. The account of the fall of Hippias at Athens does not survive in Diodorus, although it was probably covered in Book 10. It is interesting to note that, probably drawn from Timaeus, there was clearly an extended discussion of the Samian philosopher Pythagoras at the start of this book. Pythagoras was resident in Croton from about 530. It is of some relevance here since the philosopher obviously played a major role in the end of Sybaris and this connection may also have been linked in some way with the events at Athens and Rome. There must also have been some attention devoted to Croton, 10.11.1. On Croton's later decline into luxury see Aristotle, Fragment, 583 Rose, a theme which was also dwelt upon by Timaeus (see below note 49).
31. Note the frequency of settlement building on land situated between two rivers: Selinous between the Modione (Selinous) and Cotone rivers, de Angelis (2003) 129, Evans (2009) 55, Pergamum on the mountainous spur between the Selinous and Citius rivers, Evans (2011) 121, and Metapontum between the Basento (Casuentus) and Bradanus rivers.
32. The Greeks of Magna Graecia and Sicily were generally quicker to grant citizenship of their *poleis* than those of mainland Greece probably because faced with frequent wars there was a constant shortage of manpower to maintain their territories and cities. Large numbers are given for immigrants at various times but the population was clearly never on a par with Greece. The Greeks in Magna Graecia were also outnumbered by the local Italian tribes.
33. The question of size and hence importance will feature again. Here it is worth noting that Syracuse had circuit walls extending for 180 stadia, 33.2 kilometres or 20.6 miles, while the Aurelian Walls at Rome extended for 12 miles or a mere 19 kilometres. Rome in the third century AD had a population of over a million inhabitants, Syracuse approximately 200,000 in the third century BC. Bullitt (1969) 200, argued that the size of Sybaris was perhaps larger than Athens at the end of the sixth century. However, Athens in 510 was a much smaller community than it was by the middle of the fifth century by which time it possessed an empire.
34. Neither of the numbers for the sizes of the opposing armies is credible simply because of the populations available on which to levy armed forces and the land on which these huge numbers supposedly lived.
35. Winner at Olympia on no fewer than six occasions in the wrestling competition, down to about 520, Milo by about 510 was no longer a young athlete. Diodorus claims that he fought resplendent in his laurel crowns and in Herculean dress. Such an insertion into the narrative illustrates how quickly Milo's life and successes became celebrated and entered the realm of mythology, later again becoming a regular subject for artistic and sculptural interpretation.
36. Athenaeus used Timaeus exclusively for his material on Sybaris as is evident from the number of times (1.34c, 12.518d, 518f, 519b, 522a, 522c, 523c, 541c) that historian is cited in connection with the topic of Sybarite luxury. However, mention of Heracleides should alert us to an even earlier possible source since as a student of Plato he was active about the same time as Ephorus in the fourth century BC.

37. See Philostratus, *Life of* Apollonius, 10, for mention of a statue of Hercules at Ephesus that was able to avert its gaze, although this was a mechanical device not the work of the deity.

38. Timaeus, *FGrH.* 1.212, claimed that the Crotoniates themselves also fell into luxurious ways as a result of their great victory, and even tried to steal the Olympic Games from Olympia, a charge also levelled against the Sybarites.

39. Charondas is usually assigned to the late seventh or early sixth century BC, and was a resident in the Sicilian city of Catane for which city he is credited as a lawgiver, *OCD*² 228.

40. Polyzelus, recognizing the ruse, fled to Akragas instead. Scholars such as P.J. Rhodes, (2006) 9, consider that this was actually an attempt by Sybarite survivors to re-establish their city, although that does not explain the problem of the flood.

41. The Timaeus reference is *FGrH.* 566 F 93. B. ap. Schol. Pindar, *Ol.* 2.15 (29); Pearson (1987) 131–132.

42. Note that Pearson (1987) 132 considers this derived from Ephorus, although it may simply be poor copying from Timaeus.

43. Diodorus claims that the Spartans were deterred from giving actual help because of the strength of Croton at that time, which probably does point to the period about the defeat of Sybaris in 510. Unfortunately, the information is again preserved as a fragment without the full context.

44. It is probably worth noting that Thuriii did not contain a particularly large population since when requested the citizens were able to muster seven hundred hoplites and three hundred peltasts for the Athenian expedition against Syracuse in 413 BC, Thuc. 7.35. Sybaris' military capability at the end of the sixth century is therefore most probably exaggerated a great deal. The Roman colony may have had a long history but it was never a major urban centre in this part of Italy.

45. The Romans frequently renamed urban settlements, but the Greeks on occasion also renamed cities, for example, Zancle became Messene in about 490 and Catane Etna in the 470s. Himera became Punic Therma and the Romans retained both names.

46. Motya, see Chapter 3, is an interesting exception and almost parallels Sybaris.

47. For a detailed account see Bullitt (1971) *passim.*

48. Thurii had deserted to Hannibal and the Carthaginians in the aftermath of the Roman defeat at Cannae in 216 BC, but it was soon retaken and the Romans then established a colony there in 194. Unlike many of its neighbours in the region such as Metapontum it is still mentioned at the end of the first century BC, Caesar, *Civil Wars,* 3.22.

49. This work is no longer extant but may well have drawn on Timaeus as a source. For Alciphron see *OCD*² 38.

50. The story is the same as that told by Diodorus and the source undoubtedly Timaeus.

51. Athenaeus says that he read and used Herodotus but his primary source was Timaeus, although there is also a reference to Aristotle's *Wonders.*

52. Timaeus died about 250. Phylarchus probably lived down to about 215. The latter may have covered some aspects of Sybarite history in his work – Athenaeus mentions Book 25 of Phylarchus' history – or employed Sybaris as an exemplum against which to measure undue addiction to luxury. Polybius, 2.56, did not set much store by Phylarchus considering his history unreliable, although the critic was not above partiality himself.

53. For further details see Appendix II to this chapter.

54. The tale was not unique says Athenaeus who gives Aristotle as his source, Fragment 583 Rose. The Loeb edition, 344 note (a), also refers to Julius Africanus, *Cest.* 293, who provides the story of the deserter.
55. Archilochus of Paros is dated to the seventh century BC, and is one of the earliest of the Greek poets. Xenophanes a native of Colophon is dated somewhat later to the sixth century BC.
56. Pythagoras became a resident of Metapontum and probably died there perhaps about 495 BC.
57. Megara in Greece and Megara Hyblaia in Sicily have been identified as the city of Theognis' birth. Plato states the latter but this is assumed to be an error, although the philosopher knew that part of Sicily well. On the other hand, three references to events in Asia Minor might just suggest someone writing in close geographical proximity. The identification of Magnesia poses a similar problem since it could be either Magnesia ad Sipylum or Magnesia ad Meandrum, although both were in Asia Minor and neighbours. Another source for the destruction of Magnesia is Archilochus (fr. 20 West), which has led to a dating of ca. 650. For a discussion of the possible dates and the date for the calamities at Colophon and Smyrna being about 600 see Lane Fox (2000) 37–40. Herodotus, 1.16, mentions that Gyges captured Colophon, while Smyrna fell to Alyattes his great grandson. This same king was defeated somewhere in the Meander Valley perhaps following his plundering of the Magnesia situated there. All these events are considered to have occurred before the reign of Croesus (560–547 BC). Theognis of Megara, dated the sixth century BC, was a contemporary of Xenophanes.
58. Theopompus, *FgrH* 115 F 117, relates that because of their agoge the citizens of Colophon caused the rise of tyrants and then a civil war which destroyed them. The city did not disappear, however.
59. The message must be that a when people became too attached to the good life this usually ends in disaster but not necessarily one which ended forever the life of that city. Syracuse was also famous for its luxury, Ath. 12.527c, but bucked the trend and generally avoided disaster in its long history.
60. Some later resettlement occurred but not on the same scale and the site was abandoned during Antiquity.
61. The work is dated to about 360 a full decade after the loss of Helice. Ephorus may have known the dialogue but Timaeus certainly will have.
62. It is of course highly unlikely that the Crotoniates would have destroyed by water any of the temples or their precincts at Sybaris since that was also sacrilege and according to the evidence they duly observed accepted practice with regard to suppliants. In the numerous sackings recorded of Greek cities temples were usually spared out of reverence for their deities. For further discussion of the phenomenon see Chapters 2 and 3.
63. For a plan of Sybaris in Antiquity see also Bullitt (1971) 195. It is worth noting also how a river (the Euphrates), in a different way, allowed Cyrus the Median king to take Babylon, by damming the river which flowed through the city and then marching his army in along the dried up river bed, Herodotus, 1.191.
64. For an assessment of Polybius' evidence see F.W. Walbank, 'Hellenes and Achaians: "Greek Nationality" Revisited', in *Further Studies in the Ancient Greek Polis*, ed. P. Flensted-Jensen (Stuttgart 2000) 24.

65. Long, G. & R. Dinglison, *An introduction to the study of Grecian and Roman geography*, New York 1829, 196: 'The Traeis river flows into the *Sinus Tarentinus* to the east of Roscianum; it is now called Triunti.'

66. On this question see T. Jackman, 'Ducetius and fifth-century Sicilian tyranny', in *Ancient Tyranny*, ed. S. Lewis (Edinburgh 2006) 45.

67. There was a tradition, however, that Pythagoras died at Metapontum, Cic. *Fin.* 5.20, and had found refuge there when he and his followers were eventually expelled from Croton.

68. Some indeed, for example, Gelon and even Dionysius I are considered almost paragons of abstemiousness.

69. By and large, most of these commodities traded east from Greece to Magna Graecia rather than the other way around. It is possible of course that some went overland from Sybaris to the Gulf of Policastro, but again the logistics are simply untenable in either direction.

70. Etruria known for its timber especially around Pisa and some precious metals but not in abundance, and later on for its livestock farming again not producing products except for a more localized market. It does seem that the harbours at Posidonia, Scidros, and Laos were stopping places rather than entrepôts.

71. For details about the battle of the Crocus Field and the response of Philip to the sacrilege of the Phocians see Diodorus, 16.35.6.

72. In the light of recent discussions about the chronology of the earliest coins in Ancient Greece, for example by Kim (2001) 9–11, the coinage ascribed to the sixth century and before the 'end' of Sybaris probably needs to be re-dated to the early fifth century instead. If that were so then the coins of Sybaris now dated to 510 and before but which have an unmistakeable Classical appearance would confirm a continuation of settlement at Sybaris.

73. Bosworth (2002) 66–67, cites Diodorus and Arrian.

74. See Bosworth (2002) 96.

75. For a critical assessment of the numbers recorded by Livy, 37.37, drawn from Polybius, see Grainger (2002) 320–323.

76. For Cynoscephalae and Pydna see Sekunda (1989) 132–133.

Chapter 2

1. The First Peloponnesian War took place between 457 and 446/5 BC.

2. The division of the history into eight books was not an intentional decision of Thucydides but that of anonymous grammarians at the Museion (Library) at Alexandria many years after its completion and has nothing to do with the compositional framework of the history, rather a simplification of the material into more easily digestible segments.

3. Thucydides revised much of his work inserting speeches into an earlier version, but he evidently finished revising only towards the end of Book 7. Book 8 was clearly not revised before his death, which occurred probably around 400 BC. On the unfinished nature of Book 8 see, for example, Finley (1972) 26, and Warner (1954) 617–620.

4. Thucydides says that the Liparaeans originally came from Cnidos in Caria, Asia Minor, which would have made them ethnically Dorian like the citizens of Halicarnassus. The Ionians of Miletus, Ephesus and the other cities of the Ionian League lived a little further to the north along the coast of Asia Minor. Thucydides gives a brief description of the islands (Lipari, Stromboli and Vulcano), and notes that the absence of water made an

attack on the Liparaeans difficult in the summer months. Therefore this attack can be dated to October or November 427 in conjunction with autumnal wet weather. It is very unlikely that Thucydides ever set foot in Sicily or in southern Italy and here he almost certainly employed the history of the region by Antiochus of Syracuse. Antiochus is not mentioned by name, but since Thucydides presents essentially the same information as that provided by the first century AD geographer Strabo who does name this historian as his source this conjecture may be advanced with confidence, and is generally accepted. It is probably the first instance of a historian using the research of another in his composition.

5. Indeed siege engines accompanying invading armies is a phenomenon that only became common in the fourth century and afterwards.

6. These mercenaries, probably in part Campanians, had originally been settled in Catane, which Hieron chose as his personal residence in preference to Syracuse in the last years of his rule. After he died the mercenaries were expelled and retired instead to Inessa/Etna.

7. If Himera fell into Athenian hands this would mean that the coast from Messene to Himera would be under their control. To the west of Himera lay the Phoenician trading posts of Solunte, Panormus and Motya and the Elymian and Sicanian communities inland.

8. Thucydides says that the representatives of the Athenian allies sailed from Sicily, which means that they probably went via Messene or Rhegium since the Syracusans still held most of the coastal cities in eastern Sicily. The Athenians probably also provided the transport since reports about the expedition would have been regularly required by the *demos* and the various officials who oversaw the financing of such expeditions. The Athenian system was highly complex and bureaucratic with numerous checks and balances to prevent misconduct.

9. Thucydides does not say when this occurred, but had noted its surrender to the Athenians in the previous year, 3.90. The Messenians had perhaps reneged on their treaty during the winter. It is worth noting that Thucydides at 3.90 explicitly states that he will give only those Sicilian affairs that had an impact on the wider conflict.

10. Thucydides briefly digresses to give some information about the Straits, its mythical connection with the Charybdis of Homer's *Odyssey*, and the unpredictable nature of the currents that flow through this channel, 4.24.

11. Messene (modern Messina) was originally named Zankle or Dankl, which means scythe or sickle in the language of the Sicels and refers to the shape of the harbour, a shape it retains to this day.

12. Thucydides does not pretend that his speeches were actual accounts of what had happened but were rather compositions that he almost certainly added during his editing of the text and which were meant to enhance the message with content appropriate for the occasion. See the comments of Thucydides, 1.22; Finley (1972) 25–29.

13. Hermocrates was killed in 408 in the agora in Syracuse. By that time he had become the father-in-law of Dionysius, son of a Hermocrates (another citizen of the same name) one of his chief supporters, who became tyrant in Syracuse in 405.

14. Thucydides had written about the Athenian decision to send a larger fleet with Sophocles and Eurymedon as commanders earlier but had not related either its arrival or participation in the hostilities. It is possible that the reinforcements only arrived in Rhegium when the peace talks had already started. Moreover the position of the Italian cities is also neglected and nothing is said of the participation of Rhegium and Locri,

which had played prominent parts in the war and which must surely have also became signatories to the peace agreement.

15. For a more detailed discussion of Punic involvement in Sicily see Chapter 3.

16. Thucydides, 6.2, says that the Elymians were descended from survivors who had escaped the disaster at Troy. The Trojan connection is an early and important one and is exploited by many cities including Rome. This story very probably came from Antiochus' history. In fact, the entire introduction to Thucydides Book 6 is likely to have been taken from this local account almost word for word.

17. The tale of Segestaean subterfuge became famous. The leading families, none of whom was especially wealthy, were to entertain the Athenians. These envoys ate off silver plates and drank from silver cups but these apparent indicators of conspicuous consumption were actually the sum total of all the silver in the community and were handed round to each host in time to receive his guests. The Athenians went on their way none the wiser. How the Segestaeans hoped to keep their ruse secret for long is not disclosed. Their failure to pay more than two instalments for their 'aid' was nonetheless forgotten as the greater drama unfolded outside Syracuse.

18. This single reference in Thucydides is almost the only one we possess of the problem of financing fighting in the ancient world and the price associated with waging a campaign. Sixty talents was a huge sum – about 10 per cent of Athens' annual revenue from its empire in the 430s – which illustrates not only how expensive it was to wage war but also how it was becoming professionalized even by the end of the fifth century BC. It was no longer the case that citizens of one city state took up their arms to fight those citizens of another for some weeks or months during the summer. Segesta and Selinous had been belligerents for some time and neither could now afford to fight on without the help of more powerful and wealthy allies. Yet the Athenians, as wealthy as they were, still scrutinized any financial drain to their revenues and were prepared to balance this factor against any possible territorial gain or plunder to be made from the venture.

19. This peace officially lasted from 421 to 413 when the Spartans once again invaded Attica. It did not, however, prevent each side from fighting one another by proxy through interference in the military affairs of their allies who were not held to the agreement.

20. Nicias, along with Cleon who had been killed in 422, became one of the most prominent public figures after the death of Pericles in 429. Alcibiades was the son of Cleinias and Deinomache, who was a first-cousin of Pericles. Alcibiades was brought up in the household of Pericles and had studied with Socrates. For a family tree of the family see the end of Chapter 2.

21. It should be remembered that Thucydides was not present since he was then in exile. Alcibiades was in his early thirties, born about 450, while Nicias was about twenty years his senior. Lamachus was probably the oldest of the three generals.

22. Alcibiades had a reputation for extravagance and a riotous lifestyle, which Thucydides has Nicias comment on in his speech, and which forms a large part of Plutarch's *Life*, which is more concerned about the character of his subject than the events of the time.

23. As much as his connection with Pericles helped his career, people would also have remembered that he was a descendant of Cleisthenes, tyrant of Sicyon. Moreover his financing of seven chariots in the Olympic Games for which he was proud, Thuc. 6.16, also had tyrannical associations and was comparable with the rulers of Syracuse, Gelon

and Hieron, and Rhegium, Anaxilas. There would have been many who saw this as a manifestation of an ambition towards sole rule at Athens.

24. This did indeed happen mostly with the ethnic Ionian cities of Catane, Leontinoi and Rhegium, see further below, while the treaty with Elymian Segesta seems to have been maintained.

25. It later became evident that Nicias, besides his other failings, was not in the best of health and this merely added to his lack of incisive action.

26. The trireme had become almost the only type of ship to be constructed by this time. With its three banks of oarsmen it proved a fast and efficient fighting ship, but as the trireme aged within a decade and settled lower in the water the uppermost bank of oars was discarded and the space could be used to transport heavy armoured infantry as here in 415. Later still in the age of the ship the second bank of oars could be removed and the available space then used to transport horses and other goods. Pentekonters and biremes were still built but were no match for the trireme in battle.

27. Thucydides was not in Athens at the time but he may well have remembered the departures of earlier commands such as that of Pericles to Epidaurus, Thuc. 6.31, Meiggs (1972) 97–98. Thucydides also shows his interest in and an acute appreciation of the financial underpinning of such venture by exploring the minutiae of the maintenance of each trireme and its crew, and that these costs were borne by the individual trierarchs.

28. The Athenians had previously sent an expedition amounting to 200 ships to Cyprus in 460/59, Meiggs (1972) 93, which then proceeded to Egypt, Meiggs (1972) 101–104. This force had been defeated and mostly destroyed by the Persians in 454 near Memphis, but the troops had been largely those contributed by the Delian League allies rather than Athenian citizens, Thuc. 1.109–110. The Persian invasion of Greece might at first sight seem a long distance campaign, but in fact the Persian Empire possessed satrapies along the Hellespont from the close of the sixth century. In fact Darius I had crossed into Thrace nearly twenty years before the battle of Marathon in 490, campaigned as far as the Danube and left a Persian satrap to govern this region. The Persians did not have far to sail or to march when they invaded Greece. For further discussion of Marathon and the Persian invasion see Volume 2 in this series.

29. Not related by Thucydides but in Plutarch's *Life of Nicias*, 30.1, which the biographer must have obtained from an earlier source.

30. A strange recommendation and a possible example of a slip by the historian since it becomes clear from later in Thucydides' own account that the Syracusans at that stage had little in the way of a serviceable fleet of triremes.

31. Again Thucydides is presenting an argument he considers likely to have been advanced at the time. However, the Athenians were able to transport a large force of hoplites but their cavalry arm was consistently weak, which in the end was a telling factor in the defeat.

32. Each trireme had 170 rowers, one to each oar in three tiers, and thirty marines who were, in effect, hoplites. Some of the rowers would have been slaves, others metics or allies. The pentekonters were fifty single-oared galleys hence a crew of fifty each. Thucydides says (6.43) that Athenian citizens of the lowest financial class, the thetes, served as the marines in the warships, and that there were 1500 Athenian hoplites, the remainder allies.

33. These vessels contained the usual camp followers but certainly also slave traders and those prepared to buy plunder from any successful military engagement.

34. Nicias may well have visited Segesta at some point and of the three generals he alone appears to have had some real knowledge of the island and its people. Nicias, although a

prominent public figure, had business interests that may have drawn him west earlier in his life. He would at least have known merchants who traded there on his behalf.

35. The Terias River was the closest the expedition came to Leontinoi on this occasion. Note that little attempt was made now or later on to have stronger ties with Segesta.

36. Thucydides, 6.50–51, suggests that Alcibiades alone had commanded this fleet but that the other two *strategoi* were with him at Catane.

37. Thucydides, 6.54–59, has a lengthy digression on the tyranny of Hippias, which became much more autocratic after the murder of his brother Hipparchus by Harmodius and Aristogeiton in 514.

38. The Athenians were afraid that Alcibiades would use Spartan aid to make himself tyrant and a force of Spartans was known to be operating in Boeotia close to the frontier with Attica. Thucydides, 6.61, is convinced that this had no connection with Alcibiades but that it added to the tense atmosphere in Athens.

39. It is possible that he was able to elude his captors because of sympathizers at Thurii. In the summer of 413 the Thurians felt obliged to send material aid to the Athenian expedition perhaps to allay suspicions about their attitude towards the Athenian war effort.

40. It seems at least possible that there is a mistake in the text of Thucydides here, 6.62. Hyccara was a small town and so it could hardly have contained a sufficient population to raise such a huge sum.

41. It seems likely that Gela and Camarina closed their gates while the Athenians were active in the vicinity.

42. For further topographical details about this site see Evans (2009) 32–38.

43. This may well indicate that Alcibiades remained in the area for some time before he actually crossed to the Peloponnese perhaps in the spring of 414.

44. This is a puzzling piece of information and another instance of Thucydides' lack of real knowledge of the topography. Either the historian means a wall facing west towards Mount Climiti, which ran the length of Epipolai, or 'The HighGround', the escarpment that rises gradually northwards from Akradina up to the Scala Greca where there is a steep decline into the plain of Megara, or a wall from Neapolis across to the sea just above Akradina. There is no archaeological evidence for either supposition.

45. Sparta did, however, restart the war against Athens in the following spring and on the advice of Alcibiades permanently occupied the fort at Decelea in northern Attica and so disrupted the main route for supplies from the Black Sea via the harbour at Oropus on the Euboic Channel. This move intensified the struggle and made the situation more difficult for the Athenians who could no longer cultivate land in Attica and had to rely on grain being transported around Cape Sounion. The Spartans would probably not have pursued this course if Syracuse had fallen quickly. By the spring of 413 the outcome of the siege already seemed to favour the besieged.

46. The number of Spartiates or full Spartan citizens had declined during the fifth century and as the numbers dwindled due to losses in war and low birth rates, since they refused to admit new citizens, they became reluctant to place themselves in a position of great risk. The capture of 120 Spartiates at Sphacteria had illustrated their vulnerability. The decision to send even a single Spartiate was a triumph for the Syracusans not a rebuttal of their request for aid.

47. A huge sum surely not only for buying horses but any other necessary supplies.

48. Scala Greca or 'Greek Stairs' is the steep hill by which one now ascends the escarpment on top of which the land levels off into a south facing plateau that gently slopes down

to Akradina and ultimately the acropolis of the city which is on the island of Ortygia. Ortygia was joined to Akradina by a manmade mole. The city's two harbours, the lesser and the greater, lay either side of this causeway.

49. Thucydides is not very clear about this point nor probably was his source.

50. Today the main road from the west into Syracuse skirts the steep-sided plateau of Epipolai. The Athenian wall lay somewhere between the modern cemetery and the tennis club.

51. Thucydides does not say where the wood came from, but it seems that this area, although marshy, contained a fair number of farms and other buildings to be ransacked for this purpose by the Athenian soldiers.

52. Nicias had been laid up with an illness, which was the reason why he took no part n the attack on the second Syracusan counter wall. This illness was to dog his remaining time as general of this expedition and contributed in part to the hesitant leadership that can very clearly be discerned. The construction of the double wall to accommodate the Athenian expedition force is of course a direct copy of the long walls of Athens that joined that city with the Piraeus and within which for most of the war with Sparta the population of Attica lived safe from attack behind its walls.

53. Thucydides, 7.2, claims that Gylippus had captured a Sicel fortress named Ietas while on the march, but this site lies towards Segesta. It is possible that the Spartan wanted to intimidate Segesta by his actions, although it is more likely that the historian was unsure where Ietas was and was unable to check. Ietas is in a mountainous location near modern Alcamo on the north coast and would not have been an easy fort to capture without significant forces and a lengthy campaign.

54. Quite why these essential supplies could not be brought across the harbour from the main Athenian camp, which was barely more than two kilometres away, is not stated. While Plemmyrion remains a dry peninsula of limestone rock, rainfall is not infrequent and could easily have been collected and alleviated the problem. Wood for fuel was a constant worry for any army on the march and local supplies for a large force such as the Athenians would have exhausted local supplies, but the Syracusans faced the same problem.

55. The left wing of the Athenian army was probably composed of allied troops. The Athenian cavalry would have occupied the right and the Athenian citizen hoplites the centre.

56. By the time Thucydides wrote his history speeches had become an integral part of the genre but the creation of a speech within a letter was almost certainly an innovation.

57. It was unusual to send expeditions in the winter months. Thucydides expressly says it is about the time of the solstice, and certainly underlines the gravity of the situation and the extent to which the Athenians had committed themselves to this venture.

58. At the same time the Spartans invaded Attica and made a permanent camp at Decelea about twenty kilometres (14 miles) from Athens. A very noticeable escalation in hostilities throughout the Greek World had occurred.

59. Naupactus had been populated with Messenian helots ever since the siege of Mount Ithome, which had lasted for a decade and ended in 455/4. The free Messenians were allies of Athens and thus effectively blocked the Gulf of Corinth to shipping friendly to Sparta.

60. Thucydides, 7.23, says that the Syracusans lost eleven ships and their crews except for three whose crews were made prisoner, no mention however of whether the ships were sunk or captured, presumably the latter. This would suggest a total loss or fourteen warships out of eighty launched.

61. This report shows that the Athenians still had warships in the open sea and that although entry to the Great Harbour was difficult it was not impossible at this stage.
62. Thucydides, 7.33, notes that the troops from the Greek mainland suffered heavy casualties, amounting to 800 soldiers, in their march to Syracuse having perhaps made land at Selinous or Himera and being forced to cross the interior.
63. The Trojan War was of course a war/siege between Greeks and non-Greeks, although they appear in the text ethnically identical. Thucydides' enumeration of the cities and forces which were allies of the Athenians or the Syracusans, 7.57–59, is clearly drawn from Homer's naming of the Greek forces and their Trojan opponents in Book 2 of the *Iliad*. Akragas was the sole city in Sicily to remain out of the conflict as a neutral state, Thuc. 7.33.
64. It is worth noting that no attempt was made to intercept Demosthenes and Eurymedon on their way down from Rhegium, which suggests that the Athenians still had a squadron of twenty or so warships stationed near Megara Hyblaia.
65. This is actually a half circle manoeuvre since the object was to move either to the right or left of the opponent turn and ram amidships and not the stern of the enemy vessel. The opponent similarly manoeuvred hence the need for space and dexterity by the crews and pilots.
66. For a discussion of the size of this area and the improbable dimensions given by Thucydides see Evans (2009) 146–147.
67. Thucydides, 7.42, states that there were seventy-three triremes, roughly an additional 5000 hoplites, with a large number of lightly armed troops, some no doubt rowers from the ships.
68. The decision to attack appears to have been unanimous, however there is the suspicion that Nicias did not agree with the others and either because of his illness or lack of enthusiasm remained behind.
69. One wonders how much in this area was left to ransack since the Athenian forces had been stationed here about a year already. It looks as if Thucydides is filling in his narrative and what he really means is that the new troops were put through their paces.
70. Thucydides also claims that the Athenians took the same route to Eurialos as they had done in the previous spring but this is plainly inaccurate and what he means is the same direction but along the southern edge of Epipolai not the northern edge.
71. Thucydides says that these 600 were the same ones who had been assigned garrison duty during the first Athenian attack in the previous spring, but this is a slip if the writer had been correct in claiming that half of them had perished with their commander the mercenary Diomilos, Thuc. 6.97–98.
72. The paean was a chant or song that usually accompanied any triumph. Thucydides, 7.44, points out that Argive, Corcyraean and Dorian troops were all singing their chants, which added to the din.
73. There is no need, as some have done, to speculate about the nature of a specific epidemic for the sickness in the camp came from unsanitary conditions combined with the summer heat. A combination of malaria, dysentery, cholera and typhoid are all likely causes for the high death toll among the Athenians at this time.
74. The eclipse began soon after dark at 8.00 pm.
75. Plutarch also states that if a delay to any action was to be recommended following a solar or lunar eclipse it should not be more than three days but both he and Thucydides state that the Athenians waited a full twenty-seven. It is interesting to note that in a city that

produced the greatest philosophers in history, including Socrates and Plato, that the majority should remain highly superstitious and fearful of nature.

76. Thucydides has no comment on this loss to the Athenian cavalry and perhaps in light of what was to come it was a minor engagement. Still it was an ominous sign for the future. Thucydides may have known this total from one of the survivors of the expedition.

77. Thucydides, 7.56–59, interrupts his narrative to give a detailed breakdown of the composition of the Athenian and Syracusan forces following in a similar way the catalogue of ships and troops by combatants given by Homer in the *Iliad*, 2.494–759 and Herodotus, 7.60–97, 8.1.

78. Diodorus, 13.14.4, has total of 115 triremes for the Athenians and 76 for Syracuse. He may have drawn these figures from Thucydides but perhaps more likely from Philistus since Diodorus' subsequent account of the ensuing battle seems to reflect a Syracusan rather than an Athenian viewpoint. He says: 'The walls around the harbour and every high spot in the city were crowded with people since wives and daughters and all who because of age could not offer themselves for service ... were watching the battle with the greatest anxiety.' While this description is also reminiscent of the walls of Troy, he also states that the Syracusans launched numerous small boats crewed by young men whose purpose was to sail up close to the Athenians ships and cause additional damage where possible.

79. The speeches given to Nicias and Gylippus are the last of their kind in Thucydides history, 7.61–68, and almost at the point where his revision of the work ceased. Book 8 has no set speeches. Thucydides' description of Nicias' state of mind, 7.69, may well have been obtained from an eyewitness source since it is a rather unusual item in the narrative.

80. It is astonishing that when they had twenty triremes stationed along the east coast of Sicily earlier in the year the Athenians had not maintained this squadron. It had evidently also joined the rest in the Great Harbour perhaps when Demosthenes arrived. This strategy of concentrating all their forces in a single location was ill judged to say the least for had Athenian ships remained at Catane and been deployed later they could have changed the course of this battle dramatically. It is simply not credible that all avenues of communication between the Athenian camp and Catane had been lost by this time, and could not have been continued through the use of runners and mounted scouts, although the loss of Epipolai made this more difficult.

81. The obvious difference is that no violence is portrayed to the audience of a tragic play and it all takes place offstage. The historians were thus not hampered in what they could and could not describe.

82. The crews of sixty triremes plus the additional troops they carried amounts to somewhere in the region of 15,000 casualties within a matter of hours.

83. The modern Anapo River flows throughout the year in the low-lying area of Lysimeleia into the Great Harbour, having received the waters of the Ciane Spring about eight kilometres upstream, but in early autumn following a dry summer the river is dry higher up the valley near Floridia.

84. For a detailed analysis of the route of the Athenians at this stage see Evans (2009) 85–91, including a map, and 148–149.

85. It was called the estate of Polyzelos, Plutarch, *Nicias*, 27.1, perhaps originally belonging to the brother of Hieron I, former ruler of Syracuse (480–467 BC), although the name was probably a common one.

86. At Sphacteria in 425, 292 Peloponnesian hoplites were captured, 120 of whom were Spartiates, a small number in comparison to the figures at Syracuse.

87. The southern border of Syracuse is not easily identifiable but must have been roughly at the Erineos (modern Assinaro River below the town of Noto) since this would have marked the beginning of the territory of Eloros, which lies on the coast a mere five to six kilometres (3 miles) to the south. Eloros was not an independent *polis* but a satellite town of Syracuse, although it would have possessed its own identifiable *chorē*.

88. Having noted that the war had cost Syracuse at least 2000 talents Nicias was in effect offering to surrender nearly all the Athenian citizens in his army. The Syracusan rejection is understandable but indicative of emotion rather than reason prevailing for it would actually have been more materially beneficial to them than the slaughter which followed.

89. Thucydides, 7.85, states that Nicias trusted Gylippus more than the Syracusans, but was this distrust of the latter a recent revelation since previously he had considered that he had friends inside the city? Some of the Athenian cavalry did escape to Catane but whether these were with Demosthenes or Nicias is not stated.

90. A *tropaion* consisted essentially of a set of the arms and armour nailed to an available tree in the vicinity of the start of any rout. Usually any sword, spear, breastplate, shield and greaves retrieved from the dead would have sufficed. The fact that the Syracusans used the generals' arms and armour emphasized the magnitude of the victory. It was also highly unusual for the generals of an opposing army to be captured, which again shows that it was a unique event.

91. Many more among the camp followers will have died from disease or been enslaved when the Syracusans reoccupied Lysimeleia. Others will have been killed in the retreat. The total casualty figure will not have been far short of 100,000 combatants and camp followers, servants and slaves.

92. The division of the history into eight books was not envisaged by Thucydides. However, had the work continued down to 404 it would most likely have occupied at least twelve books. Thus Books 6 and 7 would have been at the central point. This is supposition of course but it is worth noting that in a work ostensibly about a war between Athens and Sparta the pivotal point lay in Sicily not in Greece.

Chapter 3

1. Servadio (2000) 19. Philipp Clüver (1580–1622) was a German antiquarian who wrote (1619) an account of Sicilian ancient monuments.

2. For the sieges of Syracuse see Chapter 2. During the second war with Carthage notable sieges by the Romans included Tarentum and Capua, both of which had deserted their alliances with Rome and gone over to the enemy as had Syracuse in 214. The First Punic War had witnessed notable sieges of Akragas (Agrigentum) and Lilybaeum by the Romans; the latter had remained in Carthaginian hands until the end of the war in 241. After 212 BC Syracuse was not sacked again until AD 878 when it was captured from the Byzantines by the Arabs.

3. The Isola San Pantaleo is now exclusively an archaeological zone with a museum containing artefacts unearthed from longstanding excavation work. The museum is housed inside the villa that belonged to a former owner of the island, the business man and viticulturist Joseph Whitaker, better remembered perhaps as a member of a family that produced Marsala wine, who became so absorbed in the history of the site that he

conducted the first excavations here and published the findings in *Motya: A Phoenician Colony in Sicily* (London 1921). For details of Whitaker's life and his interest in Motya, see also Servadio (2000) 125–142.

4. Sicily was settled, on the one hand, by a mix of Greeks who originated mostly from Megara and Chalcis, both ethnically Ionian cities. These Sicilian Greeks who lived in Naxos, Megara Hyblaia, Catane and Leontinoi are sometimes referred to as Chalcidians. On the other hand, Dorian Greeks from Corinth and elsewhere in the Peloponnese and some of the islands, including Rhodes, made up the other ethnic Hellenic group who had settled in Syracuse, Gela and Akragas. Infighting between the two was often quite vicious and as relentless as against more distant ethnic groups.

5. Herodotus, 7.157–160, claims that envoys came from Athens and Sparta requesting military aid from Gelon who was prepared to do so providing he was given command of the combined Greek force against the Persians then in the process of invading Greece. The Greeks rejected this condition and went away empty handed. In the course of the discussions Gelon is made to state that in a previous war against the Carthaginians the Greeks had neglected to send him aid. Neither this war nor the interview between Greek ambassadors and Gelon is related by later sources such as Diodorus.

6. Hamilcar was killed at Himera in battle but his body had been crucified, and so had not been returned to the defeated side as was the usual custom in such circumstances. Such behaviour was bound to cause outrage and provoke revenge. That it was so long in coming is probably due the exile of Hamilcar's son Giscon and his family.

7. Some idea of the complexities of Greek Sicilian and Carthaginian relations can be gauged by the evidence for earlier warfare between Selinous and Carthage, De Angelis (2003) 156–157, and Gelon of Syracuse's destruction of Megara Hyblaia in 483/2, the metropolis of Selinous and reason enough for a Selinuntine alliance with Carthage, De Angelis (2003) 66–67.

8. Diodorus may mean that the entire siege lasted nine days or that the final stages lasted this length of time. The duration of the siege cannot, however, have extended much beyond two weeks.

9. Diodorus also refers to a certain Empedion, a prominent citizen of Selinous who had clearly escaped to Akragas, and who returned as an envoy to Hannibal on behalf of the refugees offering ransom for any captives. This was refused but since Empedion had previously been an advocate of a pro–Carthaginian alliance in Selinous Hannibal restored his own possessions and released those of his family members who had been captured in the siege.

10. Diodorus was a native of Agyrium in the interior of Sicily near Enna but is thought to have spent much of his life in Rome.

11. Current excavation work (2012) has uncovered what is taken to be the agora of the pre-409 settlement beyond the acropolis facing north more or less at the midpoint between the city's two beaches but at some height above them. This would suggest that some market area was also available at the harbours.

12. This was probably the force already at Akragas when Selinous fell but Diodorus has them arrive after Hannibal had invested Himera. On balance they more likely arrived before the Carthaginian army. Such a small force would not have been able to force their way through enemy lines and they almost certainly came overland.

13. Diodorus' use of figures is troublesome to say the least, for while this total for Hannibal's army, 40,000, appears quite realistic he does not name his source. The earlier numbers he

gave for the Carthaginian army on its departure from Africa, which he says he obtained from Ephorus, 200,000 infantry and 2000 cavalry, and Timaeus, not more than 100,000 in total, 13.54.5, along with 60 warships and 1000 transports, 13.54.1, appear grossly inflated and perhaps were meant to enhance the threat to the Greeks. Later in his description of the siege Diodorus also attributes to Hannibal's army 80,000 barbarian mercenaries, 13.60.3, which simply adds to the confusion.

14. Tyndaris and Mylae were the closest Greek settlements along the north coast but Diodorus says that the fleet landed its refugees at Messene, 13.61.5, which must certainly have been at least a day's sailing each way and probably more. The chronology here is therefore probably vague at best to suit the drama of the moment.

15. It is worth noting that Hannibal was surely in a position to prevent this but either let them go or was quite lax in his investment of Himera. It should also be remembered that, according to Diodorus, the Carthaginians had probably arrived just two days before.

16. Both Gela and Akragas, which are noted as being sympathetic to Selinous and which were prepared to send troops for its defence, also had extensive harbour facilities and must have possessed fleets of their own. Perhaps all were cowed by the apparent Carthaginian naval supremacy.

17. Hannibal's time as a child at Selinous meant that he knew the city well, which makes understandable, therefore, the choice of this city as the first place of assault.

18. In fact, Therma became the town that in later antiquity was called Thermae Himerenses, and today Himera Thermae. The city later in 405 took in former Himeraean citizens as well, Diod. 13.114.1, and flourished throughout the Roman period. Note that a new town built in the same vicinity with a new name exactly duplicates the end and rebirth of Sybaris as Thurii.

19. Hermocrates who had been prominent in the defence of Syracuse against the Athenians in 414–413 (see Chapter 2), was sent to reinforce the Spartans with a fleet but was then exiled and served with the Persians who provided the funds for his return to Sicily. Diodorus says he had five triremes and a thousand men, which comprises exactly the crews of these warships, and later on commanded a force of six thousand, which was simply not sufficient to capture cities.

20. A propaganda exercise if there ever was one since the bodies would have long since been stripped of any means of identification.

21. Dionysius was not a relative of the Hermocrates whose supporter he was. However, he had recently become Hermocrates' son-in-law.

22. After the defeat inflicted on them by Gelon the Carthaginian interests in Sicily appear to have been dormant or, at least, the literary sources are completely silent on the issue. The invasion of 409 comes out of the blue but may have been prompted by a growing concern about Syracuse's newfound supremacy on the island. These fears proved well founded as later events show.

23. Transporting an army overseas was fraught with dangers not only from natural events such as severe storms which could easily destroy an entire army, but also because the transport ships, usually elderly triremes with two of the banks of oars removed, were slow moving and vulnerable and could easily be destroyed by enemy warships.

24. There is a lengthy digression on Akragas, which Diodorus probably knew, and a detailed account of the Olympieion which was never finished because of this ruinous war (13.82.1). Although Akragas had a long and prosperous history in the Roman period this temple, like the temple at Segesta, remained unroofed.

25. The cathedral that stands on the highest point of Agrigento today gives some idea of the building that once occupied this site. Diodorus either knew the city or his source did. It is perhaps remarkable that the citizens of this city should have entrusted their citadel to mercenary troops who had recently fought against Greeks. It is possible that they harboured real grievances against Hannibal so that their loyalty would be guaranteed.

26. At this point in the siege Himilcon has been replaced by a certain Himilcar without notice by Diodorus, 13.85.5, and is arguably a copyist error rather than a new appointment since Himilcon reappears at 13.87.1. Himilcon was to become the dominant Carthaginian general in the next decade. Meanwhile, Himilcar might conceivably have replaced Hannibal, although they are initially mentioned together seemingly in joint command, and appears in the text up to 13.91.1, but never at the same time as Himilcon, and finally at 13.114.1 and thereafter he disappears. Here I have noted Himilcar with Himilcon in parentheses as being one and the same person.

27. A large burial chamber known today as the 'Tomb of Theron' stands just below the Temple of Heracles and is therefore also close to the Olympieion.

28. Compare Alexander's ramp or mole at Tyre.

29. He is said to have offered sacrificial victims to Cronos and Poseidon not Punic gods probably to atone for the desecration of Greek tombs.

30. Diodorus states that this relief column was composed of Greeks from Syracuse, Gela and Camarina, Messene and some anonymous cities in Magna Graecia, perhaps Locri and Rhegium, but also Sicel allies, 13.86.4–5.

31. Diodorus, 13.87.5, appears to indicate that there were five generals or *strategoi* who had probably been elected to take joint command. Argeius is named as the general who was not killed in this ugly confrontation. Dexippus also escaped unscathed.

32. The text of Diodorus, 13.88.5, states that eight Syracusan ships were sunk and these are described as 'large' or 'great' vessels which the translator (Loeb edition) has rendered as warships, although it seems more likely that large ships would be the transports while the triremes or warships were smaller and more agile in manoeuvre, rather like the modern destroyer or frigate accompanying a wartime transatlantic convoy.

33. In repeating himself it is certainly possible that the writer had switched sources and that each of these had the same information.

34. The death of Tellias, although no doubt recorded in Diodorus' sources, is almost certainly not historical but again a topical element in a history where the wealthy man kills himself among his own riches or that of his city rather than let himself and them be taken by the attacker.

35. Philistus later wrote a history of Syracuse and became one of Dionysius' most trusted supporters. He is also named several times as one of Diodorus' sources. Diodorus notes, 13.103.3, that Philistus composed two histories, the first from early times down to 406, the second from 405 through the rule of Dionysius II.

36. In ancient democracies such as Athens and Syracuse and Akragas (at various times) the control over the armed forces was entrusted to a committee of elected generals who served for one year but who could be re-elected. These took turns to act as overall commander for a specified period of time within that year in office. Accusations of poor leadership or misconduct were common and could lead to deposition, fines and even execution.

37. Since Himilcon's army was quartered throughout Akragas for the winter after its fall in late December the date of Dionysius' arrival in Gela can probably be placed in the spring of 405, perhaps March or April.

38. Tyrants usually had personal bodyguards and Diodorus claims that Dionysius emulated the Athenian tyrant Pisistratus who also had a guard of six hundred, but Gelon also possessed bodyguards although he dispensed with them after his victory at Himera.

39. Among these was the general Daphnaeus whose withdrawal of the Syracusan-led army from Akragas had sealed that city's fate.

40. Diodorus, 13.108.5, actually says that while these things took place many years apart he thinks it still suitable to comment on because it was remarkable.

41. Impressive fortifications are to be seen at the east end of Gela but these are Hellenistic and date to the wars with Carthage towards the end of the fourth century when Agathocles was ruler of Syracuse.

42. Dionysius is credited with an army of 30,000 infantry, 1000 cavalry and 50 covered pentekontas, smaller ships than the usual triremes but with decks for carrying larger number of marines or armoured infantry, Diod. 13.109.2.

43. Time and time again Diodorus presents Dionysius as an innovative thinker and tactician, although his strategies did not always go according to plan. His source was probably the loyal Philistus.

44. The Syracusan casualties are given in some detail, 1000 of the Italian Greeks on the left wing and 600 Sicilian Greeks on the right wing, Diod. 13.110.5–6.

45. Camarina was the most easterly of the harbour towns along the southern coast of Sicily. It was situated above the beach and like Gela had no natural strong points. As a result it was attacked with ease throughout its history and suffered a number of sackings and removal of its citizens.

46. The total number of displaced persons can of course only be conjectured. Some of the refugees from Himera made it to Messene, but still others must have gone to Syracuse. There they were joined with perhaps 100,000 from Akragas, 20,000–30,000 from Gela and perhaps another 10,000 from Camarina. These figures are astonishing yet have given cause for little comment in modern scholarship. The evacuation of so many cities in Sicily in such a short space of time cannot be matched elsewhere in the Classical period of Greek history. It far exceeded the mass removal of people from communities such as Megara Hyblaia and Camarina by Gelon in the 480s.

47. The destruction of Naxos, which was never rebuilt, must have been an exceptionally traumatic for the Sicilian Greeks since this city was the oldest Hellenic settlement in Sicily and its temple to Apollo held a senior place in the cultic hierarchy of the region. Both Catane and Leontinoi were soon repopulated with citizens more loyal to Dionysius. Dionysius had earlier attempted to besiege Leontinoi, Diod. 14.14.3, but on that occasion a lack of siege engines forced a retreat.

48. After this episode the only other attempt to oust Dionysius occurred in 404, Diod. 14.7.6–9.8, when civil unrest gripped the city and he suffered some major reverses including being blockaded on Ortygia, but eventually again overcame the threat to his power. For the next thirty-eight years he ruled unchallenged at Syracuse.

49. For further discussion about the fortifications of Syracuse see Evans (2009) 112–113, 128–131. Diodorus records the extension of the city walls along Epipolai in his coverage of the year 401, although this may well have occurred rather later and been more closely associated with his planning for war. They were clearly unfinished in 397 when the Carthaginians besieged Syracuse.

50. Thucydides, 7.52, gives a total number of seventy-six, and in the final battle in the Great Harbour against the Athenians in 413 they lost about twenty-five of these, 7.72, but would

have been able to reuse perhaps as many as fifty Athenian ships left behind when the besiegers decided to retreat overland.

51. Regarding this issue see Oldfather (1954) 127; Tarn (1930) 130–131; cf. Van Wees (2004) 238–239 who accepts the claim.

52. With a total fleet given as 400 warships, hiring crew for 200 or approximately 20,000 men seems unrealistic and not all ships would have been in use at the same time. However, the assertion mainly serves to illustrate the power and wealth of Dionysius.

53. It is said that Doris, the Locrian wife of Dionysius, arrived in Syrcause in one of the first quinqueremes.

54. It is likely that Diodorus writing in the first century had the appearance of the Roman legions in mind when he wrote this.

55. Diodorus' claim is refuted by modern scholars who point to use of the catapult in the Middle East at least four hundred years earlier. It should be noted that the historian is clearly using two sources at this point in his narrative since he is obviously repeating information in a rather haphazard fashion, but this also indicates that his sources, a combination of Ephorus, Philistus and Timaeus, did not doubt either the energy of Dionysius and the Syracusans in their preparations.

56. It is highly unlikely that many full Spartan citizens would have made themselves available as mercenaries at this time but helots might well have been encouraged to serve away from the Peloponnese.

57. Diodorus notes Syracusans, mercenaries and other allies, which may have included Sicels. Moreover there can hardly have been significant numbers of Selinuntines or Himeraeans. The former had suffered severely in 409 while many of the former citizens of Himera had gone to Messene, which did not support Dionysius,

58. Some points of interest occur here since the Elymian town of Halicyae, 14.54.2, which had been ignored in the campaign in 397, in the next year when threatened by the Greeks came to terms with Dionysius, and this suggests that he was keen to win over the Elymians as allies rather than conquer them by force of arms. Nothing more is heard of Entella, which may have withstood the Greek attack. The citizens of Segesta on the other hand repelled their attackers during a night sortie after a siege that had lasted about a year, Diod. 14.54.2. Eryx was nominally under the control of Segesta but here acted by itself, which might point to some disunity among this ethnic group. It was retaken by the Carthaginians in 396, Diod. 14.55.4, while the Halicyaeans quickly returned to their former alliance at the same time.

59. The island of Motya can be seen easily from the summit of Eryx, the distance no more than twenty-four kilometres (15 miles).

60. For the main cities in western Sicily, see Evans (2009) 8, and 116 for a map of Motya.

61. Diodorus' text, 14.51.3–52.4, again has strong internal evidence for the historian's almost simultaneous use of two sources since the account of the dramatic events as the Motyan defences collapsed is obviously repetitive.

62. Diodorus, 14.53.1, employs the rather general word χῶμα, which can mean any sort of mound, including that for a burial, or the sort of ramp erected against fortifications, but given that there is insufficient space at Motya for building ramps this must therefore be intended to convey the idea of a mole and the one that can be observed is the causeway from Birgi.

63. Diodorus, 14.53.4, names a certain Archylus who received a monetary prize for outstanding bravery. Such action by Dionysius was designed to encourage both loyalty

and good practice but it also marks a stage in the evolution of a professional army. Honours, awards and discipline were to be a later feature in the army of the Macedonian kings Philip II and Alexander the Great and the whole principle was, of course, taken up by the Romans. Dionysius was certainly an innovator in many respects at least so the literary sources would like us to believe.

64. It is interesting to note that the garrison is said to have comprised mostly Sicel allies and not Sicilian Greeks.

65. Himilcon was a *sufes* or one of two most senior of the annually elected officials at Carthage. Diodorus describes him as *basileus*, 14.54.5, not perhaps as a king but rather as supreme military commander. Himilcon had obviously been one of the *sufetes* on a number of occasions and certainly since 405 when he had held office with Hannibal. Election to this office was clearly unrestricted like that of the office of the *strategos* at Athens or Syracuse but unlike the consulship in the Roman republic.

66. Diodorus, 14.54.5–6, rather sceptically gives figures that he says he obtained from Ephorus: 300,000 infantry, 4000 cavalry, 400 chariots, 400 warships and 600 transports, and he also says that Timaeus gave only 100,000 infantry and another 30,000 enlisted when Himilcon arrived in Sicily. Diodorus' preference for and reliance on a writer of Sicilian origin is very clear.

67. Alexander's well known attachment to the cult of Heracles and indeed to all cults should have alerted the Tyrians to the fact that the King would wish to participate in any rituals that were being held. It is interesting that far from being flattered by his interest they considered it an insult.

68. Alexander had also ordered the destruction of Thebes after a brief siege in 335. Diodorus maintains that the Tyrians expected aid from the Carthaginians, cf. Curtius, 4.2.10, but none arrived probably because in 332 they had still to recover from the severe defeats they had suffered in 340/39 at Akragas at the hands of Timoleon, Evans (2009) 126. The Tyrians are also said to have sent some of their civilian inhabitants to safety elsewhere before the siege began, although their destination is not stipulated, Diod. 17.41.1. Curtius is perhaps not far from the truth when he says that Carthage could not send relief because of a war with the Syracusans, 4.3.19–20, but a war they had recently lost not one actually still in progress. Moreover, his assertion that the Sicilian Greeks had invaded Africa is a mistake for the expedition of Agathocles in 310.

69. This causeway has remained ever since and made the island location of Tyre into a peninsula.

70. Some commentators have seen in this material Diodorus' use of a technical manual about siege equipment but, in fact, there is not much here of a truly specific nature.

71. Arrian's figure of 30,000 enslaved, 2.24, is hopelessly exaggerated, while Curtius, 4.4.15–16, says that the fleet of Sidon rescued as many as 15,000. Although allied with Alexander the citizens of this city had a common origin. If the account is accurate it may well have been sanctioned by Alexander in order to reduce the death toll and to allow repopulation of the city, which did take place.

72. Arrian, 2.24–25, notes that Tyre's king and most of the prominent citizens were spared by Alexander although a new king was appointed by him. Moreover, Carthaginian envoys visiting the cult of Heracles were also released unharmed. The extent of the casualties given by the sources is therefore probably meant to be appropriate for the savage climax of a long contested siege.

73. The main sources for Tyre after Diodorus are Curtius Rufus, *History of Alexander*, 4.2.1–
    4.21; Plutarch's *Life of Alexander*, 24–25; Arrian's *Anabasis*, 2.16–27.
74. Curtius says the siege lasted six months, 4.4.19, while Diodorus, 17.46.5, and Plutarch,
    Alex. 24.5, each give seven months.
75. That would assume, of course, that Ephorus and Timaeus were entirely independent
    of one another and this is far from certain. Timaeus probably had access to Philistus
    and Ephorus when he wrote his history. Ephorus could have accessed Philistus and
    then Antiochus for earlier material. What seems likely is that Diodorus did not use an
    intermediate writer between his own time in the first century BC and Timaeus in the third.
76. De Angelis (2003) 149.
77. Inconclusive because neither side was in a position to destroy the other, which would
    certainly have happened if one possessed a sufficiently superior military capability.
78. It is interesting that Strabo, except for a passing and rather vague mention, 6.2.1, does
    not deal with Heracleia Minoa at all, consigning this whole stretch of coast from Cape
    Pachinus to Lilybaeum as deserted, 6.2.5, but this may a fault of the writer or his source
    and clearly stems from a lack of familiarity since he also has very little to say about Akragas,
    Gela and Selinous, 6.2.6. The history of the site at Heracleia Minoa is also similar in that
    it began as a Greek-inspired settlement and subsequently became a Carthaginian fortress,
    though unlike Motya or Selinous it had a renaissance under the Romans.
79. Motya was clearly abandoned, however, and Lilybaeum became the main Punic settlement
    in this part of Sicily. Any surviving Motyans would have resettled in Lilybaeum, which
    is already mentioned in the literature as a harbour of importance to the Carthaginians.
    Why Lilybaeum should have been chosen is unclear. Later it was regarded and still is
    by modern commentators an impregnable site but the local geography simply does not
    bear that out. Modern Marsala lies on flat land with a small unimpressive harbour and
    cannot have benefited from any natural defences which it lacks, nor is it obviously easily
    defendable unless massive fortifications were constructed, although there seems to be no
    evidence for these.

Chapter 4

1. A third Germanic tribe the Ambrones is consistently missed in modern accounts,
   and there were other subdivisions among this ethnic group. The Tigurini and Volcae
   Tectosages claimed to belong to the same ethnicity as the Cimbri but had been settled
   in the Alps and in western Gaul for some time before the Cimbri arrived. Indeed, the
   Cimbri were only joined by the Teutones and Ambrones in 102, although the former had
   been in a process of migration across Western Europe for at least a decade by then. For a
   recent discussion of this campaign see Sampson (2010) 93–179.
2. During Augustus' rule (30 BC – AD 14) the porticoes adjoining the temple of Mars Ultor
   came to contain statues of those who had been granted triumphs and an inscription was
   set up describing each individual's career and honours. Marius was included here and
   also by virtue of being a relative by marriage to Augustus' adopted father Julius Caesar, E.
   Nash, *Pictorial Dictionary of Ancient Rome*, London 1968, Volume 1, 401; Evans (1994) 2.
3. For my comments then see Evans (1994) 169–174, and reiterated (2003) 12–13, 35–36.
4. Romulus was the first and Camillus the second, Plutarch, *Mar*. 27.5; Evans (1994) 169.
   Augustus was later to proclaim himself the 'fourth founder' of Rome.
5. For a fuller discussion of the Sallust's speech and its relevance to Marius' career see
   Evans (1994) 68–74, and on the question of honourable scars as an estimation of warrior
   status, Evans (1999) 77–94.

6. It is quite possible that Marius saw service in Spain for a considerably longer spell than the campaign undertaken by Scipio. He may well have been present at the notorious defeat at Numantia of the army of L. Hostilius Mancinus (cos. 137) in which Tiberius Gracchus also served as the consul's quaestor or second in command. Indeed, Marius may have served his *decem stipendia* or ten years' service in the army as an *eques* or cavalryman, as suited his social rank, in Spain.

7. For Marius' canvassing see Evans (1994) 66–67.

8. The consul who presided over the electoral process in 107 was either Ser. Sulpicius Galba or M. Aurelius Scaurus, neither of whom is recorded as having been active in a provincial command in this year, Evans (1994) 211. Scaurus was elected as a suffect following the conviction of the consul *designatus* Hortensius, probably in late 109, and so may have begun his consulship only after new elections could be convened. Galba elected at the normal time would therefore have presided over the election of his own colleague early in 108 and then also presided over the elections for their successors. Broughton (1984) 201, considers that the evidence shows that Scaurus was elected after the calendar year began.

9. Q. Caecilius Metellus Pius, the son of Numidicus, was consul with Sulla in 80, born either in 129 or 128, since he was praetor in 89/8, Broughton (1984) 41. Marius, on the other hand, was born about 157. The comment, if indeed it was historical and not the sort of politically motivated material put about later, would have caused great offence. There was certainly a great deal of animosity between Marius and Metellus Numidicus later on when they were very clearly opponents in the senate and their previous relationship may have fuelled this situation. Marius was fifty years of age when he was consul. The career of Q. Metellus Pius was retarded because of the instability in Rome in the 80s when he was a supporter of Sulla. He was consul aged forty-eight or forty-nine.

10. Metellus, however, had to wait until probably the middle of the following year, Broughton (1951) 554, to celebrate his triumph, which was delayed most likely through the jealousy of Marius and the active obstruction of his political allies in the tribunate. The date of Metellus' triumph is missing but on the *Fasti Triumphales* it is recorded as earlier than the triumph of M. Minucius Rufus (cos. 110) for his victory over the Thracian Scordsici, which took placed in the month of Sextilis, Greenidge & Clay (1960) 79. Sextilis was later renamed August after the first Roman emperor.

11. For the measures passed by Saturninus, which had probably been composed by Servilius Glaucia, and the implication of this innovative public oath see Evans (2003) 128–131.

12. He had earlier in 102 as censor tried to debar Saturninus, by then an ex-quaestor, from a place in the senate and to expel Glaucia, a former tribune, from the *ordo senatorius*, Evans (2003) 117–118.

13. Sallust, *Iug.* 65.5, states that everything favoured Marius' successful election in 108, not least the fact that there were probably not that many enterprising candidates in that particular year. No other candidates are mentioned other than the two politicians elected: Marius and L. Cassius Longinus, Evans (1991) 133.

14. Generally, the Cimbri are now considered to have emigrated south from Jutland in Denmark where they had suffered famine and a shortage of land, which had been inundated by the sea, Flor. 1.38 (3.3); '*cum terras eorum inundasset Oceanus, novas sedes toto orbe quaerebant*', 'when the ocean had swamped their lands they began to seek new homes throughout the whole world;' Evans (2005) 39 n. 4.

15. Illyria was not a Roman province before the time of Augustus but the towns along the Adriatic coast had treaties with Rome as probably did some of the tribes living more inland such as the Delmatae, Evans (2005) 39. Moreover, Aquileia in Cisalpine Gaul, as

the Roman settlement closest to Illyria, might have been a tempting goal, which would account for concern to be voiced in the senate.

16. Plutarch, Mar. 16.5; Velleius, 2.12.; Tac. *Germ.* 37. For modern references see Evans (2005) 40 n. 6.

17. Incidentally, Appian calls this tribe Teutones, but the epitome of Livy, and Strabo, 5.1.8, unequivocally Cimbri, which should be preferred. The confusion possibly arose because the Teutones later joined the Cimbri in Gaul but also may have been marauding in Eastern Europe at much the same time.

18. Noreia lay somewhere in the Austrian Tyrol and Cisalpine Gaul was a mere two hundred or so kilometres further south and within easy reach of a Cimbric attack and of sufficient proximity to account for senatorial concern. For Noreia see Evans (2005) 40.

19. A charge of *repetundae* or provincial maladministration seems unlikely, while treason or *perduelio* was an uncommon charge especially for actions outside the state, and notoriously difficult to obtain a conviction since it was held before the entire citizen body drawn up in its tribal constituencies and easily disrupted by a magistrate who might note some adverse omen or portent. It is worth also noting that the family included the famous turncoat tribune C. Papirius Carbo, cos. 120, a former ally of Ti. Gracchus and then an opponent of his brother, who committed suicide after a conviction for *repetundae* in 119 and Cn. Papirius Carbo, consul three times between 85 and 82, an opponent of Sulla who was murdered by Pompey, and had a notorious reputation, Cic. *Fam.* 9.21.3. Cicero is the sole evidence for Carbo's suicide in 113 and is perhaps, on balance, a doublet with the more famous suicide in 119. Sudden unexplained death could easily be attributed to suicide.

20. Asconius, *pro Cornelio de maiestate* = Lewis (2006) 288.

21. Livy, *Per.* 65, does not state that the Romans were forced to go under the yoke, which is a probable modern invention. Thus the painting of Charles Gleyre (1806–1874), which portrays the defeated Romans going under the yoke but which probably only occurred after the notorious defeats at the Caudine Forks and at Numantia.

22. Nothing is said about the attitude of the Nitiobroges but they presumably had little say in the matter and tried to remain neutral.

23. Caepio was praetor and proconsul in Hispania Ulterior between 109 and 107, Evans (1994) 55; Evans (2008) 85, and celebrated a triumph in early November 107, Greenidge & Clay (1960) 75, just prior to starting his consulship.

24. Flaccus celebrated a triumph the next year for victories over the Ligures, Vocontii and Saluvii, Greenidge & Clay (1960) 30. This politician notoriously became a supporter of the radical Gaius Gracchus and was murdered in Rome in 121 at the same time as his ally.

25. Calvinus also celebrated a triumph on his return to Rome for the same reasons as Flaccus, Greenidge & Clay (1960) 44.

26. The Sagusii occupied the northern bank of the Rhone before its confluence with the Saône, Strabo, 4.1.11, and the site of Lugdunum belonged to them. Strabo, 4.1.11, 4.2.3, in his description of the Arverni, says that they put armies numbering 200,000 in the field against Domitius Ahenobarbus and Fabius Maximus and even more against Caesar in the 50s. Most likely these figures are a total representing a number of tribes from this part of Gaul, including the Allobroges.

27. The *Via Domitia* was eventually meant to join the colony at Narbo with Italy. It was extended into northern Spain probably after the end of Marius' successful campaigns against the Germanic tribes and only completed during the first century AD.

28. Fabius Maximus took the name Allobrogicus for his victory. He was the grandson of Aemilius Paullus the victor over Perseus of Macedonia in 168.
29. For the dates and that the triumphs were over the Allobroges and Arverni and other Gallic tribes see Greenidge & Clay (1960) 48; Broughton (1952) 644.
30. The old Greek settlement of Nemausus (modern Nîmes), which was situated nearby, was apparently unaffected by the close proximity of the new city.
31. That peaceful conditions had been enforced here from 117 seems indicated by the lack of any mention of activity by proconsuls in the area until Iunius Silanus' command in 109. However, that is less than a decade of reconstruction after what must have been an intense period of fighting.
32. In theory provincial commands were supposed to be made public six months before the consular elections according to the *lex Sempronia de provinciis consularibus* of C. Gracchus, but its provisions had been largely overturned by Marius in 107, Evans (1994) 77–78. In the years immediately following, 107 military commands were probably being allotted by popular assemblies convened and supervised by the tribunes. It is worth noting that Rutilius Rufus is known to have served alongside Marius in Spain and Numidia so clearly had campaign experience.
33. Cicero is unduly harsh perhaps given that he too was a *novus homo* in political life. Notably, Mallius Maximus lost both his sons at the battle of Arausio and then endured exile for his failure.
34. Sampson (2010) 137–138.
35. Thus see Sampson (2010) 133–136. Orosius, 5.16.2, places the capture and death of a consular he names as Aemilius in the battle but there is clear confusion in the text and a telescoping of events from his reading of Livy, his main source.
36. On the relative status of the two generals see Evans (2005) 42. Mallius was senior by virtue of his consulship but Caepio was the more experienced and was proconsul on his side of the Rhone.
37. Granius also has Caepio boasting of coming to the help of a timid consul as he crossed the Rhone, Greenidge & Clay (1960) 83. Caepio was accused of the theft of temple gold belonging to the Volcae, which had been stored in Tolosa and which it was claimed had originally been stolen by Gallic attackers of Delphi. For the accusation and its outcome see Livy, *Per.* 67; Strabo, 4.1.13; Greenidge & Clay (1960) 85–86.
38. For further detail see Spann (1987) 12–13; Evans (2005) 42–43.
39. It does seem highly likely that there is a moralizing message in that he apparently sought safety by going in the opposite direction to Rome as he also later tried to accomplish when he led his rebellion in Spain. For a discussion of this episode and the early career of Sertorius see Spann (1987) 12–13.
40. Both were subsequently accused of misconduct and exiled. In 103 Mallius Maximus was exiled by popular vote. Caepio was convicted under the new *maiestas* or treason law of the tribune Saturninus in the same year, Evans (2003) 122–123.
41. The fact that the Romans had been commanded at Arausio by Mallius Maximus who was also a *novus homo* had no impact at all. Servilius Caepio (cos. 106) was a patrician. C. Flavius Fimbria Marius' consular colleague in 104 was also a *novus homo*, while Rutilius Rufus (cos. 105) and M. Aurelius Scaurus (cos. 108) were certainly the first consuls in their families.
42. Jugurtha had been defeated in the field on several occasions by then and Numidia had been secured by the Romans, while the province of Africa had not been threatened in

the final campaigns of Marius. There was no regional re-organization as such since the kingdoms of Numidia and Mauretania remained independent in theory. Therefore there was no reason for a senatorial commission to visit to supervise any conditions of peace as occurred after the defeat of Aristonicus in Asia in 129, which had involved the establishment of the new province of Asia replacing the kingdom of Pergamum.

43. Elections in absentia to the consulship had not occurred since the end of the second century during the war with Hannibal when senior figures in the field were granted this special dispensation so that they did not leave their armies without a commander. Q. Fabius Maximus and Ti. Sempronius Gracchus were elected consuls for 213 although they both were absent from Rome, Liv. 24.43, similarly M. Claudius Marcellus and M. Valerius Laevinus, elected consuls for 210, Liv. 26.23, and P. Sempronius Tuditanus consul for 204, Liv. 29.11.

44. Note *CIL* 1².1.195 (XVIII), 10.5782, 11.1831: '...*triumphans in secundo consulatu*'; Evans (1994) 1–2.

45. Although Terentius Varro took the brunt of the blame for the defeat at Cannae in 216 because he survived the battle his consular colleague L. Aemilius Paullus had been equally at fault but the latter's role became submerged in the literary sources on account of a general admiration for his son the consul of 182 who had been the victor over Perseus, last king of Macedonia, at the battle of Pydna in 168.

46. It should be noted that the Cimbri never reached Italy as it was defined by the Romans at this stage. The Cimbri are said to have reached the Po Valley, which was in Cisalpine Gaul. Granius Licinianus clearly had a similar situation in mind of some young men supposedly intent on fleeing from Italy in the aftermath of Cannae as related by Livy.

47. Livy, 22.53.1, retells a curious incident following Cannae when certain young aristocratic survivors suggested abandoning Italy for a life elsewhere. The tale is very probably unhistorical and may emanate from a writer such as Valerius Antias, Evans (1989) 119–120. Granius will have known his Livy and perhaps found a similar report for the aftermath of Arausio.

48. Diodorus says that 60,000 *socii* had been killed in the defeat at Arausio. For conflicting reports on the number of Roman casualties see Sampson (2010) 139.

49. Evans (1994) 25; the consul of 108 was born about 151, and a son with the same name was quaestor probably in the 90s, Sumner (1973) 79–82; Broughton (1984) 32. The moneyer M. Aurelius Scaurus associated with the foundation of Narbo Martius ca. 118 may be the consul, although he seems to occupy a subordinate position to others much younger than himself. Sumner (1973) 82 assumes that the moneyer was the consul; cf. Crawford (1974) 1.298, no. 282.

50. Welch (2007) 91, suggests without any good reason that this was a brother of the consul and that the gladiator school was situated at Capua, neither of which is stated by Valerius Maximus.

51. P. Rutilius Rufus is not known to have served in the army after his consulship, which is perhaps a little surprising considering his well attested military service in both Spain under Scipio Aemilianus and later in North Africa as a legate of Metellus Numidicus. He probably remained with Numidicus and returned with him in early 107 to be associated with his commander's triumph later in that year, an event that will certainly have increased his chances of election to the consulship in the summer of 106. He had been a praetor in 118, Evans (1994) 208, and had campaigned for the consulship at least once before in 116

when he had been defeated by M. Aemilius Scaurus, later the *princeps senatus* for more than twenty years, Cic. *de Orat.* 2. 280; Evans (1991), 118 and n. 45.

52. Service in the Roman republican infantry composed of citizen recruits required a property qualification, but Marius had waved this obligation since he was in a hurry to return to Africa at the start of 107. The property qualification could be overlooked in time of duress, but was generally observed down to the Principate of Augustus, 30 BC – AD 14, when service in the legions became voluntary and salaried.

53. '...*Italia omnis contremuit*' says Sallust, which translated suggests that the 'whole of Italy trembled violently' or was 'shaken' almost as if by an earthquake.

54. C. Flavius Fimbria presumably had a military background, although none is attested nor is he known to have been particularly energetic during his year in office. Lack of information does not mean, however, that Rome was left in unsecure hands and Marius seems to have been able to count of stalwart support at home for much of the time prior to the battle at Aquae Sextiae.

55. A late source, Arvenius, mentions the name Theline with a possible Punic presence at some stage in its early history, although it is also noted as the satellite town of Massilia with Greek citizens. Strabo, 4.1.6, notes that Arelate was a thriving town in his day but has nothing to add about its history. Indeed his coverage of the entire region is cursory to say the least with most attention, and not much of that, focussed on Massilia. Arausio is briefly noted, 4.1.11, as is Aquae Sextiae, 4.1.3, Valence not at all; and even Narbo is only deemed worth discussion in the context of its naming the whole of a province, thus Gallia Narbonensis, 4.1.1–14.

56. The epitome of Livy is quite specific: *Cimbri vastatis omnibus, quae inter Rhodanum et Pyrenaeum sunt, per saltum in Hispaniam transgressi.*' 'When the Cimbri had laid waste to everything which is between the Rhone and the Pyrenees, they crossed through a pass into Spain.'

57. See also Spann (1987) 13–17.

58. The text of Plutarch, *Sulla*, 4.1, is not reliable here since the author refers to Sulla's capture of a chief of the Volcae Tectosages, a sure doublet with the capture of Jugurtha, and he also mentions a tribe that he names as Marsi. However, this was an Italian not a Gallic tribe and must indicate some confusion between this campaign and the Social War in which Sulla was a commander for the Romans against the Italian allies, which included the Marsi. For Sulla's service in southern Gaul see Greenidge & Clay (1960) 89. Note, however, the existence of a German tribe named the Marsi who lived along the Rhine, Broughton (1984) 73, and the argument that this tribe had joined the Cimbri at some point in their migration.

59. For the argument for the timing and the proconsulship of M. Marius see Evans (2008) 77–90.

60. The ruin of Narbo is of course a supposition since there is no ancient confirmation of such a disaster, yet this proposition is almost certain. Narbo was quickly re-settled just like Colchester and London in the aftermath of the Boudicca rebellion in AD 61. The casualty figures are given for these catastrophes in the new province of Britain, and both were unfortified nearly twenty years after they were founded.

61. For the details regarding these events see Evans (2008) 84–85.

62. Conditions in Spain from 102 were highly unstable with, at first, frequent and bitter hostilities between the Celtiberians and the Romans, then with the uprising of Settorius

and then with the civil war between Caesar and Pompey. The region was only pacified under Augustus in the 20s. For a discussion of events in the 90s see Evans (2008) 83–90.

63. For a sensible discussion of this issue see Sampson (2010) 186–187.

64. For the name see Ptolemy, 2.10. However, he places the canal to the west of the delta, whereas Strabo has it correctly on the eastern edge.

65. Plutarch also claims that there were reports that the Cimbri would return from Spain in the spring of 103 and that such reports ensured Marius re-election to the consulship in the summer of 104, *Mar.* 14.6.

66. The literary sources namely, Plut. *Mar.*15.4; Obsequens, 43, seem quite sure that the Germanic tribes joined together here and again probably indicates Roman military intelligence shadowing the tribes' movements during these years.

67. Orosius says that this attack lasted three days, 5.16, while Plutarch says, *Mar.* 18.1, that since they could not take the camp the Teutones and their allies decided to push on to the Alps and Italy.

68. Plutarch also says that these had defeated the armies of Mallius and Caepio at Arausio, although they were not mentioned earlier.

69. Florus' description of the Germanic dead is highly reminiscent of the slaughter of the Athenians at the Assinarus River in 413 (see Chapter 2): 'The victorious Romans drank not more water than blood of the barbarians from the bloody stream' (1.38.9).

70. It is interesting to note that Plutarch presents a more positive picture of this battle than Florus (1.38.7–10) who not only conflates the battles into one and ignores the plight of the Ambrones but considers that it was a case of accomplishing something useful out of what was in the beginning carelessness on the part of Marius. Plutarch may well have been using a more sympathetic source, although both he and Florus probably used Livy who may have included more than one version of events at Aquae Sextiae.

71. For M. Claudius Marcellus see Broughton (1984) 55 and the suggestion, probably correct, that he had already been a praetor by the time he joined Marius' staff in about 102 and may well have replaced Manius Aquillius who left Gaul to canvass for the consulship of 101, a campaign that was successful.

72. Marius acquired considerable wealth from his Germanic campaigns and dedicated a temple to Honos and Virtus, which was presumably financed from the public sale of these spoils (*manubiae*).

73. As the epitome of Livy, Book 68, notes: '*duobus deinde proeliis circa Aquas Sextias … hostes delevit*', 'then in two battles near Aquae Sextiae he destroyed the enemy'.

74. The comment is probably not specific to Aquae Sextiae since much of the sentiment may be found in a poem of Archilochus writing in the seventh century BC that his bread and wine came from the spear, *Greek Lyrics* ed. R. Lattimore (1955) 1.

75. Florus states briefly that the Tigurini, had been posted as a reserve force in the eastern Alps, and that they dispersed after they heard news of the destruction of the Cimbri, 1.38.18–19. The Helvetii who were later destroyed by Caesar claimed descent from the Tigurini so it is possible that this tribe actually returned to its former territory rather than accompanying the Cimbri as late as 101. There is considerable uncertainty as to the wanderings of the Tigurini after their victory at Agen in 107. Caesar's excuse for killing huge numbers of Helvetii was in revenge for Agen.

76. Catulus' memoirs clearly circulated for some time, but Plutarch may have only referred to them through the autobiography of Sulla, which he certainly read and used as a source. Sulla served with Catulus at Vercellae and was on good terms with this public figure.

77. It is interesting to note that the inhabitants of Cisalpine Gaul who had been hostile towards Roman domination even as late as the first half of the second century do not appear to have shown any interest in the Cimbri and it must be assumed that the cities of the region were by then thoroughly Romanized and simply took defensive action to avoid the destruction experienced by the inhabitants of southern Gaul and northern Spain. However, it is also possible that there was as much devastation here and that it has not remained in the sources. According to Plutarch, *Mar.* 23.6, the land was left unprotected and ravaged. Implicit in his brief note is that the towns and cities of the region probably also suffered extensive damage and looting.

78. The moralizing message in Florus can also in part be explained by the time, second century AD, in which he lived. Writers of the Second Sophistic had a tendency to call into question even the greatest moments of Rome's history.

79. Marius' latest consular colleague L. Valerius Flaccus remained in Rome. Marius' army will have marched from Transalpine Gaul along the coast avoiding all contact with the Cimbri. Their general will have crossed to Rome by sea from Massilia.

80. Plutarch gives no reason for this delay, *Mar.* 15.5. If it is accurate it shows immediately the difficulty of carrying out a grandiose plan in a world in which communications were basic to say the least.

81. See the arguments concerning this issue, Evans (2005) 49–51.

82. Plutarch claims that these Teutones had been captured in the land of the Sequani and subsequently handed over to the Romans, *Mar.* 24.4. The lands of the Sequani were situated in the Rhone Valley in close proximity to Lake Geneva and therefore these fugitives were probably trying to find the Cimbri.

83. For further discussion see Sampson (2010) 187.

84. Boiorix is mentioned as being responsible for the killing of M. Aurelius Scaurus at Arausio in 105, Livy, *Per.* 67, but the epitome does not refer to this person again. However, Florus states, 1.38.18, that he died fighting in the battle.

85. Plutarch states that the third day after the challenge was issued was chosen by common consent for the battle, *Mar.* 25.3, while Florus, 1.38.14, says the next day was chosen.

86. The city lying on the Adige River may have been destroyed by the Cimbri in 102. The people of Verona were granted Roman citizenship in 89, which may signal an appreciation of its support for the *res publica* in this conflict.

87. The derogatory remarks about Marius presumably came from Sulla. They became deadly enemies. At Vercellae Sulla was still only an ex-quaestor and had yet to obtain a curule magistracy. By then he was about thirty-six years old and probably hoped to campaign for an aedileship in the following year using a successful campaign against the Cimbri as an aid to his candidacy. As events turned out Sulla was never an aedile and probably praetor only in 97 or more likely in 94, Broughton (1984) 73–74.

88. This is reminiscent of Alexander's tactics against the Persians at Gaugamela in 331 and so is perhaps not historically accurate information for Vercellae.

89. Florus, 1.38.15, gives a rather different description of this battle and claims that it was also a windy day. But it is more likely that a wind blew up later during the course of the day after the mist he describes had dissipated in the heat of August. He also makes clear that the wind was easterly and that Marius drew up his troops with the wind behind him and that the array of the legions occurred in the early morning since the sun caught the bronze of the soldiers' helmets, making them a more fearsome sight for the enemy looking into the sun. On the whole, however, his account is much more negative than that

of Plutarch who was using Sulla as a source, which might be expected to offer a hostile view of Marius' leadership qualities, but he does corroborate Festus' evidence of a battle fought from east to west. Frontinus, *Str.* 2.2.8, confirms the easterly wind.

90. The epitome of Livy has 140,000 enemy killed and 60,000 taken captive; Florus, 1.38.14, gives 65,000 enemy dead and just 300 Roman casualties.

91. On the lack of precedence for such an act see A.N. Sherwin–White, *The Roman Citizenship* (Oxford 1973) 294–295. For the ancient sources see Cicero's *Oratio pro Balbo*, 46, Valerius Maximus, 5.2.8, Greenidge & Clay (1960) 104.

92. The common Greek and Roman literary element of *hubris* and *nemesis* is present here again for Marius' triumph at Vercellae marked the high point in his career, which went downhill afterwards, at least according to his biographer and the historians who covered this period. The topical elements that were favoured by ancient writers should always be treated with some caution. Marius remained a formidable public figure down to his death in 86.

93. This fragment White (1912) 118–119 considered referred to the battle between Carbo and the Cimbri in Noricum in 113, but that makes little sense, while it makes eminent sense if applied to the aftermath of Vercellae.

94. He might have expected a command in Iberia once the threat from the Germanic tribes had dissipated since that region remained unstable throughout the first century BC and was a particular problem in the 90s. However his popularity suffered because of his political alliance with Saturninus and Galucia, Evans (2005) 54–55. On the enduring link with the Germanic tribes see Claudius Claudianus, *Bellum Geticum*, 635–647, composed in the early fifth century AD. For a discussion of this issue see Evans (1994) 12–13.

Chapter 5

1. See, for example, Suetonius, *Iul.* 52; cf. Plutarch, *Caes.* 48–49. They indicate that the relationship continued until Caesar's death in March 44.

2. Cicero, *ad Atticum*, 11,15: '*ille enim ita videtur Alexandria teneri ut eum scribere etiam pudeat de illis rebus ...*', Shackleton Bailey (1966) 5.43.

3. Shackleton Bailey (1966) 5.51. Obviously Cicero had yet to learn about the relief of Alexandria.

4. Pompey left Rome on the day that he received a report that Caesar was advancing into the mountains that separated Rome from the Adriatic.

5. Florus, 2.13.52, probably using Livy, specifies the beach at Pelusium killed 'by order of the vilest of kings (Ptolemy XIII) and the advice of eunuchs'.

6. Caesar was evidently trying to emulate Alexander who after Gaugamela in 331 had set off in pursuit of Darius III whom he hoped to capture alive. Like Pompey, Darius was murdered shortly before the victor arrived.

7. Appian, *BC* 2.89, states that he called in at Rhodes and that the sailing time from there to Alexandria was three days.

8. Plutarch says that Pompey's ashes, but not his head, which Appian, *BC* 2.90, says was buried near Alexandria, were eventually interred by his widow Cornelia in Pompey's villa at Alba Longa just south of Rome. Caesar, *BC* 3.104–106, mentions Pompey's death briefly and only in passing, and characteristically of the author not his reaction to his rival's end.

9. Roman intervention at this time may have been contemplated by the senate, but the revolt of Aristonicus in Asia and the continuing instability in Iberia following the destruction

of Numantia precluded such a move. For a discussion of the possibilities and the sources including the epitome of Livy, see Lampela (1998) 204–205.

10. Caesar, *BC* 3.108, mentions only Pothinus, whereas other writers note the influence of the Theodotus who is said to have presented the head of Pompey to Caesar on his arrival in Alexandria. Plut. *Caes.* 48.2, adds the additional detail of two other members of the King's household, whom he names as Dioscorides and Serapion. Caesar may well have omitted the episode of the ghastly gift quite purposely, not wishing to be seen to dwell on the fate of his rival. Plutarch notes that Theodotus was a citizen of Chios, *Pomp.* 77.2.

11. Caesar does not mention a specific building, but it may be inferred from the fact that the King and his entourage later appear to have been with the Romans that this was indeed the palace of the Ptolemies. That it was close to the harbour is suggested by the attention Caesar gives to the Pharos Island and that his place of residence was targeted in later fighting that spilled out around the port.

12. Appian, *BC* 2.89, places the King at Casium, which was close to Pelusium. Appian, a native of Alexandria, should probably be preferred to most of the sources for topographical information, although writing two hundred years after the event. For Casium see Walbank (1957) 1.610 and for other ancient sources.

13. The Etesians blow north to south down through the Aegean and directly to the Egyptian coast.

14. Florus, 2.13.56, has Cleopatra as suppliant before Caesar but no theatrical entrance.

15. Ptolemy XV Caesarion had a birth date of 23 June 47, in fact, late April or early May. If he was the son of Cleopatra and Caesar and was born after a full-term pregnancy this would date their affair from early August and with a week or two of their first meeting.

16. Dio is the sole source for Ptolemy's behaviour. It not to be found in Caesar's *Bellum Civile*, understandably perhaps since the author was in the habit of suppressing material detrimental to his own character; and this reason would also apply to the *Bellum Alexandrinum* if authored by Hirtius, Caesar's friend. However, it is also absent in the works of Plutarch, Appian, Suetonius and Florus, which may indicate some invention in the source used by Dio at this point. The historian and politician Gaius Asinius Pollio is a good candidate as a historian who may have written some negative material about Caesar's activities in Egypt. Some of the sources place Achillas at Pelusium, but Dio states that he was in the palace conspiring with Pothinus and when Caesar was alerted and had had the eunuch killed, Achillas fled to the army, took command and led it back to the city.

17. This may well have taken place before Achillas arrived in the city.

18. However, it should be noted that while Caesar's legionaries may have been Roman citizens, his cavalry was from Gaul and his fleet, including rowers, was mostly Ionian or Asiatic Greek,

19. In 55 Ptolemy was restored after being an exile for three years in Rome, during which time his daughter Berenice had ruled. Roman support had come because Gabinius had marched down the coast and took Pelusium and defeated the fleet and land forces of the queen on the same day or very soon after, Dio, 39.58.1. He was later accused of treason for leaving his province without permission from the senate and though acquitted on that charge was later convicted and exiled for extortion. Dio says disparagingly, 39.58.2, that not only was the Ptolemaic army not a match for the Roman legions but as a whole the Egyptians had no ability when it came to conventional warfare.

20. They had, in fact, been raised in the usual way of a levy of citizens and were not employed as professional soldiers so probably found life in Egypt simply more congenial than in Italy.

21. Dionysius used larger variations of the tireme, the quadrireme and quinquereme, which probably indicates that they had a similar beam and length to be accommodated with the smaller galleys in the boat sheds.

22. This harbour was evidently named after Eunostos, the king of Soli on Cyprus, who was a son-in-law of Ptolemy I Lagus.

23. The wording, *BC* 3.111: 'The contest was as keen as one would expect, since one side saw that a swift victory, the other that their safety, depended on the result' is highly reminiscent of Thucydides, 7.71, and the description of the sea battle in the harbour at Syracuse between the Athenian led attackers and the besieged in August or September 413 BC.

24. Caesar says (*BC* 3.112): 'On the island is the Pharos, a tower of great height, raised by astonishing ingenuity, which takes its name from the island.'

25. The Pharos Island gives protection against northerly winds. The *Diabathra*, roughly translated meaning the opposite pier, was a manmade construction extending from a bluff on the eastern side of the harbour, which partly enclosed the Great Harbour and both protected against winds from that quarter and provided the facility with a narrow and manageable entrance and exit.

26. It is worth noting here the similarities between the harbour area at Alexandria and that at Syracuse where the island of Ortygia was joined to the mainland and the agora in Akradina by a causeway, also forming an almost impregnable harbour. It is certainly possible that Ptolemy II Philadelphus during whose reign the lighthouse was built had this fact in mind when he ordered its construction and link with the mainland. For a map of the harbour at Syracuse see Evans (2009) 81 and 84.

27. Caesar is vague here and it is certainly possible that only the lighthouse was garrisoned since the author of the *Bellum Alexandrinum* recounts fierce fighting on Pharos weeks later.

28. She was probably younger than Cleopatra but older than Ptolemy, hence a young adult rather than a child. She was evidently captured at the end of the war and paraded in Caesar's great triumphal procession in Rome in 45. After this she was imprisoned, but later murdered on the order of Cleopatra in 41 in her place of detention, the temple of Artemis at Ephesus.

29. Caesar himself adds that by restraining the King it made it appear as if the war was being engineered by some private individuals rather than backed by the ruling family, *BC* 3.109.

30. '*Haec initia belli Alexandrini fuerunt*' was obviously not the place where Caesar intended to finish his Commentary and this briefest of sentences reads like a gloss and was inserted by the continuator, a scribe or a scholiast.

31. As events indeed unfolded for many of those who lived in the city at that time for Egypt was incorporated into the Roman Empire less than two decades later. In 30 BC it fell with hardly a fight to Octavian who as Augustus became the first Roman emperor.

32. Appian, *BC* 2.90, clearly telescopes events here and merely says that once Caesar had sufficient troops he had both Pothinus and Achillas executed for the murder of Pompey. Theodotus escaped but was executed some years later.

33. A notable topographical fact emerges here, *BA* 5, that Alexandria possessed no public fountains in its streets. The city is after all low lying and built on the silt brought down by the river. However, individual houses may have possessed private wells.

34. This may have been a deliberate obfuscation of the truth in order to inspire the troops seeing that very soon afterwards the Alexandrians are not only reported as having a fleet but one that was capable of taking on the Roman warships.

35. It is quite unusual for an author to be so precise in dating events in ancient historiography and this suggests either personal experience of the events in Alexandria or this is based closely on the report of someone who was there with Caesar.

36. Gardner (1967) 298, suggests that Caesar had been somewhat economical with the truth when he described a total destruction of the Egyptian fleet in the harbour, *BC* 3.111, and that some must have escaped. However, it is perhaps more likely that some had been stationed all along at Pelusium, cf. Plut. *Pomp.* 78 and 80, and that these were utilized in the siege later.

37. On another battle in which small vessels are noted see Thucyidides, 7.23, 7.25 and especially 7.40: 'even more damage was caused by the Syracusans who went about in small boats, ran in underneath the oars of the Athenian warships, sailed against their sides and from there hurled javelins at the sailors; cf. Diod., 13.14.4. This was undoubtedly commonplace and mostly escapes comment by ancient writers because it was so.

38. Note that biremes are not mentioned among the Alexandrian fleet but evidently made up a substantial part of Caesar's force. The bireme was an open-decked galley with a double bank of oars relying on a single oarsman to an oar. Smaller than the trireme they would have had about a hundred oarsmen and perhaps twenty or so marines on board. Like the triremes they could be highly effective in shallow waters and tight spots where the larger vessels might be hampered.

39. It is also possible that the Romans managed to retain a presence in the lighthouse but nowhere else on the island.

40. As its name *Heptastadion* indicates, the causeway was approximately seven stadia in length, thus 7×606 feet = 4242 feet = 1414 yards, or a little less than one and a half kilometres, and roughly the same distance between Ortygia and the mainland at Syracuse, and Motya to the mainland at Birgi. At either end there was a structure described as an arch. An arched gateway at the Pharos and the city seems quite plausible, less so is an arched bridge since this entrance–exit to the Great harbour could be opened and closed and so it is much more likely that here, as in Messina, there was a form of pontoon bridge that could block the passage from one harbour to another but also allow the movement of traffic from the mainland to the island and vice versa.

41. It is impossible to reach even an approximate figure for the numbers under Caesar's command here. By the early Roman Empire the cohort numbered six centuries, each with about eighty legionaries bringing a total of 480 for each cohort. But in Alexandria Caesar did not have 4800 legionaries, which means that the information is given loosely or that the units were considerably less in total than the later ideal. It is possible that there were roughly 200 men to a unit termed by the author here as a cohort and thus a total of 2000 legionaries, which seems a more plausible total for the attack in question, given the numbers mentioned by Caesar earlier in the expedition, *BC* 3.106, and perhaps represents about half the total manpower available to him.

42. The quadriremes and quinqueremes are often described as decked ships since unlike the smaller and lighter triremes and biremes the oarsmen rowed below an enclosed deck space. The provision of a deck allowed a greater number of troops to be carried for fighting. The triremes carried thirty marines or *epibatai*, mainly posted at the stern of the open boat, but the quadrireme–quinquereme design could allow for far more, perhaps as many as 120 soldiers plus catapults or small ballista; and so in the event of close quarter combat through boarding enemy vessels a battle on water was transformed into a fight on land.

43. It is probable that Caesar was with a number of his immediate staff who would also have given him advice on how to save himself, although doubtless that route would have become

obvious. It is also curious that Ptolemy XIII eventually died in similar circumstances at the end of the siege, which must throw some doubt on the historicity of this episode, which was exploited and much embellished by later writers especially Plutarch, *Caes.* 49. 4–5; Flor. 2.13.59; cf. Suet. *Iul.* 64, with less detail but Caesar's actions no less heroic; App. *BC* 2.90, has Caesar lose his cloak.

44. The Alexandrian mob had a poor reputation even in antiquity on account of its often volatile and violent behaviour, but the political leaders especially those close to the ruling dynasty, frequently eunuchs, draw especially negative comments from various writers, for example, Florus, 2.13.52.

45. *BA* 23–24, has the Alexandrians tired of having a young woman and a eunuch as leaders, and has Caesar characterize the leadership as one of foreigners and runaway slaves. Arsinoe and Ganymedes may have been outflanked here but retained influence with Ptolemy, perhaps an alliance of convenience. Ganymedes was apparently killed fighting in the battle at the Nile, after which Arsinoe was captured.

46. Ti Claudius Nero, father of the later emperor Tiberius (AD 14–37), was Caesar's quaestor, hence officially his second-in-command, and praetor in 42.

47. This is likely to have been the same route that Caesar had sailed in the previous expedition to save the beleaguered transports and probably the reason why he felt there was no need for his presence.

48. There is something not quite right in the text here, 13.4.3, for either Strabo or his translator is in error. If Mithridates VI was, in fact, the father of this Pergamene noble then his mother must have been Adobogion and not a daughter of Adobogion who would have been his contemporary, perhaps a sister.

49. Evans (2012) 67–68. A Roman army commanded by C. Flavius Fimbria besieged and stormed Pergamum and Mithridates was lucky to escape.

50. Caesar spent some time pursuing philosophical studies in Rhodes, a common enough pastime for young Romans of the ruling elite, either in the 70s or rather earlier according to Plutarch, *Caes.* 3.2.

51. Caesar had appointed Cn. Domitius Calvinus as proconsul of Asia when he was in Ephesus, but he had obviously not made appointments for Cilicia or Syria, which were left to govern themselves. The cities of the region and their governments had to step in to provide stability until new appointments could be made.

52. Strabo, 13.4.3, seems to suggest that he also had a reputation for philosophy and rhetoric being compared favourably with Apollodorus, another native of Pergamum, who was a noted rhetorician and taught the emperor Augustus.

53. Highly effective cavalry units are noted as early as 240 BC in a battle between Antiochus Hierax and his brother the Syrian king Seleucus II near Ancyra, Evans (2011) 11.

54. Alexander defeated the Persians at Granicus in the summer of 334 and then went on to besiege Miletus and Halicarnassus, before defeating the Persians again at Issus in November 333. The siege of Tyre occupied six or seven months, January to July/August 332 (see Chapter 3) and the capture of Gaza after a brief siege occurred in October 332 before Alexander advanced into Egypt in the winter of 332/1.

55. The partisan nature of Josephus' work is quite clear, but will have been derived from earlier records of Antipater's exploits, probably from a court historian of that time. It is unlikely to have featured in a purely Roman account. Antipater, a former supporter of Pompey, was obliged to show his newfound loyalty to Caesar and to have these recorded

for the new ruler. As also an ally of Cleopatra he was well rewarded afterwards and his family ruled Judaea and various parts of the region for over a hundred and forty years.

56. *BA* 27. Townend (1988) 51 places the town of Delta at the apex of the triangle from which the many streams of the Nile Delta start. Josephus, *BJ* 1.4.191, says that the battle took place at a settlement called the 'Camp of the Jews' and seems to place it a little to the south of Memphis.

57. Josephus claimed just fifty Jewish dead in the battle when he repeated the episode in his *Antiquities*, 14.135. Antipater received Roman citizenship and Hyrcanus was confirmed as High Priest. Caesar passed through Judaea after the left Egypt in about May 47.

58. The description of steep-sided banks and the Roman side crossing to attack their opponents has distinct similarities with Alexander's crossing of the Granicus River before engaging with the Persian on the opposite bank in 334. At Issus in 332 Alexander also crossed the river to attack the Persian left wing aiming for Darius in the centre.

59. D. Carfulenus was tribune of the plebs in 44 and may be the same person. If so in 48/7 perhaps a military tribune of one of the legions, possibly the Thirty-Seventh, since D. Carfulenus was not a supporter of Caesar or may have been an equestrian officer serving on Caesar's staff, Broughton (1984) 50.

60. Florus: '*Regis ipsius corpus obrutum limo repertum est in aureae loricae honore.*'

61. Broughton (1984) 50.

62. The ten-year Roman siege of Veii the Etruscan city between 400 and 390 is obviously something of a construct based on this event, although the event took place when reputable historians were writing.

63. The civilian population had been removed at the start of the war in 431 BC, so the besieged area may, in fact, have comprised only a fraction of the former urban site since it was effectively held for so long by such a small garrison.

64. Following the successful reliefs of Kimberley and Mafeking the British were able to advance on and capture Pretoria then the capital of the Transvaal Republic with little opposition (see plate).

65. The siege of Leningrad is generally regarded as the longest on record, after the probably unhistorical decade long sieges of Troy and Veii.

66. Cape Town to Kimberley, still the direct rail link to Johannesburg, is precisely 1000 kilometres (800 miles). From Kimberley to Mafeking the distance is a further 364 kilometres (225 miles).

67. The British force consisted of 11,000 mounted troops and 30,000 infantry, but it was the cavalry led by General French that was instrumental in lifting the siege, covering the last 192 kilometres (120 miles) in four days but leaving the infantry under General Roberts well in the rear to catch up later.

68. For example, the British had problems in the advance to Kimberley crossing the Orange River, which was evidently flowing strongly as a result of the summer rains.

69. See Broughton (1984) 51 for Cassius' quaestorship in 55 and the argument that he was proquaestor throughout the Carrhae campaign. He was praetor in 44 and assigned Syria after Caesar's death.

70. Cassius' whereabouts are not attested between July 48 when he attacked Messina and Vibo Valentia with Pompey's fleet, Caes. *BC* 3.101, and his reappearance as a legate of Caesar's in the campaign against Pharnaces of Pontus in the summer of 47. Cassius was with Caesar in Cilicia probably on the return from Egypt, which suggests that he had

accompanied the dictator to Alexandria, Cic. Phil. 2.26; Broughton (1951–52) 2.290. It is probably significant, however, that after Caesar's assassination Cassius returned to Syria as proconsul and while there raised funds and recruited troops for the campaign, which led ultimately to Philippi and his death along with Brutus in 42.

71. These troops may well have already been near Pelusium and represent those forces that Cleopatra had employed in her invasion of Egypt just a few months beforehand. Josephus also claims that it was through Antipater's good offices that prominent individuals in Coele-Syria had lent support to Mithridates, although these would have been encountered earlier in the advance unless supplies in arms, troops or money caught up with the relief at Ascalon.

72. Pharnaces was a son of Mithridates VI and succeeded him as king of the Bosporus after his father's suicide in 63.

73. Mithridates seems to have died about 45, before Caesar's assassination a year later.

74. He took with him the Sixth Legion, leaving three legions – Twenty-Seventh, Twenty-Eighth and Thirty-Seventh in Alexandria to prop up Cleopatra's regime, and probably other troops as well. Plutarch, *Caes.* 49.5, has no doubt about the paternity of the child. The fact that Caesar appears to have awaited the birth of this child is highly suggestive particularly as later Cleopatra and presumably her son were with the dictator in Rome. Caesar's only other child to have survived into adulthood had been Julia who had died in childbirth in 53, wife of Pompey.

Bibliography

Ancient sources

Aelian, *Historical Miscellany*, trans. N.G. Wilson, Harvard 1997.

Appian, *Appian's Roman History*, (4 volumes) trans. H. White, Harvard 1913.

Archilochus in *Greek Lyrics*, trans. R. Lattimore, Chicago 1949.

Arrian, *The Campaigns of Alexander*, trans. A. de Sélincourt, Harmondsworth 1958.

Asconius, *Commentaries on Speeches by Cicero*, trans. with Introduction and Commentary R.G. Lewis, Oxford 2006.

Athenaeus, *The Deipnosophists* (7 volumes) trans. C.B. Gulick, Harvard 1933.

Caesar, *Civil Wars*, trans. A.G. Peskett, Harvard 1914.

Caesar, *The Civil War*, trans. J.F. Gardner, Harmondsworth 1967.

Cassius Dio, *Dio's Roman History* (9 volumes) trans. E. Cary, Harvard 1914.

Cicero's Letters to Atticus (7 volumes) edited and translated by D.R. Shackleton Bailey, Cambridge 1966.

Curtius Rufus, *The History of Alexander*, trans. J. Yardley, Harmondsworth 1984.

Diodorus Siculus, *Diodorus of Sicily* (12 volumes) trans. C.H. Oldfather/C. Bradford Welles, Harvard 1939.

Florus, *Epitome of Roman History*, trans. E.S. Forster, Harvard 1929.

Frontinus, *Stratagems, Aqueducts*, trans. C.E. Bennett, Harvard 1925.

Herodotus, *The Histories*, trans. A. De Sélincourt, Harmondsworth 1954.

Josephus, *The Jewish War* (volume 2) trans. H. St. J. Thackeray, Harvard 1927.

Plutarch, *Lives of Pericles, Nicias, Alcibiades, Marius, Sulla, Pompey, Caesar*, trans. B. Perrin, Harvard 1917–1919.

Plutarch, *The Rise and Fall of Athens: Nine Greek Lives*, trans. I. Scott-Kilvert, Harmondsworth 1960.

Polybius, *The Rise of the Roman Empire*, trans. I. Scott-Kilvert, Harmondsworth 1979.

Sallust, *Sallust*, trans, J.C. Rolfe, Harvard 1921.

Sallust, *Jugurthine War, Conspiracy of Catiline*, trans. S.A. Handford, Harmondsworth 1963

Strabo, *Geography* (3 volumes) trans. H.C. Hamilton and W. Falconer, London 1892.

Strabo, *The Geography of Strabo* (8 volumes) trans. H.L. Jones, Harvard 1929.

Suetonius, *Life of Caesar*, trans. J.C. Rolfe, Harvard 1913.

Tacitus, *The Agricola and the Germania*, trans. H. Mattingly & S.A. Handford, Harmondsworth 1970.

Thucydides, *The Peloponnesian War*, trans. T.E. Wick, New York 1982.

Thucydides, *History of the Peloponnesian War* (4 volumes) trans. C.F. Smith, Harvard 1919.

Thucydides, *Historiae*, (2 volumes) (eds.) H.S. Jones & J.E. Powell, Oxford 1955.

Thucydides, *The Peloponnesian War*, trans. R. Warner, Harmondsworth 1954.

Thucydides, *The Peloponnesian War*, trans. W. Blanco, New York 1998.

Xenophon, *Hellenica* (2 volumes), trans. C.L. Brownson, Harvard 1921.

Modern sources

Balot, R.K., *Greek Political Thought*, Oxford 2005.

Bosworth, A.B., *The Legacy of Alexander: Politics, Warfare, and Propaganda under the Successors*, Oxford 2002.

Broughton, T.R.S., *The Magistrates of the Roman Republic*, volumes 1–2, New York 1951–52.

Broughton, T.R.S., *The Magistrates of the Roman Republic* (volume 3) (supplement) Atlanta 1984.

Bullitt, O.H., *Search for Sybaris*, London 1971.

Cartledge, P., *Ancient Greece: A History in Eleven Cities*, Oxford 2009.

Caven, B., *The Punic Wars*, London 1980.

Ceserani, G., *Italy's Lost Greece: Magna Graecia and the Making of Modern Archaeology*, Oxford 2012.

Chaniotis, A., *War in the Hellenistic World: A Social and Cultural History*, Oxford 2004.

Compton, W.C., *The Athenians in Sicily*, London 1940.

Cook R. & Cook K., *Southern Greece: An Archaeological Guide: Attica, Delphi and the Peloponnese*, London 1968.

Crawford, M.H., *Roman Republican Coinage* (2 volumes) Cambridge 1974.

De Angelis, F., *Megara Hyblaia and Selinous: The Development of Two Greek City-States in Archaic Sicily*, Oxford 2003.

Di Lampedusa, G.T., *The Leopard*, trans. A. Colquhoun, London 1988.

Durrell, L., *Sicilian Carousel*, Harmondsworth 1978.

Ehrhardt, C.T.H.R., 'Crossing the Rubicon', *Antichthon* 29, 1995, 30–41.

Evans, R.J., 'Was M. Caecilius Metellus a Renegade? A Note on Livy, 22.53.5', *Acta Classica* 32, 1989, 117–121.

Evans, R.J., 'Candidates and Competition in Consular Elections at Rome between 218 and 49 BC', *Acta Classica* 34, 1991, 111–136.

Evans, R.J., *Gaius Marius: A Political Biography*, Pretoria 1994.

Evans, R.J., 'Displaying Honourable Scars: A Roman Gimmick', *Acta Classica* 42, 1999, 77–94.

Evans, R.J., *Questioning Reputations: Essays on Nine Roman Republican Politicians*, Pretoria 2003.

Evans, R.J., 'Gaius Marius and the Consular Elections for 106 BC', in *Literature, Art, History: Studies on Classical Antiquity and Tradition*, (eds.) A.F. Basson & W.J. Dominik, Frankfurt am Main 2003, 295–303.

Evans, R.J., 'Rome's Cimbric Wars (114–101 BC) and the Impact on the Iberian Peninsula', *Acta Classica* 48, 2005, 37–56.

Evans, R.J., 'Gaius and Marcus Marius in Iberia and Gaul: Family Affairs and Provincial Clients', *Acta Classica* 51, 2008, 77–90.

Evans, R.J., *Syracuse in Antiquity: History and Topography*, Pretoria 2009.

Evans, R., *Roman Conquests: Asia Minor, Syria and Armenia*, Barnsley 2011.

Evans, R., *A History of Pergamum: Beyond Hellenistic Kingship*, London 2012.

Feiling, K., *A History of England*, London 1966.

Finley, M.I., 'Introduction', in *Thucydides: The Peloponnesian War*, Harmondsworth 1972, 9–32.

Flamarion, E., *Cleopatra: From History to Legend*, New York 1997.

Flensted-Jensen, P. (ed.), *Further Studies in the Ancient Greek Polis*, Stuttgart 2000.

Forster, E.M., *Alexandria: A History and Guide*, New York 1922; republished Oxford 1986.

Freeman, E.A., *The History of Sicily from the Earliest Times* (4 volumes) Oxford 1891–1894.

Froehlich, R., 'The Location of Archaic Greek Sybaris', *AJA* 73 (1969) 261–273.

Gelzer, M., *Caesar: Politician and Statesman*, trans. P. Needham, Oxford 1969.

Grainger, J.D., *The Roman War of Antiochos the Great*, Leiden 2002.

Greenidge, A.H.J., & A.M. Clay, *Sources for Roman History 133–70 B.C.*, revised E.W. Gray, Oxford 1960.

Griffin, M. (ed.), *A Companion to Julius Caesar*, Oxford 2009.

Hornblower, S., *A Commentary on Thucydides*: Volume III: Books 5.25–8.109, Oxford 2008.

Isserlin, B.S.J. & Taylor, J. du Plat, *Motya: A Phoenician and Carthaginian City in Sicily*, Leiden 1974.

Jackman, T., 'Ducetius and fifth-century Sicilian tyranny', in *Ancient* Tyranny, (ed.) S. Lewis, Edinburgh 2006, 33–48.

Johnston, S.I., *Ancient Greek Divination*, Oxford 2008.

Kamm, A., *Julius Caesar: A Life*, London 2006.

Kim, H.S., 'Archaic Coinage as Evidence for the Use of Money', in *Money and its Uses in the Ancient Greek World*, (eds.) A. Meadows & K. Shipton, Oxford 2001, 7–21.

Lampela, A., *Rome and the Ptolemies of Egypt: The Development of their Political Relations 273–80 B.C.*, Helsinki 1998.

Lane Fox, R., 'Theognis: An Alternative to Democracy', in *Alternatives to Athens*, (eds.) R. Brock & S. Hodkinson, Oxford 2000, 35–51.

Long, G. & R. Dunglison, *An introduction to the study of Grecian and Roman geography*, New York 1829.

Meier, Ch., *Caesar*, trans. D. McLintock, London 1995.

Meiggs, R., *The Athenian Empire*, Oxford 1972.

Mommsen, T., (ed.) *Corpus Inscriptionum Latinarum*, Berlin 1863–.

Morton, H.V., *A Traveller in Southern Italy*, London 1969.

Nash, E., *Pictorial Dictionary of Ancient Rome* (2 volumes) London 1968.

Pearson, L., *The Greek Historians of the West: Timaeus and His Predecessors*, American Philological Association, Atlanta 1987.

Pedley, J.G., *Paestum, Greeks and Romans in Southern Italy*, London 1990.

Rhodes, P.J., *A History of the Classical Greek World, 478–323 BC*, Oxford 2006.

Rhodes, P.J., *Alcibiades*, Barnsley 2011.

Sabin, P., 'The mechanics of battle in the Second Punic War', in *The Second Punic War: A Reappraisal*, (eds.) T. Cornell, B. Rankov, P. Sabin, Bulletin of the Institute of Classical Studies 67, London 1996, 59–79.

Salmon, E.T., *Roman Colonization under the Republic*, London 1969.

Sampson, G.C., *The Crisis of Rome: The Jugurthine and Northern Wars and the Rise of Marius*, Barnsley 2010.

Sekunda, N., 'Hellenistic Warfare', in Hackett, Sir J., *Warfare in the Ancient World*, London 1989, 130–135.

Servadio, G., *Motya: Unearthing a Lost Civilisation*, London 2000.

Sherwin-White, A.N., *The Roman Citizenship*, Oxford 1973.

Slater, N.W., 'Shaw's Caesars' in (ed.) M. Wyke, *Julius Caesar in Western Culture*, Oxford 2006, 228–243.

Spann, P.O., *Quintus Sertorius and the Legacy of Sulla*, Fayetteville 1987.

Sumner, G.V., *The Orators in Cicero's 'Brutus': Prosopography and Chronology*, Toronto 1973.

Talbert, R.J.A., *Atlas of Classical History*, London 1985.

Tarn, W.W., *Hellenistic Military and Naval Developments*, Cambridge 1930.

Trevett, J., 'Coinage and Democracy at Athens', in *Money and its Uses in the Ancient Greek World*, (eds.) A. Meadows & K. Shipton, Oxford 2001, 23–34.

Townend, G.P. (ed.), *Caesar's War in Alexandria, 'Bellum Civile 3.102-112, Bellum Alexandrinum 1–30,'* Bristol 1988.

Van Wees, H., *Greek Warfare: Myths and Realities*, London 2004.

Walbank, F.W., *A Historical Commentary on Polybius* (3 volumes) Oxford 1957.

Walbank, F.W., 'Hellenes and Achaians: "Greek Nationality" Revisited', in (ed.) P. Flensted-Jensen, *Further Studies in the Ancient Greek Polis*, Stuttgart 2000, 19–33.

Welch, K.E., *The Roman Amphitheatre: From its Origins to the Colosseum*, Cambridge 2007.

Whitaker, J., *Motya: A Phoenician Colony in Sicily*, London 1921.

Wilson, J.-P., '"Ideologies" of Greek colonization', in (eds.) G. Bradley & J.-P. Wilson, *Greek & Roman Colonization: Origins, Ideologies & Interactions*, Swansea 2006, 25–57.

Index